MORE THAN THE MADNESS

JOHN KANIECKI

More than the Madness
Copyright © 2016 by John Kaniecki

Disclaimer: Some names and identifying details have been changed to protect the privacy of individuals. The author has tried to recreate events, locales and conversations from his memories of them. None of the information in this book is intended as medical or psychological advice, nor is any information in this book meant for any purpose other than for the author to tell his personal story. The publisher and author assume no liability for any damage or disruption caused by the contents of this book.

Cover Art
Macario Hernandez III
Editors
Kristi King-Morgan
Connor MacDonald
Editor-in-Chief
Kristi King-Morgan
Formatting
Niki Browning

Printed in the United States of America

First Printing, 2016

ISBN 13: 978-1539430131
ISBN 10: 1539430138
Dreaming Big Publications

www.dreamingbigpublications.com

DEDICATION

To my wife, Sylvia.

CONTENTS

ACKNOWLEDGEMENTS

Special thanks to Vivian Francis.

Thanks to Doug Lemon, Marianne Warren, Anne Marie Jones, Jerry Caprio, Alice Marks, and Pat Kenschaft for their help in working through this manuscript.

Thanks to Kristi Morgan for making my dream come true.

INTRODUCTION

People like me don't come from any one particular place; in fact, we are all around the world. We live in every country. We don't have any particular skin color; we share them all. You can't tell that I am any different by looking at me. What sets me apart is what is going on in my mind. I belong to a dreaded world that most people fear and don't understand. There are many names for my state: crazy, lunatic, crackers, nuts, insane, and mentally ill.

I didn't specifically set out to write a book. I started by writing stories for myself to express what is so deep within my soul. When I shared these stories with friends, we laughed together and reminisced about our common experiences. This book that you hold in your hands was born. It is the story of my life.

You will never completely know what I am by simply reading my tales, but perhaps you will begin to understand. When Jesus was asked, "And who is my neighbor?" he didn't answer the question. Instead he told the story of the Good Samaritan. The parable did more than answer the question. In the same way, I hope my story will help answer the question of what mental illness looks like and feels like.

My illness is called manic depression and is caused by a chemical imbalance in the brain. I was diagnosed when I was twenty. The year was 1987. Now it is called by the milder name bipolar. Psychiatric disorders are often misunderstood; I was a leper with a hidden disease. One can't simply look at me and see something wrong, yet my existence has been far from normal.

An x-ray reveals a broken bone, and anyone can see the cast on a leg. Nobody would expect a person with a broken leg to run a marathon. But when someone suffers from an illness like depression, the reality is denied. "There's nothing wrong with you," or "You're just lazy," are typical comments. The compassion of loved ones seems missing due to frustration. They can't see the problem because they can't get into the person's mind to experience the battle raging inside. They can't see the living hell. I've walked in those shoes. This is a book of my footprints.

This book is about mental illness, written by one who suffers from it. I open my life with candidness and honesty. I am not afraid to reveal my soul.

Mental illness needs to be better understood. There are mountains of misinformation. Is it treatable? What are the symptoms? Are there different kinds? How does it affect you? There are textbooks that you can read to answer those questions. My book is not a clinical book filled with facts and figures, but a book of humanity to touch not just the mind, but the heart. It not only shows the illness with all its ugliness, but it also reveals the fact that I am a human being, just like you. The illness makes up part of what I am, but it does not define me.

Unlike most physical ailments, there is a stigma attached to mental illness. We hide it from our neighbors, coworkers, acquaintances, and even friends. It's the dirty little secret that the rest of the family doesn't like to talk about. In my experience, if you're poor, they will call you "crazy" and most likely you will wind up in a state institution or worse, a prison. If you're middle class, you suffer from a "chemical imbalance," and you will most likely get adequate treatment. If you are rich, you will be called eccentric and you will get the finest treatment. Whatever you call it, most people would like to brush it under the mat, somewhere out of sight.

This book, I hope, will help change some of these negative perceptions. The purpose of this book is to heal and not to hurt. Therefore, all of the names except my own have been changed, even my parents. It is sufficient to say that our home life was unpleasant. Some information I have purposely left out; I have no desire to air dirty laundry.

I am a devout Christian. Without God, the pain of the darkness of night would have crushed my soul and destroyed me. I bore my cross, and many have helped me carry it along the way. It has indeed been a long strange trip. I am not what the potential of my gifts may have promised, but what are the criteria to judge? I know without a doubt that I am a better person for what I have gone through. Remember, the measure of a man is not determined only by the distance he travels, but the nature of the road must be considered as well.

I am forty years old and happily married. I have a bachelor's degree in mathematics. I work full time as a civil engineer, and I support myself financially, with my wife Sylvia doing her share. I have come a long way from lying in bed all day thinking of how I was going to kill myself. I must humbly submit that I have overcome those demons. I am not one hundred percent out of their grasp, but they no longer dictate the terms and conditions of my life. I have progressed beyond many who have suffered from the same malady and even some who do not.

There is more to me than the madness. I am a human being just like you. The illness is just another dimension in a complex picture. I hope after reading this book, you will realize that I am not a creature who needs to be locked away from society, as some would demand. I hope you will understand that I am not a bizarre phenomenon. I hope that you will see some of yourself in me and realize that we really aren't too far apart after all. Most of all, I hope that when you encounter an individual who suffers from a mental illness, you will not ostracize them and consider them second class or worse.

Many have helped and supported me in this work and I give them my thanks. I hope you enjoy this book as much as I have enjoyed writing it. It has indeed been a labor of love. Be prepared to be challenged. Get ready for your horizons to be broadened. I am going to show you my life, a life that is probably very different from yours. Or maybe very similar to yours and, if so, I hope this helps you feel not so alone in your struggles. In sharing my experiences, I have exposed the shadows of deception with the brilliant light of truth. I hope it will set you free. I hope the shackles of prejudice will be unfettered.

My First Hospitalization An Angel Named Tim

Being in a psychiatric hospital was a traumatic experience for me, especially the first time. Mountains of anxiety, fear, and doubt made it hard to believe that it was happening to me. "After all, I really can't be crazy, can I?" I asked myself hundreds of times. "There must be some mistake," was the constant reply. The thought that I was insane hit me like a flood. It was savage and relentless. I tried to deny it and pretend it was all a bad dream. My self-worth was crushed, my ego diminished to nothing. I was something dirty, something less than human. At least that is what society had taught me about the mentally ill, and I believed it. At only twenty years old it seemed as if my life was over.

I've been in psychiatric wards on seven different occasions from what is considered the best, Heaven House, to what is considered the worst, the New Jersey State hospital called Bluerock. Each held their own advantages and disadvantages, but no matter how pleasant the surroundings were, there was a constant feeling of confinement. This is not a good thing, especially to a free spirit such as me. You don't realize how much is lost by being locked up until you have experienced it. No sunshine, no wind blowing on your face, and no talking to neighbors. You can't walk to the store if you want something. I couldn't go anywhere but into my room, the radio room, the television room, or the hall.

My first hospitalization was in Saint Anna's. It was a cruel and harsh experience, and I needed help in the worst way. My mindset was that I was locked up with a bunch of crazies. I don't know if I was scared, but I was definitely stunned and confused. Fortunately, the good Lord sent me an angel, so to speak, to help me. My angel's name was Tim. He had neither wings nor a halo, but he had a heart of gold and a kind spirit.

Tim was a little taller than six feet. The top of his head was bald with just a few strands of red hair, while over his brow the hair was thick. When he smiled or laughed, which was often, he revealed a mouth full of gapped, yellow, rotted teeth. The perfect word for Tim's look was goofy, but don't judge a book by its cover.

One thing the ward at Saint Anna's provided was structure. I was in the committed ward, as opposed to the volunteer ward. Supervision was excessive. There was a watchful eye observing me at all times. Patients are only sent to the committed ward if a psychiatrist decides they are a threat to themselves or someone else. A doctor thought I was a threat. I was literally out of my mind. The volunteer ward, which I would experience later, is a little more open and less controlled, but it's a matter of degree. A prison is still a prison even if one is more tolerable than the other.

Everything was done by a prearranged schedule. There was a time to get up, a time to eat, a time for medicine, a time for group therapy, a time for doctor's appointments, a time to meet with the social worker, a time for recreation, and a time to sleep.

There are two locked doors between the committed ward and the volunteer ward. A thick glass was in the midst of the barrier. Sometimes the mildly crazy would stare at us, the severely crazy, through the glass, but this was frowned upon by the staff. We could never leave the ward under any circumstance; strict control was implemented. We were not allowed to take a walk on the hospital grounds, nor were we allowed to go to the hospital restaurant. Both of these things were allowed for the voluntary patients. We had to eat hospital food. While better than nothing, it was not something to boast about. When there's so much boredom, mealtime became a time of excitement. I looked forward to anything to break the monotony.

Every morning at eight o'clock the loudspeaker would blare out a hideous rendition of the Our Father. This was a Roman Catholic hospital. There were statues of saints on the hospital grounds. Perhaps if the saints were alive today they would have been locked up with me. After all, we shared many things, like hearing God's voice and a deep devotion to the Christian faith. The priest would visit and give us communion on Sundays. I still recall him dispensing the Eucharist, which is a bread wafer, and saying "body of Christ" in a pious manner as he placed the emblem on the tongue. Though I had left the Catholic faith, I still took the host. It was a personal expression of my faith in God. My belief in God was one of the few positive aspects of my psyche that remained. All other self-worth and confidence had vanished. Rarely would the priest visit with us during the week. The holy man never came to hang out or talk with us. I guess he had better things to do, like recite the Rosary or pray.

The main avenue of escape was watching television. This was a window to the world away from the hospital. However, it was kept off limits, locked up in a cabinet with a glass window. We were forbidden to touch the television and needed special permission to change the channel. The staff then took their own sweet time in doing so and, if they were watching with an interest, they might even refuse to interrupt their show despite the patients' wishes. In small ways some of the staff were very selfish. Not changing a channel might seem trivial to most but, with the limited number of things to do, it was not so minor to me at all. One day, as I was watching the news on the television, I learned that the stock market had taken a tumble and, in my delusion, I thought I was responsible for the crash. Insanity doesn't make sense.

There also was a room called the music room. It had a radio, and we were allowed to listen any time we wanted. However, listening to the Christian station, which was called Family Radio, was forbidden. They, somehow, perceived it as being unhealthy for us. The radio did have a tape player, so I used to play Neil Young's album, Comes a Time. As I listened to the title track, I prayed there would come a time when I could leave the hospital. There are indeed times for all things, the song taught me. So I was filled with hope by the encouraging message. Since it was my first hospitalization, I didn't know the system. The structure of psychiatric hospitals appeared quite complex, with many players and policies. I had an awful thought that I would never get out. This notion filled me with horror. It was the "music" room that helped me cope. In addition to Neil Young, I also listened to James Taylor. Taylor's song "Fire and Rain" is about his own stay in a psychiatric hospital when he was overcoming his heroin addiction. The soothing voices of these singers kept me mellow and transported me to another realm. Music is a healer.

At that time the patients were allowed to smoke in the hospital. However, we were not allowed to carry matches or lighters, and were restricted to one cigarette per hour. One could always tell when the time to smoke was approaching. All us crazies would get out our cigarettes, ready to have them lit. It always seemed coldhearted and authoritarian to me when the ones who were in charge would wait until the exact second to light the cigarettes. They would bring their arms close enough, so that they could observe their wristwatches and refused to light the cigarettes an instant before the proper time. It was like counting down to New Year's Eve.

I had smoked only a handful of times before I was admitted to the hospital, but to alleviate the incredible boredom I took up the habit. After all, I was too drugged up and anxious to read. I was medicated with Thorazine and Haldol, drugs that slowed down the thoughts in my mind. They can also bring on serious side effects, including anxiety. My hourly cigarette was something to look forward to in a bleak environment. It was something to do every hour. It gave me a psychological thrill and, as a new smoker, I literally got high off the nicotine. I, however, had no cigarettes of my own. It was Tim that gladly supplied me with Marlboro.

Providing me with cigarettes was very generous on Tim's part. He had neither friends nor family to visit and keep him supplied. I never learned if his parents were dead or if they had just forsaken him. If he ran out of cigarettes, he would have to go cold turkey, and this just added to his misery. He gave me something precious and asked for nothing in return. Every hour he would give me a cigarette. Tim often broke the rule of one cigarette an hour; he would quickly and fiendishly smoke the first one in hurried puffs, and then use the butt to light the second one. He smoked that one in a more leisurely fashion. This was a serious breach of the rules, but he never got caught. The staff would accuse him, but he would deny it. Tim could refute the charges with a perfect poker face, giving no sign of guilt and, without proof, there was nothing they could do.

Tim and I just clicked; we were friends right away. We were both Christian warriors and both out of our minds. I was convinced that I was a prophet from God. I don't know what they thought was wrong with Tim though. He seemed completely normal to me. But I also thought God was speaking to me, so I guess I wasn't one to judge. On my first day in the hospital, Tim showed me a special cross. He took a piece of paper and drew it for me. The word LOVE was drawn vertically, and GOD was written horizontally. The two words shared the letter O and also made a cross. Around the words an outline was drawn with small lines representing emanations of light. I invented my own cross based on Tim's. In my cross the word SATAN was vertical and the word WAR was horizontal. It was a little long on the bottom, but who cares?

As I mentioned before, one of the drugs given to me was Thorazine. In my experience, this is an awful drug, which is sometimes even used as a horse tranquilizer. I experienced what is commonly referred to as the Thorazine Shuffle. My limbs tightened rigidly, causing me to shuffle like a Zombie. When I got anxious, my tongue stiffened and stuck out of my mouth. The realization of being in a psychiatric ward was enough stress to trigger my awful reaction. My tongue would extend as far as it could which was extremely painful. My jaw felt like it was going to disconnect from my skull. Whenever this happened, the staff would give me a shot of Cogentin. Cogentin relaxed me, but it took a couple of minutes to work. I would be in excruciating pain and a spectacle to the other mental patients and staff members. To prevent this adverse reaction, I eventually received a pill of Cogentin with the Thorazine which helped control the spasm attacks. I wrote a song about it. "I got the Thorazine shuffle. I got the Haldol blues. When they overmedicate you, it ain't nothing but bad news." Tim and I often laughed together about it.

Every morning the staff checked our blood pressure. At first, every time my blood pressure numbers read high, I would get very upset. I thought that if my blood pressure numbers came out to one hundred twenty over eighty, I would be let out of the hell of the hospital. To me, having the proper numbers would prove that I was, at long last, normal. Every day the numbers got lower and lower and, finally, I met the goal. I smiled enormously as the nurse announced one hundred twenty over eighty. Sadly, my hopes were dashed. It was not yet time for me to exit the hospital. The next time I got my blood pressure taken, I had lost all interest in the numbers. What did it matter?

Doctor Rug was my doctor. In my opinion, he was an evil and wicked man and by far the worst doctor that I have ever encountered. I am sorry I have to change his name. He was paid a substantial amount of money, around two hundred dollars a session, for his daily meetings with me. Our sessions were supposed to last an hour but lasted less than one minute and were identical.

"How are you doing?" Doctor Rug would ask, not appearing to care the slightest bit about me.

"Fine" I would reply, "Can I get out?"

"Not yet," he would answer.

That was it. The cruel man even refused to shake my hand. He made me feel guilty, as if I did something wrong. Being sick is not a crime, I later realized. Two months later, when I was finally released, he shook my hand. I really didn't want to shake his hand, but I felt completely at the mercy of the psychiatrist. There was no point in angering him. It was impossible to get out without his approval. So as we shook hands "goodbye and good riddance," I thought.

I've been hurt by many people in my life. You learn to forgive and forget, but I felt this man really did me a disservice. If he had treated me as he was being paid to, I would perhaps have understood more about my illness. When I was finally released, Doctor Rug wanted to continue to see me as an outpatient. I had never had one session with that man as competent doctors would give me in the future. I thought, "What was the sense in seeing a psychiatrist? After all, they do nothing." As a result, I didn't have the support of a good doctor upon my release. It cost me plenty. With a good caring doctor I would probably have avoided an enormous amount of suffering and pain. A good doctor could have steered me around the pitfalls. I was especially vulnerable, as I was very uneducated about mental illness. For doctors to work effectively, there needs to be trust between them and their patients. I didn't trust Doctor Rug; it's hard to trust someone you despise. Good doctors are caring and nurturing. Good doctors take an interest in their patients. Dr. Rug took no interest in me. I barely would have noticed his presence if he had not been the one in charge of my release.

Tim was another glowing example that the system really didn't work. Selfish staff and doctors performing inadequately are just some of the cracks. Through these deficiencies the patients get lost in the shuffle. Tim himself had well over twenty stays in the hospital; he had lost count. He knew all about the negligent treatment akin to Doctor Rug and others. It is a reality that mentally ill people have to face. It's hard enough fighting your demons, but to do so alone is terrible. I was blessed to have family and friends to look out for me. Tim was not so fortunate. I had the choice to ditch Doctor Rug. Tim, being a product of the system, was at the mercy of what was dished out to him.

Years later I would attend a support group for bipolar patients and their families. When I mentioned Doctor Rug, there was a general consensus. He was evil and negligent to the point of being a criminal. He never showed any compassion or concern, and he made the patients feel they were subhuman. I recall my friend Rolf telling me that Dr. Rug refused to see him without a security guard present. Rolf had gotten angry over the thoughtless way the doctor was treating him. I imagine many of his patients wanted to give him a pop in the mouth with a fist. This rotten doctor is probably retired, which is good for the patients. Based upon what I heard, he must have severely hurt hundreds of people in his tenure as a psychiatrist, while being paid a good salary. I have never met anyone who has anything good to say about the man, only stories of hurt and harm.

Most of the time Tim and I hung out and just talked. I'll always remember one story of his. While walking in the woods, Tim met an angel. The angel objected to his smoking and told him to get baptized. Tim was in awe. He tried to obey the angel, but he couldn't find enough water to baptize his whole body. So Tim just baptized his feet in a small creek. It was a strange story, just like Tim.

I can't remember any of the names of the other patients, but I recall the faces of a few of them. There was one woman who was a waitress. She had been physically abused by her mother, who burned her with a pancake griddle when she was a child. Most of the time this woman was more than okay; she was a pillar of strength, support and courage. She would help me walk up and down the halls when I was suffering from the Thorazine shuffle. Sometimes when she would take my arm to assist me, things would seem to get to her. Suddenly the woman would revert to a child being burned by a wicked mother. She would stop walking, break down and weep like a baby. My heart went out to her whenever the awful memories manifested themselves. I could only look on with pity, though I wished so badly I could have helped. After all, she helped me, if with nothing else but the love of her friendship.

In addition to the waitress, there was a middle-aged man who built houses for a living. The three of us would walk up and down the hall continuously back and forth, like a marathon. I sometimes took breaks because the pace was exhausting, though the waitress always encouraged me to continue on. Both of these patients seemed completely normal to me. I think the homebuilder got in trouble because he quit taking his medicine. This problem would haunt me as well later in life, and is the primary reason that psychiatric patients relapse.

It has been my experience that if you get help in a psychiatric hospital, it almost exclusively comes from your fellow patients. After all, they are going through the same ordeal. They are the ones on your side, your brothers and sisters. The people in authority are often seen as the enemy. They are the ones with the power to release you and since you're still in the hospital, they can't be on your side. If they were, you would be free. At least that's how a patient sees the dynamics. That was the way I saw it. That's why the friendship between Tim and I flourished. We needed each other to help each other in the struggle against the drudgery the hospital inflicted upon us. In the psychiatric ward there is no stronger desire or hope than getting free.

Fortunately, there were two staff members who did help me. One was an older nurse. I can still picture her face. She sat me down and explained to me that I had a chemical imbalance. She said that it is very similar to diabetes, and that people with diabetes feel good and normal when they take their insulin. However, when they stop because they are feeling better, they get themselves in trouble. So too was my illness. I believe this advice helped me tremendously, though it took me a while to be totally convinced.

A social worker named Sally also helped me. She was very nice to me and tried making arrangements for me after I was released from the hospital. It was thought that the college fraternity where I had previously been living would be very bad. The wild life and partying would be unsuitable; it wouldn't be good to be around alcohol and drugs. However, I didn't want to go to my parents' house. I was fragile and had bad feelings about both my parents, as they had already caused me a great amount of pain. I did not want to live with them. Sally tried to arrange for me to stay with an older friend named Roger, who was the Vice President at Edwards Institute of Technology where I had attended school. I thought we were very close, like a father and son. However, he let me down in a tremendous way, refusing to let me stay with him. Sally was unsuccessful, and I ended up returning to my parents' home. Regardless, her great efforts and her care and compassion were a tremendous blessing. Sally cared about me and treated me like a human being.

Tim was going through his pains as well. My friend really had no options, and his fate would eventually lead him back to a group home. Still, despite the older nurse and Sally trying to help, there was more than enough drama. This came in the form of a cold psych tech, a low ranking employee, who acted like he was God's gift to psychiatry. The position of psych tech is a lowly office. They are ranked at the bottom, below doctors, psychologists, nurses and social workers. Some psych techs are very decent people, but some get off on the itsy bitsy piece of power they have over the patients. He clearly thought he was hot, though I just recall his stupid mustache and funny hair.

We were all gathered at a group therapy session in the television room—attendance was mandatory. Group therapy, to me, was a very humiliating process. I was supposed to share the thoughts going on in my head. In other words, I was expected to reveal, to complete strangers, my deepest feelings and fears. And the others were supposed to provide me with help, based on their past experiences. Would any human being like to tell their deepest and most embarrassing secrets? The psych tech analyzed our confessions, and then gave us feedback. They sometimes spoke as if they were the absolute authority, which is extremely pompous. We couldn't question their conclusions. If we did, we were labeled as being in denial. In this microcosm, they were the experts. The patients were not to question authority. This created a power differential and gave me an unhealthy feeling of inferiority.

There was one particular session when the psych tech gave us an elaborate story to consider. It went like this:

There was a man who had a drinking problem. The man drove his car to the bar. At the bar he couldn't control his drinking, and he promptly became drunk. Then he had to drive home. Since he was drunk, this would be very dangerous. He could even get arrested, or worse, get in a terrible accident. The question put to us crazies was, "What was the man to do?"

The answer the psych tech wanted to hear was that the man should quit drinking. Tim, thinking out of the box, had another idea. The solution was that the man should drink at home instead of the bar. Not only would it be cheaper, but he also wouldn't need to worry about driving. It seemed like a reasonable answer to me.

The psych tech was furious. His carefully laid plans were destroyed. Tim had come up with an alternate solution that destroyed his own. The tech yelled at Tim like he was reprimanding a child. "Tim, you'll never get out of the hospital with that attitude." He was serious. "Before you're released, the psych techs are consulted."

When I was in Saint Anna's for a second hospitalization, I heard the same psych tech tell us the same stupid story. I'll bet everyone passing through the hospital hears that stupid story. I wish I'd had the guts to repeat Tim's answer.

There was another psych tech taking classes for his master's degree at Edwards Tech. When I was in the hospital, he refused to talk to me. Instead, he studied his books and told me to be quiet. Why that behavior was allowed, I don't know. I later ran into this individual at a fraternity party. This person, who was presumed to be a wise expert on life, was a joke. All he did at the party was slowly sip on a beer and look terrified at the other people at the party. He had no courage to talk to a stranger or to let loose a little. I tried to introduce him to people and put him at ease, but he couldn't escape his inhibitions. He was too timid to socialize. And this was a person who was supposed to guide me to a better life!

There was a woman in the hospital, a fellow patient. She was a beautiful singer. She was dating the bass player from the rock band Blondie. He came in and played guitar and she sang a beautiful song about a bird. It was an original song and it seemed like it could have been a hit. I recall talking to her about John Lennon being an Anti-Christ. Her boyfriend had told her that, and she was convinced of it. It was a strange conversation and, at the end of it, we agreed that not only was John Lennon an Anti-Christ, but that many others were too.

In addition to her strong views on music and musicians, she

was also a self-proclaimed strict vegetarian. However, I think she was actually a vegan. Every time she filled out her menu, she wrote clearly in big letters that she wanted no meat. And, without fail, every morning she would carefully open her food dish and every morning without fail, to her horror, she would discover eggs.

The woman would react like her mother had just died. She would cry in agony, go silent and then weep bitterly. I think some of the staff got a kick out of it and made sure her wishes weren't met. Some mentally ill people can feel the woes of this world with such intensity, our souls mourn over the slightest injustice. You can understand why patients stick together like Tim and I. It's a matter of mental survival.

Throughout my hospitalization, I received many cards and letters from people in my church. I received so much correspondence that the staff was amazed. In fact, I don't think any patient received more mail than me. Each piece of mail was a precious treasure: windows to a pleasant place. I smiled at the funny ones and was touched by the sentimental ones. But, above all, I felt like I wasn't forgotten or alone. Moses, the man who led me to Christ, said that he tried to visit me, but the hospital would only allow family to come into the committed ward. No one from my fraternity bothered to write me. So much for their brotherly love. My mother and father came to see me. My sister Matilda got married when I was in the hospital, but she still managed to visit as well. Poor Tim didn't get a single card or a single visit.

I served my thirty days in the committed ward and near the end of my stay they sent Tim to Bluerock Hospital, a state institution. After serving my time as a committed patient, I spent another thirty days in the voluntary ward. It was more of the same but had improvements. We were taken for brief walks on the grounds of the hospital. I never heard the birds sing more sweetly or the clouds look so lovely. When my parents visited, I was allowed to go down and eat at the hospital restaurant. I finally got some good food. It had been a long time since I'd had a cheeseburger. You learn to appreciate things when you are forced to go without them.

The voluntary ward is really a misnomer. It's really not voluntary, though you are technically allowed to sign yourself out. After signing out, the hospital has three days to go through the release process. During this time the psychiatrists will review your case. Their automatic conclusion will be to commit you, which means going back to the more restricted ward. This is common knowledge and the staff explained it to me plainly and without any pretense. The message was clear: if I signed out, I wouldn't be leaving. I would only be prolonging my stay. I would have signed myself out without hesitation if it meant freedom. I was desperate to leave.

It was in the voluntary ward that I met John. One day he and I were staring at the rain through the window. He was rocking slowly back and forth, and out of nowhere he announced "I'm Jesus and I'm making it rain." I looked at him strangely. It was the first time I had met someone who thought he was Jesus, but certainly not the last. My thoughts instantly returned to my friend Tim. He too was a prophet of God as well. Or at least he was in his own mind.

Three years later, after getting out of Bluerock psychiatric hospital myself, I was attending a day center. This was a place where people with all kinds of mental illnesses met. We'd hang out, do gardening, cook lunch and do other things. I was happy to see Tim there; it's always refreshing to see a friendly face. We continued our friendship. Another client named Jerry looked up to Tim and imitated him exactly. They walked the same and talked the same. When Tim said he was going to California because it was nicer, Jerry said the same thing word for word. This upset Tim greatly. Jerry was stealing Tim's best ideas. Jerry would literally follow Tim around like a lost puppy. In Jerry's mind, Tim was a superstar, an idol to be emulated.

Tim was in a group home at the time. I eventually left the center, but I occasionally heard about Tim's progress from mutual friends. There is a whole mentally ill community that we belonged to, a subculture. For a while, Tim was a heavy alcoholic. He had left the group home because they didn't allow drinking, and resorted to living under a bridge. I was devastated to hear this news. Then

I heard he was living in the woods of North Carolina and was smoking a lot of crack. I felt extremely sorry and distraught to hear this as well. Tim was definitely addicted to drugs and alcohol. He had become the classic town drunk.

Tim had been like an angel to me. He was caring and gave to the point of sacrifice, never asking anything in return. In the world's sight he was a crazy loser who couldn't control his drugs or liquor, but I have found few people as good-hearted or as genuine as Tim. Tim made hell bearable. I will always remember Tim with fondness, gratitude and love. He was indeed an angel.

Whenever I see a person rummaging through the garbage for food or witness a drunk passed out on a park bench, somewhere in the recess of my mind I think of Tim. I look at them with compassionate eyes. They may be angels as well.

SNOB HILL

I was the third child of Betty and Stanley Kaniecki. My sister Matilda was the oldest and my brother Bert was the middle. Between Matilda and Bert my mother suffered a miscarriage. For some reason my father only wanted three children. If the miscarriage hadn't happened, I wouldn't have been born. Therefore, I consider myself a child of promise. My father named me John because John was the disciple closest to Jesus. It was also his middle name. Today my father is an agnostic, but at one time he considered becoming a Catholic priest. He became a chemist instead. What a great contrast from having faith in the unseen spiritual world to accepting only what can be examined and investigated. He lost his faith to science.

I was born in Brooklyn, which makes me a native New Yorker. It is a fact, but I have no memories of New York at all. I was a baby when we moved to Illinois; my dad's job transferred him there. My mother didn't really want to leave her social network in New York. The entire extended family lived there. It was all she knew and she didn't know anyone in Lagrange, Illinois, but she went along anyway. Maybe she wasn't even consulted. Interestingly enough, the one thing my parents found difficulty adjusting to after the move was the quiet. They couldn't sleep because they were so accustomed to the noise of traffic right outside the door.

My first memory is of a giant black hand trying to crush me. This happened before I even learned how to speak. I was an infant in my crib. To avoid the dark specter, I buried myself under the large amount of stuffed animals surrounding me. I do not understand the origin of this disturbing vision. My second memory is that of my mother potty training me. It was done in the basement, as I recall.

I also have memories of preschool. I used to jump through the windows of a large dollhouse that was intended to be for the girls. Perhaps that was my first sin. I knew it was wrong and that we weren't supposed to do it. But even after a scolding, I continued to jump through the window. I recall wetting my pants during Spanish lessons at the same preschool. I don't even think I was embarrassed; I was so young.

One day there was an eclipse. My mother felt that viewing the sun on that day would have catastrophic results. First she refused to let us out of the house. Then she relented on one condition: we were instructed to take books and hold them over our eyes like they were visors. My brother, a friend, and I walked around all day with one hand holding a book on our heads. We were all too young to realize how stupid and foolish it was. Children listen to their parents and do as they are told. Children, likewise, learn by what they see: good or bad.

A sad event occurred in Illinois. I had a friend who lived two houses away. One day I walked over and rang the bell, wanting my friend to come play with me. An adult answered the door. I didn't catch on right away, but my friend had moved away and was no longer there. I rang the bell the next day and the nice woman explained again that the boy no longer lived there. It still puzzles me as to why he never said goodbye. The loss of a friend was very difficult to comprehend.

We moved from Lagrange, Illinois to Pequannock, New Jersey when I was five years old. This must have made my mother happy because it brought her closer to New York City. Dad bought a house in an upscale area of town on Munson Drive. This area, nicknamed Snob Hill by the rest of the town, boasted bigger houses and property sizes than anywhere else. As a result, there was animosity and ill feelings against our whole family. My brother Bert and I, being younger, felt it the most. We started out with one strike against us, unfairly so.

To make matters worse, we didn't even fit into Snob Hill. Our moving in must have been seen as an intrusion or even an invasion. Upon reflection, there are probably many reasons why we didn't belong. We were city folks coming into a rural environment, and there was hostility towards our Polish ancestry. I was the brunt of many ethnic jokes. In addition, I believe we lacked certain basics in hygiene. As children, we weren't taught to shower daily. One bath a week was pretty much the extent of our bathing. This was definitely a negative. Finally our clothes were of the inexpensive variety. One day the mischievous children in the neighborhood glued a picture of my mother on our front door. It was a hand drawn cartoon depicting her yelling, as she often did. Written on the note were the words "shut up and take a bath".

There was a whole host of bullies living on Snob Hill, a bunch of miserable people. They would constantly harass Bert and me by calling us names, which often led to fist fights. One bully that sticks out in my memory is Roy. He was six or seven years older than me and was huge in size, compared to me. There was no way to stand up for myself. One day Roy threw a rock through our living room window. My mother suspected Roy because she looked out quickly and saw him running away. My mother confronted him. She told the troublemaker, "That rock broke the window and glass shattered; somebody could have gotten seriously hurt!" Roy apparently acted remorseful enough for my Mom, but this didn't stop his antics.

Later in life I discovered Roy's parents had divorced, and he was staying with his grandmother. As a child I didn't understand why Roy was such a bully. Years later, Roy ran into my mother and apologized to her for his actions. He told her of his change of heart after becoming a born-again Christian. He said that his faith in God had helped him realize that the pain and anger he felt due to his parent's divorce was what fueled his behavior back then. I believe all people are capable of change.

Our house was very close to a farm owned by some Dutch people. Their children were also older than my brother and I. Our mailbox was blown up with firecrackers about seven times. We suspected the Dutch kids because they always had an ample supply of firecrackers. One time my sister even found firecrackers with a stuffed animal in the mailbox. Apparently, they decided to start a fire using the toy's flammable insides as kindle. Matilda was so scared that she insisted that my parents call the police, which they did. The police came, but did nothing.

These children were raised in the strict Dutch Reformed environment. There were many rules in this sect, but I guess they skipped the lessons on Christian love. One rule was that they weren't allowed to own a television. When I invited two of the children, Paul and Bruce, to a birthday party, my mother expected them to cause trouble. Instead, they sat silently glued to the TV set, fascinated. I believe it was the first time they had ever watched television.

Paul and Bruce would always call us names, and my brother and I called them names in return. Then they would chant, "Sticks and stones may break my bones, but names will never hurt me." They were so wrong; words are powerful and can bring great pain. Psychiatrists believe that mental abuse can be more detrimental than physical harm.

Because I rode the bus to school, most of the kids knew where I lived. They were the ones who informed me that I lived on Snob Hill. The bus was torment, especially because of a boy named Horace. Horace had the foulest mouth that I had ever heard. It was from him that I learned how to curse. He was always calling me names, until one day I turned around and punched him in the face. His lip started to bleed and swell up. Another child said, "I'm not going to bother John any more. Look what he did."

Horace answered, "It's only a fat lip. It's no big deal." That statement diminished my act. He seemed glad that he got me to hit him. Years later Horace would prank call our house repeatedly and use his filthy mouth to torment my mother. Despite the police trying to trace the call, the episodes continued for a long time. The authorities eventually caught him. They couldn't reveal his name because he was a minor, but we heard it was him from another source. Later on in life, I would meet Horace's mother at a support group for people with mental illness. Through her, I learned of Horace's past abuse by his father and his struggle with mental illness. He was in and out of prisons frequently. He would even show up to his parole meetings drunk, which was a violation of his parole. I was very sad to learn that Horace suffered from mental illness. It's not something one would wish on anybody. Not even somebody who was abusive.

There was another older boy in the neighborhood named John. He didn't like the fact that we had the same name. So to differentiate our names I was referred to as John John, because the other John was much older. It was my first nickname, and I hated it. "Why did I have to change my name?" I thought to myself. I never understood why I had to change my name.

Melvin was a bully in the neighborhood who had a much younger brother, Herman. Herman was younger than me. I didn't like him. He was very competitive, especially at sports. He came across as obnoxious, to the point of arrogance. One day we were playing whiffle ball in my front yard, using a stone in the ground as home plate and another stone as second base. First base and third base were trees. I was pitching, and Herman hit the ball. I called it a foul, but Herman said it was fair and declared it a home run. To make his point Herman started to trot around the bases. He was cheering and whooping it up, despite my protests that the ball was a foul. When he rounded third base and made his way to home, I punched him from behind. My fist somehow arched around his head. I would lie later and claim that I had hit him from the front.

My fist found Herman's eye. Herman cried like a baby for over an hour. I never saw anyone cry so much. Part of me felt bad for Herman, but a small part of me felt glad that he got what he deserved for acting so arrogantly. But, as the boy continued to weep, I was truly and completely remorseful. My mother tried to comfort him and put ice on his eye, but he went home with a black eye, still weeping. I wished that he would shut up; the guilt I felt was agonizing. The next day Arnold, from up the block, came by and hit me; his was revenge in order to even the score. Never mind all the unfair abuse my brother and I endured with no retribution! Herman later became a basketball coach at a college. I hope he teaches his team good sportsmanship, but I doubt it.

In the midst of all the bullying, I visited the emergency

room three times. Each time was because I was hit in the head and a big lump developed. Each time I got x-rayed and then sent home. I can recall only one of these three incidents. When I was about five years old, Arnold and I were at his house sitting at the top of his driveway, playing with his plastic army soldiers. We set up the miniature plastic soldiers as if there was a battle with two opposing sides. We faced each other with our respective armies lined up between us, and we started tossing rocks to knock them over. The idea was that the winner would be the one with the soldiers standing the longest. Arnold picked up a rock and threw it as hard as he could at my face. I was seated only two or three feet away. In hindsight, I realize the attack was both vicious and cruel. It resulted in a large bump on my head. I ran home crying. My mother immediately took me to the emergency room. The diagnosis didn't reveal any serious damage.

Dan and Neal were two brothers who lived up the block. I spent many days playing with them. One day we went to the creek to catch frogs. I was terrible at catching frogs because I was slow and I was afraid of getting my feet wet. Dan, who was quick and nimble, caught them all. After hunting for frogs all morning, Dan and I had a disagreement, and I swiftly beat him up. Neal, the younger of the two, became enraged that I hurt his brother and attacked me by swinging the bag of frogs at my head, but that did nothing but kill the frogs. I then promptly beat up Neal. We were all upset that day; the frogs got crushed. Neal blamed me for that because I had a hard head. Dan was a good friend, maybe my best friend at the time. I did to others what I hated to be done to myself. I realized I was far from being an angel, and far from being good or nice.

Bill lived up the street, the last house before Rockledge Terrace. We often went into the woods where there was a little clearing. "This is my fort," Bill declared to all of us. Then he pointed to a wooden board. "That's my throne," he boasted. Then the king sat on his throne. The weight of Bill caused the board to crush a beehive that was underneath it. When we realized what had occurred, we all ran with terror from the angry bees and into Bill's house. The bees stung all of us several times, so Bill's mother rubbed some soothing paste on our stings and pulled the stingers out.

Bill and I were friends until we had one final disagreement. We were the same age, but even though I was short, I was tough for my age. So when Bill and I had a fistfight, he was the one who went home crying. I was sorry that we fought because Bill was always nice to me. I had been taught to communicate with my fists, and so after that day our friendship diminished. I recall that same day my sister Matilda had one of her boyfriends over. He witnessed the fight and, knowing a little about boxing, he told me to keep my thumb outside when I made a fist, because my thumb was tucked inside my fist when I punched Bill. I learned that I could break my thumb that way when throwing a punch.

We had woods in the back of the yard at that time. The woods, though small, had trees and bushes thick enough to give the feeling of an undisturbed wilderness. We loved to play there. However, the Dutch kids would cause trouble by claiming that a certain apple tree was theirs. The tree was on the border of the two properties. I never learned why they were so obsessed with the tree. I think part of it was because the Dutch people used to own the whole area. They resented new people on their turf. The apples were no good to eat, but they were perfect for throwing at each other. This wasn't a fun game; this was conflict. It's just another example of violence in a childhood full of hostility.

Now all the woods are gone. My parents' house still has trees in the back yard, but it is nothing like the uninhibited growth which once flourished. The people who moved into the neighbor's house next door had the wilderness removed when they put in a pool. The Dutch people cleared a lot of the area to build new homes. The woods I knew were a taste of undisturbed nature. In a sense, they were sacred to me. All throughout the world nature is on the retreat. Destruction of the wilds is labeled as progress. I strongly disagree with this title. In the Garden of Eden man was given the responsibility of caring for nature. What he has done instead is dominate and destroy. I can hear Mother Earth crying to me in anguish. Of course the psychiatrists say that is all just a delusion. Whatever the case, I view what man has done to Earth as a violation of his duty and a grievous sin, and the disappearance of the woods behind a house in some way violates the memory of my childhood.

One pastime we had was particularly brutal when we were playing a game called Kill the Guy with the Ball. The idea was to tackle whoever had the ball as we passed it around. The holder of the football would run and dodge the tacklers for as long as he could. One day the game became particularly violent. For some reason Melvin singled me out and threw the ball over and over to me, so that he could tackle me over and over. At first I didn't mind; I wanted to be seen as tough. After a while though, I came to realize that this was no longer a game. It was a lesson in survival, since I felt the others were trying to seriously hurt me. I couldn't leave and be considered a coward, so I accepted my punishment. Later during the game when Melvin was tossed the ball, I hit him quick and hard and, despite his larger size, my blow flattened him. Melvin complained, "You didn't give me time to catch it." Yet he was doing the same thing to me constantly.

Later that day, already in a bad mood from my conflict with Melvin, I made it home to see Mother was in a particularly foul mood as well. To escape her screaming, I retreated to my bedroom and cowered in my bed. The screaming continued and, though it was only the middle of the day, I pulled the covers over my head. I wished I was dead, and that I could kill myself. It was no fleeting thought; I had an intense desire to end my life. I was too young to understand how to go about it, and that realization only upset me more.

Don't get me wrong, life wasn't always grim and we had a lot of fun. Snob Hill became a giant sleigh-riding park when the snow came. It was situated on a dead end so we never had to worry about traffic. One year, Ron and Joe, from Rockledge Terrace, got a toboggan for Christmas. We hauled it to the top of the hill where there was a golf course, and spent the rest of the day running up the hill and sliding down. The hill was bumpy which made the rides more exciting. It was great exercise and great fun. Ron and Joe's mother made us all hot chocolate on that day. It was nice to be together as friends, instead of at odds with one another.

Unfortunately, the following year, the golf course stopped the sleigh-riding over concern that someone might get hurt, and they would be liable. It was another treasure of my youth that would be, sadly, unknown to future generations.

Years later I would realize how abnormal my childhood was, especially the amount of fights I was in when I was young. After graduating from Montclair State University, I started applying for jobs. Some required a personality test. One of the questions asked how many times I had gotten into fights with the following choices: zero, one, two to four, four to six and more than six. I could easily remember a dozen and a half fights without thinking hard at all. I lied on that answer. I knew that if I answered truthfully, it would have been viewed negatively, but I didn't get hired anyway.

I learned hatred early on as a child. That was the lesson of my youth. Now I realize that children don't know the consequences of their actions. This is true about adults as well, who really aren't any better. I have forsaken hatred now, deciding that love is a much better path. With love comes forgiveness and with forgiveness comes healing.

But as a child, the damage had been done. I was not getting supportive love at home; I was receiving the opposite. The seeds of my mental illness were being sown. But there was the smile; I always smiled. Photos of me during that time show an enormous smirk. My friend Alexander called it a "shit-eating grin." I was a child and I knew no other life. I made the best of it. I didn't realize the horror I was going through because I had a limited perspective to draw from. I was strong and I survived...with a smile. I would later lose the smile, and have to fight to have it return.

GRANDPARENTS

My Mother's father was a short and compact man named Robert, or as the family called him with affection, "Grandpa Bobby." With a quick glance one might think that he was pudgy, but a closer examination would reveal a muscular frame. He reminded me of Popeye the Sailor Man.

My earliest memories of him were the letters I would write to him telling him about my grades in school. He would reward my efforts by sending me money. The better the grade the more money he sent. I did very well in school, so I collected a lot of loot. What a thrill it was to get a letter with a five-dollar bill in it! It never occurred to me to lie to him about my grades. While my Grandfather's rewards did not directly drive me to get good grades, it was an encouragement.

My mother would take us to Brooklyn where he lived. At that time, she would never drive into Brooklyn as she did in later years. My father scared my mother about the horrors of New York City traffic, so instead we took the bus and rode the subway to Brooklyn. I understood that New York was a tough town, especially the subway. I felt macho because I was brave enough to ride New York's subways, especially at a very young age.

Grandpa Bobby had no telephone, so we never knew when he would be home. Mother would write him to tell him of the day we were coming, usually a Saturday. We had other relatives in the Brooklyn area that we would also visit on the same trip. There was Grandma Maggie, my father's mother, Aunt Gloria, my mother's aunt, and Grandma Anna, my mother's mother.

Grandpa Bobby and Grandma Anna were separated. I don't know if they were officially divorced, but they lived apart and had no interaction. During one particular family gathering, the two of them were at our house in New Jersey at the same time. My brother Bert pointed out Grandma Anna to Grandpa Bobby, but the two refused to acknowledge one another.

Grandma Anna had psychological problems. To make matters worse, she liked to drink beer. It is very bad to mix psychotropic medicines with alcohol. I'm sure this took its toll on the marriage.

Grandma could function fine when she took her medicine, but her behavior would become erratic and things could get out of hand when she stopped taking them. My mother would have to pay her a visit to convince her to take her pills. I recall one incident in which she threw things out of her apartment window at people six stories below. My mother and I traveled to Brooklyn to take care of her. I recall the intense fear and dread as we drove her to the hospital. Later in life, I would learn why she dreaded going to a psychiatric ward the hard way. The poor woman repeatedly screamed, "I don't want to go!" The panic intensified the closer we got to the hospital. Upon our arrival, Grandma attempted to flee. It was fortunate she didn't get violent, although she did resort to a little pushing.

All of that aside, Grandma Anna was a really sweet woman whom I knew loved me. She always sent me cards for birthdays and holidays. Yet even as a child, I could tell there was something wrong with her. She never talked in complete sentences. Usually any conversation with her would involve asking her a question to which she wouldn't reply. Her clothes were often dingy and her appearance disheveled. But still I knew Grandma was concerned about her appearance. One thing my mother frequently did on our visits would be to fix up Grandma's hair, cutting it and putting it in rollers to make it curly.

Grandpa Bobby, on the other hand, was very masculine. He worked in the shipyards as a welder. This was physical work and Grandpa was strong. I remember he had a problem with a young man who lived in his apartment building, a multi-story complex with no elevator. According to Grandpa, this young punk was on drugs. As a result of his addictions, he needed money. On several occasions he tried to threaten Grandpa, hoping to get some money. Grandpa, though much older, wasn't scared a bit. Stuff like this didn't bother someone like Grandpa Bobby. He had an iron pipe to defend himself, and in case he needed more help, he had a gun. I'm sure it was illegally owned and not registered.

As you can tell, Grandpa Bobby was a fighter. When he heard my brother and I were having trouble with neighborhood bullies, he was incensed. He wanted to buy us a huge German Shepherd to attack our antagonists. Sometimes I wished he had. Whenever we visited Grandpa, he would cook us dinner. He wasn't a great cook, and many of his meals were influenced by his Polish culture. The food always had a strong smell, which meant the whole complex floor knew that he was cooking. The odor would discourage my appetite. I never complained about the food, but I was always relieved when we went to McDonald's or Burger King instead.

Grandpa Bobby was very proud of his Polish heritage. He instilled in me a pride to be Polish. My fellow students in school would cruelly ridicule my culture and told an endless amount of Polish jokes.

"How many Polacks does it take to remove a light bulb?"
"Four! One to hold the light bulb and three to turn the chair."

I believe people try to make others feel inferior so they can feel superior. Whether this is because of race, color, or anything else doesn't matter; they cause the same thing. Prejudice is actually a sign of weakness and insecurity, and it comes from doubts of one's own adequacy.

Grandpa would play a trick with me as a child. He would grab my nose with his two fingers. Then with his thumb sticking between his two fingers he would claim that he had taken the nose off of my face. I would then quickly feel my nose to reassure myself it was still there. It always brought a smile to me when he did this. I do the same trick on the children in my church.

Grandpa Bobby had a large family back in Poland, and he

would write back and forth with them. The Communists at that time were in power, and Grandpa hated the Reds. He viewed them as oppressors. The Soviets were viewed as foreign occupiers, largely due to the fact that Russia dominated the Eastern Bloc countries. Also, the system in Poland didn't work; there was much corruption coupled with shortages in goods. There was no free speech and the mail was censured. Apparently every package and letter from overseas was opened to see if it contained any forbidden material. Grandpa would complain that the government officials would steal the stuff he sent in packages when they examined it for contraband. To avoid this thievery he would send shoes in different packages. One package would have the left shoe and a package sent later would have the right shoe. This strategy worked. It was no good stealing just one shoe.

Years later Lech Walesa would bring worldwide attention to Poland. As a union leader in the shipyards, Walesa stood up to the communist government, as he demanded democratic reform in Poland. The situation became intense, and it was thought that the Polish government, or even the Soviets, would crush the brave union workers who were on strike. The strike eventually led to free elections in Poland, with Walesa coming into power. Poland was instrumental in the collapse of the Soviet Union. During these events, when the whole world had their eyes focused on Poland, the pride of my heritage swelled. Instead of being dumb Polacks, we had been proven to be brave and strong.

Grandpa was quite the craftsman. He would make picture frames and simple furniture. I recall several chairs he created that used to sit on our porch. They weren't elaborate or ornate. They were sturdy and made out of steel and wood. The chairs still sit on the front porch at my parents' house. They are over twenty-five years old and as sturdy as the day they were made. He also made cabinets that had secret compartments on top. An almost invisible metal lever opened a secret drawer. Grandpa even had a decoy drawer. This drawer had a piece of metal like the secret compartments, but it was just a fake; there was no drawer to open. I guess a thief would lose precious time trying to enter a secret compartment that didn't exist. As a child these secret compartments fascinated me. I loved to open them and examine the clever construction. It was here that Grandpa hid his most valuable things, including his gun. My saddest memory of Grandpa Bobby was when he was dying. I recall going to his hospital room. There was Grandpa lying in bed. He had cancer, and we all knew he was going to die soon. At one point Grandpa needed to use the bathroom, and I was the only one in the room. I had to lift him up, help him walk to the bathroom and hold him up as he urinated. The worst thing was the look in his eyes. He had a haunting gaze of desperation and fear. Here was a strong man and, despite all of his strength, the thought of facing death made him weak. It hurt to see a pillar of strength turn soft.

The only part of the funeral I recall was that the family rode in a limousine. We were all quiet and sad, especially my mother. At this same time I had a history book report due for history class. Perhaps because of my preoccupation, I did poorly on this assignment. My teacher, Mister I, asked if there was something going on that made me do so poorly. I lied and told him that nothing was wrong. I thought I was being strong, like Grandpa Bobby.

I found out a little later that Grandpa Bobby had left the family some money. However, our cousin Alfredo was left out of the will and got nothing. Grandpa heard he was doing drugs. My mother asked me if I wanted anything from Grandpa's house. The only thing I desired was his gun. "No, you can't have that," she said. Uncle Mort had already given it to the police. I'm sure she wouldn't have given it to me under any circumstance.

I wrote a song about Grandpa Bobby. He was what he was; someone who was always good and nice to me. Whenever he was near, I felt a genuine love from him. Somehow, he is still a part of me.

FOURTH AND FIFTH GRADE

As I take my journey through the past, I am amazed how certain things remain crystal clear, yet some things I cannot recall at all. I have slight memories of first grade and kindergarten. Second and third grade draw a total blank. I cannot even remember my teachers' names. On the other hand, fourth and fifth grade are vivid. Even as I write, I recall things that have been hidden for over thirty years. My journey through the past and dealing with those painful memories lurking in my subconscious has helped me in the present,

My fourth grade teacher was Mrs. B and, having such a position, she played a major role in my life. In all honesty, if I could evaluate fourth grade with a pass or fail mark, I would readily give it a fail without a doubt, and here's the evidence as to why.

Mrs. B had a habit of getting angry. Small insignificant things like talking or laughing would set her off in a rage. Most of the time, I couldn't figure out what the class had done wrong. Love is patient and not quick to anger. When she got angry I'd be full of fear and terror. I always had great respect for authority figures, so when Mrs. B went into a rage, I would sit wide-eyed, staring at her with tears of anguish forming in my eyes. I always wanted things to go smoothly and by the book, with no waves or wrinkles. Stability was something that home didn't offer, so I found comfort in the rigors of school. When my teacher got angry, I would retreat into myself.

There were varying degrees of her anger. It went from bad

to worse. If she was somewhat angry, her face would turn red. If the anger increased, she would turn bright purple. Finally, at her ultimate rage, she would turn bright red again. She sat in the front of the class with all the students neatly lined up in rows. The children had small desks consisting of a connected chair and table. Mrs. B had a huge desk with a wooden top and metal drawers. One day she got so angry, she kicked her heavy desk and moved it several inches. It was the angriest I had ever seen a human being. In her fit of fury, she broke the tiles on the floor that day. This was the woman to whom parents entrusted their most precious little ones.

Mrs. B had a way of making the most interesting things seem terrible and boring. Take poetry for example. I've come to love poetry now, despite Mrs. B. Poetry for her consisted of generally selected love poems, which I considered to be boring and meaningless works. I cannot recall one poem or poet, but what I do remember is her writing the poems on the chalkboard, line after line. Then, in unison, we would recite the poem over and over. We had a special poetry notebook, and we were forced to copy the poem exactly, word for word, all of which was dull and boring to me.

Other things were also tainted by my instructor, including the Bible. I don't know how, but one day we got off the subject of the lesson and began talking about the Bible. We were discussing the Psalms in particular. Mrs. B asked the students if they knew a particular Psalm. To her horror only one student, Kathy, raised her hand. Kathy could, in fact, quote it completely. I, however, didn't even know what a Psalm was. I had never read the Bible at all. Mrs. B criticized and condemned all of us as ignorant heathens for not knowing much about the Scripture. What a blown opportunity! If the teacher had simply taken out her Bible and read to us rather than condemned our ignorance, I believe I would have started to read the Bible at a much earlier age.

Another area she bungled was geography. I loved geography. In fact I was in possession of two atlases. One was a gift from my Grandpa Bobby, and it was my favorite book in the world. It was a great little leather-bound atlas from the period between World War One and World War Two. My Dad also owned a large current atlas, and I was fascinated when comparing the two. Being from different times in history the borders of the countries were drawn and redrawn. I was especially fond of the maps of Poland, where all my Grandparents had lived.

But again my teacher made this subject dull and boring. Our geography lessons consisted of memorizing the names of all the counties in New Jersey. We never did anything interesting like look at pictures of the places we were studying. Mrs. B would never tie in history like Washington's battles from the Revolutionary War or the Native Americans' lives. No, all we were left with was a faceless list of sinister names to commit to memory. And of course spelling was counted.

I'll never forget the day Mrs. B looked at my hand and asked, "Is that a mood ring?" Mood rings were the rage of the time. They would turn different colors, supposedly revealing your mood.

"Yes it is," I said.

Mrs. B retorted, "I have an obsidian ring," upon which she flashed her black stoned ring on her finger. "My friend asked me if it was a mood ring. I can't believe she thought it was a piece of crap like that."

Black was indeed a good color for Mrs. B. Where was her compassion? Where was her nurturing nature? Where was the love? That comment has stuck with me this long. It's amazing the impact a few negative words can have on a person.

But despite all the bad, there was good. Mrs. B, I believe, found me to be her favorite student. She seemed to like the fact that I was interested in geography, and one day she called me to the front of the class to display my knowledge. I gave a talk about the two Chinas: the mainland known as Red China and the Island Formosa known as Taiwan. I drew the two different flags on the chalkboard, and I also compared the sizes of the world's countries in area and population. I still remember the Soviet Union is the largest in area, followed by Canada, China and the United States. China is the largest in population, followed by India, the Soviet Union and the United States.

One day I brought the complete works of O. Henry to class. To be honest, I actually thought it was about the baseball player

Hank Aaron. Mrs. B asked me if I was reading the book. Indeed I was. She was amazed. Then she flattered me in front of the whole class. "John" she said, "is reading a high school level book and he's only in the fourth grade." I soaked up the praise and attention willingly. I felt smart, and it felt good. I actually read a few of the stories. I vividly remember "The Gift of the Magi," a story about two poor young lovers. The woman had beautiful hair, and, in order to buy her husband a gift for Christmas, she cut and sold it. She used the money to buy him a beautiful chain for his beloved watch. Unfortunately, her husband had sold his watch in order to buy her a set of expensive combs for her hair. I guess that was my first lesson in irony.

I also recall a shameful time in my life from the fourth grade. I was by no means a popular person, but I did have my own little gang. It was Pete who later moved away, but Kevin, Pete, and I terrorized a fellow classmate named Jess, often beating him up. At three against one, it was very cowardly and unfair. We'd twist his arms and give him nuggies. A nuggie is smacking the top of the head with a fist and then rubbing the hard knuckles against the head. In order for us to stop the torment and torture, he had to recite a saying: "I am slime, slime is the lowest form of life, there is nothing lower than slime. I am slime." I feel awful for what I did, and I often wonder why I would do that to an innocent person. My early childhood was very violent to say the least. My life at home was far from pleasant and stable. I believe I lashed out because I was hurting inside. It somehow helped me to make someone else suffer. That is the only answer I can come up with.

When I was about twenty-two years old, I happened upon Jess. He was working for the water company reading water meters. I apologized for my behavior in the fourth grade. He graciously accepted my apology. I'll never forget his response: "I always considered it just part of growing up." Jess actually became a very good friend of mine, though from time to time, with great disgust, he'd remember our past.

My fourth and fifth grade experiences were as different from each other as night and day. As wicked as Mrs. B was, Mrs. F, my fifth grade teacher, was the opposite. Whereas I had been Mrs.

B's favorite student, I believe Mrs. F didn't like me at all. I was quite a nasty person. But where Mrs. B would attack and alienate a student she didn't like, Mrs. F did none of those things. She was quite the professional.

Mrs. F encouraged us to study. She would allow students to make a bet on their test grades. The terms of the covenant were as follows: If the student got an A, you were rewarded with an ice cream from the teacher. If, however, the student got a D or worse, the student had to give Mrs. F a Marathon bar. In order to make the bet, you simply had to write your name on the chalkboard. I won at least once, maybe twice, and never lost. Some of the girls lost but they made good on their bet. The idea was to encourage us to study. I didn't study; I was just good at school. I attribute this to the fact that I enjoyed reading and read a great deal. I also paid attention in class and had a remarkable memory.

I was usually the first student to finish and turn in my test. While waiting for the other students to finish, we were allowed to work on a jigsaw puzzle. There was a girl named Joelle who had a crush on me, but I never knew that she liked me until the sixth grade. She would hand in her test early just so she could be with me doing the puzzle. I was incredibly shy, especially around girls, so nothing ever came of it. My self-esteem was so low that it never occurred to me that a girl would have affection for me.

However, I did have a crush on a girl named Veronica. I didn't think she was nice looking or that she had a great personality. I liked her because she was smart. Like me, she got excellent grades. To me, we were two gears on the same machine. I thought I was superior to everyone else because I was smart in school. Veronica, being smart as well, was worthy of my affections. I attribute this attitude to my father's influence. He placed a great deal of importance on education. He would boast in arrogance about his PhD. I never asked Veronica out though; I only thought about it.

One of the things we did in class was read aloud from a book. Some of us would read as fast as we could get the words out. Each student would read one paragraph, then the student who had just finished reading would pick the next reader. It became a popularity contest. I was usually selected near the end. Each student could read only once so there was no other choice. However, one classmate named Donald would choose me to read all the time.

One time Donald and I, along with the rest of the class, were in an assembly. The entire school was gathered in the gym to see a play. At the time, there was a popular song sung by the rock group Queen called "We Will Rock You." Donald and I were imitating the song, banging our knees twice and then clapping. Mrs. F told us to stop. Donald wisely stopped but I foolishly continued to have my fun. Our teacher was extremely upset. Unlike Mrs. B in fourth grade, I couldn't tell that she was upset by her demeanor but only by her punishment for my infraction. Mrs. F's method of discipline was writing out the entire spelling list multiple times. The punishment was usually five or ten copies, but for my rowdy clapping I had to write the spelling list fifty times. To make matters worse, that week the words were very complicated.

The playground in particular was a place of torment for me. The cool kids wore Levi jeans and purple Puma sneakers. I was constantly teased for wearing hand-me-downs, cheap shoes and floods. Floods are pants that are too short and look like someone's expecting to walk through floodwaters.

I was quite the violent child. One day during lunch, for no good reason, I started a fight with my friend Kevin. I have no idea why I did this; Kevin never did me any wrong. Though I was a lot smaller, I got the better of the fight. I pounded Kevin with punch after punch until he dropped. I didn't stop until an old woman named Grandma, the lunch aide, broke up the conflict. Because the fight happened at the end of lunch, we were ushered back into class instead of the principal's office. Though not one punch hit me, I started to cry. The tears came from a deep pain and aching in my heart. It was another miserable day in a miserable life. When we got back to class, Mrs. F was informed about the fight. "Kevin, you should be ashamed of picking on someone John's size," she said.

A student named Craig interrupted her and said, "Are you kidding? John killed him." Mrs. F, out of character, snapped, "Why you little…" but then abruptly became silent.

In that moment she presented an air of discipline. It would have been right to chastise me for the fight because I had provoked it. Furthermore, I believe Mrs. F thought I was somehow faking my tears. But as a professional, she kept her cool and responded with stern discipline. Mrs. B would have bellowed and screamed uncontrollably.

The school was collecting Campbell Soup labels. There was a promotion going on that schools could receive equipment and supplies for exchanging the labels. My Grandpa Bobby ate a great deal of Campbell Soup and he'd been saving the labels for a long time. The clever Mrs. F had a method to encourage us to bring in labels. For every five labels we would get a small piece of candy. I turned in hundreds of labels. After Mrs. F counted my collection, I received my booty of candy. I nearly took all the candy from her large jar. All my fellow students lined up. They each took a piece of candy from me. Greedy as I was back then, I wanted to keep it all for myself.

Fourth and fifth grade are, of course, distant memories. Looking back, I see the kindness and nobility in Mrs. F and the contrasting nastiness of Mrs. B. It is ironic that the one I remember with fondness most likely held a lower opinion of me. On the other hand, the one who seemed to care about me, I really didn't like at all. We can't always control how we perceive people, and we definitely can't control how people perceive us. This is another lesson I would have to learn later in life.

Sixth Grade and Talking to Girls

Sixth grade involved going to a brand new school, commonly called PV, an abbreviation of Pequannock Valley. It was a classic red brick building with two floors. There were also portables in the back, large trailers used as classrooms. It was in these trailers that the sixth grade classes were held. Not only was the physical environment different from fourth and fifth grade, but there were new kids in our classes as well.

One of these new students was Merlin. He had a mole on his cheek about the size of a nickel. Most of the kids looked down on him, labeling him as one of the dreaded "dirt bags," a term which was used to describe dirty kids. True to form, one day it was announced that Merlin was going to miss school for a while; he had gotten lice in his hair. Everyone was horrified. We had studied lice in health class, and had learned how nasty these tiny beings were. To realize these things actually existed in real life was quite a shock to me. As an adult I realize that all kids are susceptible to lice, even clean ones, but at the time it was horrifying.

The tough kids crowd, from which I was excluded, used to give kids wedgies. It's a both painful and humiliating form of bullying. I speak from experience when I say a wedgie can ruin your day. To add insult to injury, after the deed was done, the bully would often scream "wedgie! wedgie!" Then the whole class would stare, point fingers and laughter would flood the air. I was the shortest kid in the class, which made me a very tempting target. But still, Merlin was the more desirable target. One day he received the king of wedgies. Not only did they pull his underpants up, they hung him from the metal fence by the extended underpants. There was poor Merlin, six feet high struggling with violent twists and turns in a futile attempt to get free. He flopped like a fish out of water. The whole class gathered around laughing hysterically. I laughed too; I was glad it wasn't me up on the fence.

Merlin was very strange. I guess that was the reason for most of the abuse. He would throw quarters and dollar bills on the ground, and then laughed as the children scrambled to grab the money. Usually, when this was going on, a large crowd would gather and Merlin would toss the quarter right in the middle. We would dive and fight for the little bit of money. Merlin would get a good chuckle out of it. One day he was throwing silver coins around. They were old, and we all knew they were valuable. But he wasn't throwing them in his usual fashion. He was just randomly tossing them around. He threw them so quickly that we couldn't even find them. My friend Freddie suggested that we return after the school day was over to continue the search, so that's what we did. We returned and started walking on the black asphalt surface where the coins lay hidden. Every few minutes, I would say, "found one," and pick up a coin. Freddie would get mad and we'd continue looking. I found a handful of coins but I don't think Freddie found any.

Unfortunately, Merlin and I ended up fighting. I have no idea now what it was about, but I remember the fight clearly. For some unknown reason, I closed my eyes. I had been in plenty of fights before, and I had never done this. I blindly threw punch after punch. Even with my eyes shut, I struck Merlin in the face over and over. I must have landed a dozen good blows. Merlin didn't even get one shot in. Finally, a teacher came and broke up the fight. As we were escorted into the principal's office, the other kids started cheering. I don't know if they cheered because I had just beaten up Merlin, or if they were cheering because they were getting rid of both of us. Freddie commented to our friend Donald that I had gotten lucky in the fight because my eyes were closed.

Donald quickly replied, "yeah, but he beat him up good." As usual, I couldn't but cry after I calmed down. I always felt great remorse after fighting; I didn't like it when I hurt others.

I got brave one day and asked out a girl named Lana. She was, of course, taller than me, and she had short brown hair. She had a nice figure, at least for what you could expect in the sixth grade, and boy did I have a big crush for her.

I just walked up to her and out of the blue said, "Lana will you go out with me?" She looked at me and started laughing. I took this as a bad sign. But then she quickly said, "Yes." Needless to say, I felt amazing. It should be said that Lana claimed to be a witch. When the kids found this out, they would torment her by asking her, "Are you a good witch, a bad witch, or a sandwich?"

My friends, of course, started teasing me because I had a girlfriend. The fact that it was a good thing and that they didn't have girlfriends didn't matter. I remember the little rhyme that they sang.

"John and Lana sitting in the tree. First comes love, then comes marriage, then comes little John in the baby carriage. Sucking his thumb, wetting his pants, doing the hoola hoola dance."

They would sing this song over and over, but it really didn't bother me. I'd had way worse things happen to me already.

Freddie made fun of my relationship with Lana. I remember Freddie, Donald, and I were hanging out in Freddie's back yard. He started to rip me about Lana, but Donald came to my defense. "At least he's got a girlfriend," he said. This line of reasoning finally silenced Freddie, who had no girlfriend.

Lana and I, alas, only had one date, and it turned out to be a group thing. We met at an ice cream place called Friendly's. Lana brought her friends Agnes and Joy. We ordered some food, talked and had a nice time.

Soon after that, Lana and I broke up. I don't recall why or even if there was a reason. We got so mad at one another that we literally got in a spitting fight. She would spit at me, and I would spit back at her. Then she dumped an ice cream bar over my head; so much for puppy love. I felt like crying, but I never did.

Mrs. P taught the majority of my sixth grade classes. One of the fun things we did was an assignment to build a spacecraft. The spaceship would be tossed off the roof of the school, to simulate a landing from outer space as the vessel returned to Earth's gravity. Inside the spacecraft we were to put an egg, which represented the astronaut. If the egg survived the impact without breaking, then we were successful in our design. I was determined to keep my astronaut safe, so I built a wooden box with four nails on each of the bottom corners. The nails were meant to absorb the energy of the fall. On the day of testing the janitor climbed to the roof, and, one by one, dropped the ships, all of them crashed fast to the ground. It was an exciting day. Almost everyone's spacecraft was a success. In addition to the egg not breaking, it was also tested for internal damage. The eggs were cracked open to see if the insides were intact. Only one girl's egg was damaged internally. She immediately started crying when she saw her damaged egg. Mrs. P rewarded everybody with an ice cream, even the girl with the Humpty Dumpty astronaut. Merlin didn't even bother to make a spaceship. At first Mrs. P wasn't going to give him an ice cream, but she relented. Mrs. P had a kind heart.

I also had a math teacher named Mrs. L. We called her Like a Witch, it was a word play of her last name, but it accurately described her personality. Both my sister and brother had her as a math teacher when they were in sixth grade. Neither of them liked her. She was nasty and complained constantly. I remember her complaining about her husband and, for some strange reason, her alarm clock. Her husband must have been some poor soul to have married a woman like that. She even resembled a witch physically, at least the stereotypical version of the ugly witch.

One day she handed out math books, and instructed us to thoroughly examine each page and record each mark and defect. This was so we wouldn't be fined for damaging the already soiled books. I, unfortunately, made the mistake of writing the information in the front cover of the book. I may have been very intelligent, but simple things baffled me sometimes. My friends, particularly Freddie, would always say that I had book smarts but no common sense. Freddie was right. When Mrs. L. found out that I had written in the textbook she was livid. She screamed and hollered and was so angry she sent me to the principal's office with a pink slip, which was a notice for inappropriate behavior that required a parent's signature. I was immediately in tears as I took the long walk to the principal's office. In hindsight, I realize what a miserable woman she was. All she needed to do was say I did something wrong. There was no maliciousness in my action; it was a simple mistake. Usually pink slips are reserved for bad grades or improper conduct. And, despite all the fighting in my youth, this was the only warning notice that I had ever received.

Coach F made sixth grade memorable. He was the health teacher, the one who told us about lice. He was very athletic and muscular, but very short. I think he might have been around five feet tall. To match his short stature, he also had an extremely short temper. He would yell and scream at the slightest infraction. I think he had some psychological complex because of his height. I think he felt people weren't doing what he wanted because he was so short. Whatever the reason, he was a tyrant. One day the class was chattering while he was teaching. Sixth graders have a short attention span, especially when they're bored. In a wild burst of fury Coach F grabbed a wooden beam that was holding the window open and slammed it down as hard as he could on a desk. Unfortunately for me, he had chosen my desk to whack the wooden stick on. I was so startled that I sat up straight and erect like a soldier coming to attention. I'm lucky my fingers weren't smashed to a pulp as he could have accidentally hit them. Then he began to rant and rave. I was quite traumatized.

Wrestling began for me when I joined the team in sixth grade at P.V. The so-called professionals on television, especially Dusty Rhodes, inspired me. Dusty Rhodes was a blonde-haired wrestler who was heavy but muscular. He would always fight the bigger and stronger Superstar Bill Graham. Dusty would consistently lose these fights, getting bloodied up in the process. But Dusty had spirit, always ready to make another go at it.

I was very small and I was in the lowest weight class possible. A wrestling match at this level is only six minutes, and not even six continuous minutes. There are three two-minute periods with many breaks. But you can't even begin to imagine how much this could tire a person out unless you've experienced it yourself.

The teammates weren't mean but they weren't very nice. I wasn't ostracized, but I certainly wasn't accepted. One day the coach made an announcement after practice, "From now on nobody goes home without a shower; somebody didn't shower last night." That somebody was me and I was glad that the coach didn't mention me by name. It would have humiliating for me. I recall the other wrestlers' reactions of disgust and disbelief. I had never been taught at home that I should shower every day.

I eventually left the team. I wasn't really that interested in it and I began to miss more and more of the practices. I practiced with different people, but all of them seemed to quit. This discouraged me. Finally the coach called me in and asked if I was on the team or not. He wanted a firm commitment, was I in or was I out. He didn't try to persuade me to continue; if he had, I may have stuck with it. I told him that I quit, but the practices weren't wasted. I was in good physical shape and could do push-ups with ease. That year, during gym class we wrestled, and I was able to pin my opponent rather quickly.

Freddie's grandfather would always pick him up from school. He was affectionately known amongst us friends as Gramps. He cursed like a drunken sailor, frequently using God's name in vain, and would complain chronically about his grandson being spoiled, but whenever Freddie needed a ride, he was always there in his silver car. It was like Freddie had his own private limousine driver. Without fail, Gramps was always the first in line. He would come an hour early and sit in his car reading his newspaper. Why he came so early, we never did know. But we found it funny, and it gave us a chuckle every day. "There's Gramps," we'd say at two o'clock, looking out the window.

My English teacher's name was Mrs. C, and she had a great dislike, if not an outright hatred, for me. She would criticize me and ridicule me. In her eyes, I could do no right. Every answer I gave had some fault, and her replies were seasoned with insults. In my opinion, she would give me lower grades than I deserved, which always left me feeling a great apprehension in her class. Fortunately for me, Mrs. C got pregnant and a substitute teacher, Mrs. A, completed the year. She treated me fine. I recall one day

I answered something about a boyfriend. A student mocked me teasing, "John has a boyfriend." Mrs. A cut the laughing short by saying she had many girlfriends and that it was just an expression. It felt good to be defended; Mrs. C most likely would have just laughed at me.

Why Mrs. C was so vindictive, I will never know. Nurturing is good; dislike and hatred destroys, especially when it comes from a teacher. I held teachers and authority figures in high esteem. I think somehow I connected them to God; they were people to be obeyed and not questioned. Thus it was more painful when I was met with their rejection. The negatives at this point in my life greatly outweighed the positives, and I wasn't receiving love and support at home either. It was during this time that my self-esteem sank, and I felt insecure about myself. It was as though I was never worthy.

MYRON

I wasn't very popular at school, and I didn't have another girlfriend until after high school. I never even had a date. In the seventh grade, I had a crush on a girl named Daisy. She had lovely long red hair, and, more importantly, she was short like me. Daisy liked to hang out with the girls who smoked cigarettes and went to parties. I never went to parties, mostly because my classmates disliked me. I never once received an invitation. I was very shy around girls and quite awkward. I told my friends, the few that I had, that I liked Daisy. Somehow one whisper led to another whisper, and word got out. The rumors came back to me one day before math class. Gertrude, one of Daisy's friends, gave me a warning. "You'd better leave Daisy alone if you know what's good for you," she said, in a very threatening manner. My hopes were dashed, and I retreated into my private realm of terror, a domain where I felt everybody detested me. I'm still not sure these feelings were accurate today. What I do know, however, is that I experienced a fair share of cruelty.

In the eighth grade, I had affections for a girl named Maggie. She sat on the opposite side of the room from me in English class and I had a good view of her. It took me months to get the courage to ask her for a date. My friend Alexander walked me over to Maggie one day after school. Alexander wasn't necessarily being nice. He was just making sure I wouldn't chicken out. I meekly blurted out, "Maggie, will you go out with me?"

Maggie stared me down and without a moment's hesitation

said, "No." The quickness and abruptness with which she reacted rang the rejection hard to stomach.

When I made it to high school, things deteriorated even further. First of all, I was the shortest kid in the class. I may have been tough, but a tough seventy-five pound high schooler really didn't cut it. Secondly, my brother Bert, who preceded me, was very unpopular. All the upper classmen knew Bert and associated the two of us. I got a black mark just for being a Kaniecki.

Possibly the worst moment of my high school career came in my first year. In gym class the sophomores and the freshman were grouped together. One day, when we were walking in from the day's activities, a sophomore named Conway walked up to me and said, "You don't look like a John. You look like a Myron." Everybody heard the comment and laughed at me. A chorus of "Myron, Myron, Myron," followed me in as we went to change in the locker room. The nickname spread through school like wildfire, blazing as if it were in a forest that hadn't had rain in a year. As innocent as the name was I hated it with a passion; it was far worse than John John. I cringed every time I heard it, which was frequently. Nobody called me by my real name anymore, except teachers. It wasn't a joke; it was a mockery.

Without a doubt, I suffered from paranoia. Perhaps it was also true that a lot of the kids had it out for me. But it went further than that. I always thought others were talking about me. I was in a constant state of panic. I was conscious of the way I walked, the way I talked, the clothes I wore and how my hair was combed. I would fix my hair a different way each morning, just begging to fit in. I had no sense of self-worth. I thought I was dirt and no good. I thought almost everyone hated me. This was especially true when someone shouted out the name Myron, and everyone would laugh hysterically. The paranoia was a pressure cooker. I was tense, nervous and could not relax. I was constantly on edge; I was afraid somebody was going to physically strike me. In hindsight, the concern about being beaten up wasn't realistic, but the verbal mockery was constant, as were the ill feelings from others. I dreaded going to school every morning.

Like most high schools throughout the country, the students

separated themselves into cliques. The athletes, better known as The Jocks, made up one group. Some of them bullied me and they definitely didn't want me in their company. Another group was made up of band members, better known as The Bandies. They were very tight and had broken down the barriers of age. Freshman, sophomores, juniors and seniors interacted with one another. They were connected by shared experiences in music classes. They sat together in one group at the tables during lunch, and they tended to be preppy, dressing nicely with dress shirts and sweaters. They also tended to take school seriously and get good grades. A lot of The Bandies were in my classes because I took a number of honors courses. But still, The Bandies rejected me. I wasn't in the band, and I didn't dress like them. My attire was simple, consisting of jeans and t-shirts. While they weren't violent, they were cruel. They would ignore me and look down on me. They socially excluded me. The only interaction we had was full of derision; they gave me the impression that I wasn't as good as them. In other words, I was mocked and ignored.

There was also The Burnouts. These were the people who drank alcohol and used drugs; they always considered themselves to be cool. They would brag about their wild weekends getting high. They used the term Weekend Warriors to refer to themselves. I, on the other hand, didn't party at all. In fact, I didn't attend a party until my senior year. A couple of The Burnouts didn't like me. I didn't fit in well with this group either because we had nothing in common. They tended to take the easiest courses, so we never shared classes.

In high school society, the kids who were left out tended to find each other. Therefore, I ended up with a handful of friends. They, like me, really didn't fit into any of the groups. They were my island of comfort in a sea of turmoil. But even my friends would call me Myron, especially when they were around others outside our little clique, and that always hurt.

I'll always remember the cliques at my school. I'll especially remember a handful of the students that caused me pain. There was a kid named Paul in my study hall freshman year. He was a senior who was, of course, much bigger than me. He was also extremely stupid, perhaps bordering on being retarded. I knew it bothered him because he would often criticize a girl from his history class for being dumb. Then he would say, "I'm not retarded like her." But his argument was never convincing; I still didn't think he was any brighter. He was a big drinker; he mostly hung out with The Burnouts. He was nice to me in a way; he would talk to me and act friendly. Most people wouldn't even talk to me, unless it was to insult me. But Paul was very sociable and talked to everyone, including me.

However Paul did have a very unpleasant ritual in study hall. When I arrived to class, the teacher wasn't usually there yet, so Paul would pick me up and drop me out the window. Thank God the high school only had one floor. I would then have to run to the door to get back into the building. I ran as quickly as I could, so I would beat the ringing of the tardy bell. While I was outside, Paul would push all the desks around. The desks were always in a very neat row, but after Paul was done they were in chaotic disarray. The teacher who proctored the study hall would walk in and have to spend fifteen minutes carefully putting the desks together. She didn't realize it was Paul who had made them messy.

This went on for a while until I finally had had enough and simply refused to get thrown out the window. Instead, I threw an eraser at Paul, and ducked when he threw it back. Then I tossed a container of cleaning powder at him. As the can sailed through the air, all its contents spilled on the floor creating one giant mess. Paul picked it up and threw it back at me. The fight only escalated from there. By the time the teacher arrived, the room was a disaster. She was livid and quickly told me to go to the principal's office. Paul, on the other hand, wasn't reprimanded at all. I believe the teacher was afraid of Paul. If Paul were told to go to the principal's office, he would have refused to go and would have thrown a fit. On my way to the principal's office I ran into Conway, the same boy who gave me my nickname. When I told him what had happened, he told me to just hang out in the hall and not go to the principal's office. I did exactly that and never got in trouble. I was upset and embarrassed but at least I didn't get thrown out the window that day.

It seemed the people I felt were friends consistently proved otherwise. I had another friend named Craig who had just bought a car. He and I were hanging out one afternoon, when we decided to get some pizza. I, of course, didn't have a car, so I asked for a ride in his new wheels.

Craig looked at me and said, "Are you kidding? Someone might see you." I was crushed by the rejection. Was I that embarrassing? I guess he wasn't a real friend after all. I took French my sophomore year. I sat next to a football player named Bernard. He was very heavy and most kids called him Grimace, after the character in the McDonald's commercials. One day, for some reason that I can't remember, I called him fat.

Another classmate, Alvin, reprimanded me, claiming I wasn't being nice. I realized that Alvin was right, and I felt bad about what I had said. That's when I began to think about the other students and how they treated me. There was a great injustice in it all. After all, why didn't Alvin ever defend me if he was so righteous? Where was Alvin every time some kid called me Myron? The more I ruminated on my own guilt for calling Bernard fat, the more frustrated I became with my being bullied every day. I began to feel more and more helpless. The same Alvin was in my gym class senior year. We were playing football in gym class. I was an excellent receiver because my friends and I played football a great deal. My team was doing well and I was catching ball after ball. Alvin got frustrated and punched me in my face. Though he hit me as hard as he could, it didn't faze me and I just stared at him. Alvin was a lot bigger than me, so I just turned around and walked away. But I think my evil look, coupled with the fact that he had hit me as hard as he could and I just shrugged it off, disturbed him.

There was a skinny punk named Michael who liked to call me gay. He said I went to a gay bar in New York City called the Ram Rod. In truth, he really didn't bother me much. I just ignored his rants. I could have easily beaten him up, but I had lost my belief in violence. After the seventh grade, I realized fighting wasn't the best way to solve things. I was the smallest boy in my class, and I was smart enough to figure out that I couldn't compete physically with the larger boys. I just took the insults, and let them slide when I could. I later heard that Michael got married, and then divorced only a year later. I sometimes wonder if he was a homosexual himself and mocked me because he was in denial about being gay. Years later, I would discuss this issue with a psychologist. He explained that calling someone gay could simply be an expression of hostility. This talk helped me gain a better understanding of my past. Talking things over is a great remedy. It offers both insight and puts things in perspective.

I must admit that, like most abused kids, I abused others as well. In particular, there was a skinny kid named Ralph. He was lactose intolerant, so he couldn't drink milk. He also had huge lips that stood out, especially due to his gaunt frame. My friends and I used to call him Moo Lips.

I mocked him every day at lunch. I had no excuse except that I simply followed the crowd. I never liked being ridiculed but when I made fun of someone else it made me feel a little better about myself. I never had a good example to follow; everyone picked on someone and to some degree, everyone got picked on.

My teachers never reached out to me, with the exception of Mr. M. He was my teacher for both geometry and calculus. Somehow we just clicked. He was very kind and always encouraged me to work hard. I recall calling geometry angles crazy names like double zero and negative double zero. He just took it in stride and laughed with me. The class sizes were small, so he was able to give me a good amount of attention. In my senior year I was happy to have him again for calculus. Mr. M made math enjoyable. He even influenced me to go into engineering school. I eventually earned a mathematics degree from Montclair State University. Mr. M was, without a doubt, the most influential teacher in my life.

Mr. W was a French teacher. During my senior year, he called me to his office. Though I had taken French, he had not been my teacher. He sat me down and gave me a lecture. He told me I should take life more seriously and be more responsible. He shared with me how wonderfully responsible he was. He was a good baseball pitcher in college, so a major league ball club eventually drafted him. However, he abandoned his dreams of playing baseball in the big leagues to, instead, become a high school French teacher. I walked out of the lecture thinking that he was a loser to give up on his dreams. Perhaps if Mr. W had been kind to me and nurtured a relationship with me, I would have listened to him. But he treated me very coldly and was not in the least bit nice, so his giving me advice seemed inappropriate. I had no respect for the man at all, so his words carried no weight.

Over twenty years later, I would be a temporary worker at UPS. I worked with a man named Don. We had plenty of time to talk things over as we drove around in the brown truck. One day I told Don about my odd experience with Mr. W. He claimed the teacher was full of shit. Don was a good athlete in high school, the captain of his football team. Don believed that everyone who played a sport seriously had a dream of making the big leagues one day, and Mr. W abandoning that chance did not make any sense at all. In reflection, I agree that he was a fake.

Some of the teachers had a great dislike for me. One in particular was my physics teacher, Mr. B. All the other students mocked him; they called him Chucky B. I never mocked him and always treated him with respect. For some reason, I had sympathy for him. He was extremely short, so that may have won my compassion. Upon graduation, I needed a written recommendation for acceptance into Edwards Institute of Technology. And, since Edwards is an engineering school, I asked Mr. B. His reply was, "You're one student who never lived up to your ability."

"But I got a B plus in your class," I responded, a little hurt and confused. He remained adamant in his refusal to write the letter. All he accomplished was losing the little respect I had for him. In the end, I got into Edwards anyway, but I would never understand why Mr. B felt that way about me.

One of the worst things I've done in my life occurred senior year. There was a highly intelligent and hardworking girl named Hannah in my AP Chemistry class. She was a genuinely nice person. I would sometimes copy her homework assignments. She was a bit socially awkward and awfully shy. One day, out of nowhere, Hannah asked me to the prom. I replied with a cold, "No." I was so insecure with myself that I couldn't accept the invitation. I was and am deeply sorry for my action. Later in the psychiatric hospital, I felt particularly guilty about this. When I told Ned, one of the psychiatric nurses, the story, he told me not to be upset. Rejection is something we all deal with. In reflection, I realize Hannah was one of the best people in my high school. She never made fun of me and always accepted me as I was. There is a short list of people whom I truly feel deserve my apology, and Hannah is certainly at the top of that list.

High school had done its damage. It hadn't made me angry, but it did, however, make me bitter. I felt life was a dreary prison, and I needed to escape. I longed for college or, for that matter, any place where I wasn't known as Myron.

BUSBOY

My first employment was at Solomon Hospital, in Pompton Plains when I was fourteen years old. My title was Junior Volunteer, the male counterpart of the candy striper. The young ladies with whom I worked with all wore red dresses and white stripes, thus the nickname. I, however, was spared the dress and wore a yellow dress shirt and brown slacks.

It was my friend Jess' idea to volunteer. I only worked one night a week, although sometimes Jess and I would go simply to hang out with our new friends. We basically worked as waiters in the hospital restaurant. It was rarely busy, so we worked at a relaxed pace. Even though we had to remain responsible, we did have a good amount of fun.

Jess, being a smooth talker, made a great impression with all the candy stripers. They all had crushes on him. Jess had a good heart and was a generous person, but I still think his true motivation for volunteering was to be around the candy stripers. I remember a few years later when Jess and I were walking in Manhattan by the Port Authority Bus Station, a man in dirty disheveled clothes approached Jess and asked him for money to buy food. Jess took out a couple of dollars and ordered a hot dog from a nearby street vender. I naively objected saying, "Jess don't do that."

Jess simply replied by saying, "The man is hungry." I was seventeen and so naive. It never occurred to me that truly hungry people existed. It never occurred to me that there were people who didn't have nice homes with warm beds. Everyone I had ever known was similar to me and shared the same comforts. By objecting to Jess feeding a homeless man, I only proved my insensitivity and lack of compassion.

As I mentioned already, all the girls loved Jess. I was only accepted as a friend. He was a smooth talker and good looking enough. He always had a girlfriend and never had trouble meeting new girls. I was the opposite. Being around girls made me nervous. The problem was that I really didn't understand people, male or female. There was a great disconnect between other people and me, even my friends. I found it difficult both to love and to feel love. This was a painful separation, always causing me to feel all alone in the world. Nobody in my life had ever told me that they loved me. My parents never uttered the words. The first person to give me a genuine hug was my friend Sam, and it wasn't until I was eighteen and in college.

After a great deal of self-reflection and healing, I can now talk to any stranger, male or female. I hug and kiss people without awkwardness or inhibition. Human beings need love expressed to them both verbally and physically. Feeling unloved crushes the spirit, and I am sure it contributed to my psychiatric problems.

Even though I was shy, I was able to become friends with the candy stripers and the other workers in the hospital. I felt comfortable at work, and I enjoyed it a great deal. I flourished in the collegial environment. A proper atmosphere is very important. For those who suffer from psychiatric problems, I would say that a change in scenery to a wholesome and safe environment is as vital as medicine and counseling. After a year of volunteering at the hospital, I graduated to my first real paying job.

Vito's Fine Restaurant was a drab and dull restaurant with poor lighting. It was run down and never seemed clean or tidy. But the food was amazing, so it was always packed with hungry customers. On the weekends, the lines would extend well outside the building. Everyone called it Vito's.

Vito's didn't take reservations; we worked purely on a first come, first served philosophy. The crowds would hang out and talk, sometimes getting drinks from the bar while they waited. The noise filled the entire facility and customers had to yell over the cacophony. Despite the physical drawbacks the place was packed every night; the food was just that good. The smells from the kitchen permeated the dining room and was enough to make mouths water.

In front of Vito's was a Chinese restaurant; we drove by it every night we had work. Night after night, the parking lot was dark and empty. The name constantly changed, indicating yet another new owner. But try as they might, they never succeeded. Vito's, however, would have people waiting for an hour to get in. This held true in rain, snow, heat and cold.

My friend Joe was the first to get hired at Vito's. Like the true friend Joe was, and still is, he helped me land a job too. I can still recall the thrill and anxiety of my first night. It was exciting to finally have a real job. The pay was only minimum wage, three dollars an hour at the time, but it seemed like a great deal of money to me. The idea that I was working for a living made me feel like a man at the young age of sixteen.

Being a busboy was simple. When customers finished eating their food, I would politely take their dishes away. It was important to stay alert and watch to see when they finished. The appetizer plates needed to be removed before the main course arrived in particular. We collected the dirty dishes in a plastic bin, and when the bin was about to overflow with grimy plates and cups, we would unload it at the dishwasher's station.

My friend Peter was the dishwasher. We shared a history class, and he was also on the wrestling team with me. We called him Ace Fireball. Peter took pride in washing dishes and worked as quickly as possible. If there weren't enough dishes, the cooks couldn't serve their food. We used to play a nasty trick on Peter. We would load our bins to the point of them toppling over, and then dumped them in rapid successions, trying to overload Ace Fireball. Sometimes all four busboys would go in one right after the other dumping dirty dishes like an overloaded garbage truck. But try as we might, Peter would always keep up. The cooks would cheer Peter on, chanting his name. I never saw a dishwasher with more pride in his job. Every job has its dignity.

In addition to removing dishes, we had to set the tables up

for the next customers. The tables were covered with white linen cloths. When they got dirty and soiled, usually with tomato sauce, we were supposed to change them. However, Vito's owners were cheap and didn't like spending money for the laundry. So instead of changing dirty linens, we hid the stains by cleverly positioning the napkin holders and bottles of ketchup over the dirty spots. Like I said, the place was a run-down dump, but the food was a heavenly delight at bargain prices.

I'll never forget my first night. I was in the back working hard and sweating away. Customers saw me struggling and would hand me money, mostly just a dollar bill. This happened a few times throughout the night. Joe was working next to me and, near the end of the shift, I asked him how much he usually made in tips. He looked at me bewildered and said, "Tips, what do you mean tips?"

I explained that people were giving me dollars. He was shocked; this had never happened to him in all his time at Vito's. I don't know why I got tips and Joe didn't. Part of it may have been that I looked much younger than him, but that is purely speculation. Perhaps I just worked harder. I continued to get tips, but Joe never did.

An oil painting of Vito hung like a shrine on the wall. He had passed on and left the restaurant to his children, Anthony and Frank. Anthony was the bartender and handled the money, while Frank was the head cook and handled the food supplies and deliveries. They both worked very hard and were good at what they did.

Anthony was more business-like and kept a distance from the employees. He was more like the boss. Frank was a hulk of a man, over six feet in height, and solidly built. His heart was in proportion to his size, though. Frank was a warm and friendly guy. He'd always joke with the workers and sometimes flirt with the waitresses. Frank was even nice to us lowly busboys. We were both professional wrestling fans, so we'd often talk about the latest matches and the wrestlers.

One of the best things about Vito's was that we got a free meal after our shifts. During this time we had some simple chores to attend to, but the food more than compensated for the work.

Our favorite meal was lasagna, which we ordered every night, unless the kitchen ran out of it. I believe heaven itself could not produce better lasagna. Just smelling it was satisfying. It had sausage, chopped meat, and the perfect balance of other ingredients. We'd take the hot plate the lasagna came on and lift it up with napkins, so we wouldn't burn our hands. Then we'd place butter underneath the hot plate. In a minute the butter was melted, ready to be poured on our bread. We then enjoyed our free meal along with our free soda.

The head waitress, Jan, also happened to be the oldest, probably around sixty years old. She was a feisty character with a ton of spirit, and moved surprisingly quickly and nimbly for a woman of her age. She was in charge of the busboys, and for some reason she didn't like Joe all that much. Joe worked hard but she would always accuse him of being lazy. I remember her muttering her mantra in disgust, "What's that Joe doing now?" Somehow she always spotted Joe whenever he wasn't occupied. Joe could never understand Jan's dislike for him, and felt it unjustified. I concurred.

On the other hand, Jan loved me. I worked hard and did a good job. It wasn't long before I was promoted from the back section to the middle. Then, just as quickly, I was in the front. Joe, meanwhile, stayed in the back, even though he had been working there longer than me. The middle was easier than the back and the front was easier than the middle. The back had more tables, and it was a farther trip to the kitchen to unload dishes. The front only had six tables, all of which were Jan's. I enjoyed working the front, mostly because I also got to hang out with the salad girl.

Her name was Cherri, and she was both kind and good looking. She was a year younger than me and had been dating a guy my age for a long time. Cherri was polite to me, but took no interest in me beyond that. One day she asked for some ice, so I pulled out a large bag of ice that was all stuck together. "Could you break it apart?" she inquired. In an effort to impress her, I took the bag and smacked it several times on my forehead, breaking the ice all apart. Cherri said nothing, but her look said it all. It was a look that said I was something other than human, a lingering glance full of apprehension and wonder reserved only for outcasts. And being an outcast, I can testify that it is a cruel look. I would get that look many more times in my life.

In addition to the usual work, the busboys in the front helped cut the bread and make the coffee. The bread was free with all meals, but like I said, the owners were so cheap, so we recycled the bread. Instead of throwing the leftovers away, we saved the larger pieces and served them again. I used to eat the bread with a fierce hunger. Five years after I had left Vito's, I returned to visit. Frank remarked at how big I had gotten. He jokingly attributed it to all the bread I used to eat. There was some truth in his humor.

Working in the front, I got a little spoiled and a little lazy. I took things for granted and slowed down. I also got comfortable as the challenge of the job dissipated with experience. I got bored and my work suffered. Joe and I helped our friend Freddie get a job as a busboy. It was nice to work with friends, and it strengthened the bonds of our relationship. Freddie would eventually replace me in the front. He worked harder, much like I had earlier on. He deserved the promotion. I still stayed in the middle, the second best spot. Joe, despite working there the longest, was doomed to hustle in the back.

Vito's definitely helped me make a good amount of money. The waitresses easily made over a hundred dollars a night in tips. Back in the early eighties, that was a huge amount of money. They had to work hard for their money; they were constantly on the move, carrying heavy trays and attending to customers. All the workers at Vito's were constantly busy with no rest and no breaks. We busboys didn't get a percentage of the tips, as is customary in many other restaurants. Instead, the owners paid us. We would have made a lot more money if we got the percentage. We got paid in cash every night. Anthony kept records on all of our hours and he would take out money for taxes. It was all on the up and up.

Every night Frank took a bag of cash home to deposit when the bank opened the next day. One night two punks approached Frank with knives, intent on robbing him. Frank threw the money into his car. Then the giant of a man turned to face his assailants. Very wisely, however, the criminals turned and ran away. Frank was more than a little intimidating.

Anthony could also be a daunting figure. I'll never forget the day he sat me down. I could tell that he was angry, angrier than I had ever seen him. "Did you take a bottle of liquor?" he questioned me.

"No," I answered honestly.

Anthony had happened to do inventory of the liquor that night. He found that a bottle of Jack Daniels was missing. Suspicious, he went out to the dumpster to investigate. Upon looking around, he found a liquor bottle hidden in the dirty linens. Immediately he suspected the busboys.

He asked Freddie the same question, and Freddie had the same answer. Then he turned to the third busboy. We only knew him through the restaurant. He lived in Lincoln Park and went to a different high school. Fortunately, he admitted to taking the bottle. After the confession, Anthony fired the busboy right away. He didn't even finish his shift, nor did he get paid for the night. He left with his head hung low in disgrace. Freddie and I were exonerated.

My friend, Chester, was one of the cooks. He was a short little guy, and he took a liking to me. He considered me his good luck charm. He would insist that I bet him a dollar on the Ranger's games. Despite my reluctance, I was forced to make the bet. For some reason, Chester would always give me more goals than the spread. As a result, I never lost a bet. However, Chester would bet the other way with his bookie. During the night, Chester would get nervous and give me a quarter, so I could call the sports hotline to get the scores. He'd bet serious money on the hockey games, maybe fifty to a hundred dollars a night. He won most of the time. I was glad because he was very nice to me.

A lot of the customers would tell me that I looked like John Denver. When people said that, I'd reply, "I wish I could sing like him."

There was only one problem with Vito's and that was the location. It sat right on the bank of the river, and, as a result, water would get into the restaurant when it flooded. They would have to wait until the flood dried out. Then the place had to be thoroughly cleaned.

One time the restaurant flooded badly. Instead of the normal couple of days, we were all out of work for weeks. Freddie, who was always more ambitious than me, was diligent in his search for other work, and he quickly discovered an advertisement in the newspaper for busboys.

Freddie called me up, excited to tell me about it. We were both too young to drive, so we had Freddie's grandfather, Gramps, give us a ride, since he lived in the first floor of Freddie's house. And, like I said, he was Freddie's personal chauffer, driving Freddie anywhere he wanted.

So Freddie and I both went to the interview. The restaurant was called The Grayforest, and it was attached to the Happy Inn. Unlike Vito's, it was a very elegant place with a fancy atmosphere. Freddie and I interviewed with the manager, Dan. We both had the same background when it came to our work experience. The only difference was that Freddie had longer hair than I did. Mine was short and proper while Freddie looked like a hippie-wanna-be. Though I didn't know for sure, I believe that that was the reason I was hired. Freddie, unfortunately, was not needed. But I would eventually convince Dan to hire Freddie. After all, he was my friend.

THE GRAYFOREST

The Grayforest was an upscale restaurant. It served most of the people that were staying at the Happy Inn. It was a place where a suit and tie was the rule, not the exception. The food was very good but very expensive, often costing thirty-five dollars—during 1985 that was a lot. The busboys wore white dress shirts, black bow ties, black aprons, black dress pants and black dress shoes.

Other than the classy setting, the job was very similar to Vito's. The tables were more elaborate, with more utensils, glasses and a neatly folded napkin. At the Grayforest we would never use the same tablecloth twice or multiple times as we did at Vito's. Even if the cloth was unstained, we would change it. In addition to taking care of the customers, there was a huge salad bar that needed our attention. It had over a hundred items, so it kept us pretty busy.

It was at the Grayforest that I met a Muslim busboy named Shah. He was born in Palestine and somehow ended up living in Paterson, a rough place where locals were considered tough. To the children in Pompton Plains, where I lived, Paterson was a faraway, a foreign land. It was known by only reputation. Shah was a little shorter than me, had a brown face and a large nose. We quickly became friends.

It was with Shah that I first experienced racism, or should I say I became witness to the injustice of racism. It is true that people had made fun of my Polish heritage. There had been constant jokes, but they mostly came from people that I knew. Even my friends would joke about my ethnicity. I felt that my classmates either liked me or disliked me because of the person I was, not my heritage. The fact that I was called a dumb Pollack was just another way to insult me, like calling someone gay. Yes, the insults hurt and made me feel little. I knew, or was convinced in my mind, that many of my peers hated me. However, I never thought my Polish heritage was the deciding factor.

I recall being given a test in history class my senior year. It was designed to measure our acceptance of other races, cultures and character traits. The test listed a various number of traits. We were to score how much we liked that race or trait. A score of one was equal to hatred, while a score of five was equal to full acceptance. The questionnaire was broad and included many different descriptions. I remember I scored homosexuals with a one. I was homophobic, not really understanding what that meant at the time. As a teen, calling somebody gay was equivalent to saying that you didn't like them. I was proud to see that my test results showed that I had no problem accepting other races.

One of the categories on the test was Arabs. I saw that one classmate scored them at a two, meaning they thought very little of them. I couldn't understand it. Shah was a great friend. He accepted me as a person, something many other people didn't do. I definitely thought more highly of Shah than I did this classmate, so I questioned him about his grading. He replied, "I just don't like Arabs."

I'm not a hundred percent sure, but I'm confident that he had never met an Arab in his whole life. Yet he had the nerve to reject them, purely on the basis of their background. Unfounded hatred like this is wrong and I felt real pain that day. Ask people what they think of mentally ill people, and I believe many would give us a low score. It is easy to hate and fear the unknown.

Shah had some friends who were also Palestinian. One was an everyday guy named Rick. He was, like Shah, just a little reserved and quiet. But then there was Sid and Mel, who were both older and both totally insane. I say insane in the sense that they were both sociopathic and dangerous to society.

I still recall my outings to Willowbrook Mall with my newfound Palestinian friends. We would walk up Route 46, about half a mile from the Grayforest. We had to cross the highway, which was dangerous, but fortunately we never had any close calls. The first stop was always the department store, where we would go to the cologne section. Shah would open an expensive box of cologne and take out the bottle. He and the others would then apply a generous dose, so the smell would waft off of them all day long. I felt nervous when they did this; I considered it stealing. I always had a notion and a desire to do the right thing, and would agonize over trivial things that shouldn't have bothered me at all. This was a constant source of stress for me. Finally, they would put the bottle away, and we would walk out like nothing had happened. We never got in trouble, though I was certain we would get caught every time.

Trailed by the scent of expensive cologne, we would cruise the mall, walking up and down the busy walkways. Even though Shah could be reserved, he was far from being shy. He would make a "psssing" sound to all the girls that walked by. I can't remember it actually working, but it sure got their attention. It embarrassed me every time, but, on the other hand, I admired his courage and boldness, both qualities I lacked. Of course, I had always hoped to meet a young lady who would love me, or even just like me. It was the biggest dream of my life, my deepest desire. I felt that if I had someone special love, it would make all the others problems disappear.

Shah knew a girl that he'd take to the basement next to the Grayforest to have sex with. He would often meet her at the mall before doing their deed. One day he wanted me to accompany him, so I could have sex with her as well. I was deeply troubled by the whole idea because I had a myriad of hang ups in regards to sex. I believed, and still believe, that sex should accompany love. I was terrified by the idea of having sex in such a crude manner. As things worked out, Sid was with us that day, and the girl didn't want three guys. Fortunately, I was the one left out. I'll never forget Sid's crude words to the young girl, "We have big cocks and cum quick." Shah was sixteen at the time; the girl was only thirteen. Even worse, Sid was around twenty three. It was hugely inappropriate for Sid to have sex with this young girl, and I clearly thought it was wrong. But I never voiced my opinion. The girl was from my town, but since she was so much younger I didn't know her. I recall she mentioned attending the Catholic school. I'll always regret not speaking up and voicing my disapproval.

Sid and Mel were older, but both were less than five feet tall. Sid was a seventy-pound pipsqueak, and Mel was a short ball of pudgy fat. Just looking at them, you would consider them nothing in a fight. I could have easily beaten the two of them up without breaking a sweat. However, I feared them because, as I said, they were crazy. Not crazy like so many of the friends I've made since, but they were clearly social deviants. They had no regard for anything except their own desires.

They openly sold drugs at Willowbrook Mall. They were bold, without fear, and, in my opinion, very stupid. One night they went to 42nd street, a shady part of New York City, and picked up a hooker. After fulfilling their needs, they took off without paying. The poor girl's pimp chased them, desperate to get his money. But Mel pulled out a gun and shot the pimp's tires, ending the chase.

That's why when Sid would threaten to beat me up, I felt real fear. He did it in a playful manner, while at the same time still meaning it. I always feared he would pull a gun and blow my brains out. I certainly felt he was capable of doing such a thing.

The rest of the odd cast of characters at the Grayforest was harmless. Like the waitress, Diane, who loved to give customers oral sex. The staff would always joke when she hit on the customers, using the most colorful choice of words. Shah boastfully claimed that he had sex with her, but Diane always denied the allegation. But when she denied it, she would always laugh and blush. I didn't know what to believe; I just knew that Diane was always nice to me.

Jack was the homosexual waiter. One evening his transvestite boyfriend showed up at the bar, totally decked out in makeup and a dress. I had a good look at him and didn't even realize he was a man until someone told me later. Jack was an extremely nice person and was the first openly gay person that I knew. I learned to like him as a person, even if he was a strange person and different from myself. I enjoyed listening to him spout his conspiracy theories. Carl was the burned out drug-using banquet waiter. He would put in eighty hours a week, and I am not exaggerating. He was working constantly. He was always tired and had a haunted look on his face. His eyes had a distant stare to them, probably from the drug use. He was very friendly and liked to talk to me, though he wasn't always coherent and tended to ramble on, but one day he just disappeared.

There was also a stupid waitress whose name I've forgotten. She'd go around constantly saying "You know what I mean, jelly bean." I really disliked her. When it was time to divvy up the tips, she always gave us less money than the others in the wait staff. The busboys were supposed to get fifteen percent, but she would always cheat us. It was plain old stealing. Furthermore, she was a snitch. She would go to the manager and tell them anything we did wrong. She tattled on the whole staff. I would often over hear her talking to the manager; she would be implicating some other worker in an act she felt was wrong.

Dotty was a nice waitress whom I knew from high school. She used to ride the bus with me when I was small. At the time, I thought she didn't like me but, to my surprise, she was extremely nice to me when we worked together at the restaurant. I grew to like her as a friend.

There was a second manager named Jeff. It was rumored that he snorted cocaine. I remember being in an exceptionally fine mood one day; I spent the entire day just laughing and grinning. At the end of my shift, Jeff sidled up to me and said, "John, I don't care what you're on just give me some." He was in serious need of a chemical high, while I was just high on life.

The receptionist was an older elegant lady. She was always kind to me. One day I asked her the time. She replied "I got the time, do you got the place?" This made me a tad nervous; I wasn't sure if she was kidding or not. She would always flirt with the older customers, and I suspect, on occasion, carry it further.

The bouncer was shorter than me, but was covered in taught muscles. I liked talking to him. One night he threw out an agitated drunk customer who was looking for a fight. The bouncer kept his composure and replied, "We'll fight, sure, but right here, where I'm doing my job. That way when the police come, I won't get in trouble." The two never fought, but his calm, cool demeanor always impressed me.

The craziest one at Grayforest was, by far, Oliver the Cook. There was no competition; he was way out there. He once had a scheme to win the lottery. When the pot got huge in Ohio, he collected money from the staff and actually got on a plane and flew halfway across the country to buy a thousand tickets. Unfortunately, we all lost. Oliver kept the wait staff supplied with uppers that gave them energy and removed the edge caused by the troubles of the job. Waiting on tables is a difficult job, and one bad customer can completely ruin the day. So the pills helped the hours go smoother. One day Freddie and I were standing around in the kitchen. When the manager turned his back on Oliver, the crazy cook took a glass, raised it up and then lowered it quickly, smashing it on the counter. Freddie and I started laughing uncontrollably. The manager turned and said, "He dropped a glass. What's so funny?" Did he break a glass for no reason? Or was it just to make a couple of high school boys laugh? Either way, he was one weird guy, and I've known my share of weird guys.

This next story is interesting; anyone can learn a lesson from it. One day a customer ordered a steak medium rare. When the waitress gave him his food, he went ballistic. He yelled that the steak wasn't prepared right and treated her like dirt. The customer carried on and demanded to speak to the manager. The manager got his share of the man's wrath as well. Because the employees were providing a service, neither the waitress nor manager was able to tell the customer off. If they were to tell the customer off, they would have lost their jobs. The waitress was shaken as she returned the steak to Oliver to have him cook it more. Oliver took the steak, went to the toilet and wiped the bowl with it. Then he cooked it up and it was served to the customer. To this day, I am very careful in showing respect to the wait staff. I try to be kind to people in general. I've worked in the business, so I have sympathy. This incident stays in my mind, and I cringe every time I'm at a restaurant with someone that hassles the wait staff. You never know what extra ingredient their food might contain.

The weirdest moment of all was when Oliver drove his car to

the back door and proceeded to drive forward and strike the wall. Then he backed up and struck the wall again. He did this several times repeatedly. I watched in awe and horror. Whenever somebody did something wrong, it grieved my soul, yet the breaking of the conventional rules had a strange and powerful attraction.

Oliver eventually got a job in another restaurant. He didn't have time to give an official two weeks' notice because he needed to start in a couple of days. But Oliver had a plan. He took a whole side of beef and put it in his car. When the manager found the beef missing and investigated, he had no choice but to fire Oliver, leaving him free to start his new job. Oliver was everybody's friend, and we were all sorry to see him go.

Chris was another cook, but he seemed totally normal, at first. One day he threatened me with a large cooking knife. I couldn't tell if he was serious, but I assumed he was. Needless to say, I was frightened. From that time on I walked on eggshells around Chris, never forgetting the threat. I think he later regretted his actions, but couldn't bring himself to apologize. He was always nice to me from that point on. He eventually quit and got another job, but he would return to eat in the restaurant. When he saw me, he called me over and asked how I was doing and told me about his new job. I dismissed what happened as a stupid joke, or at worse a bad moment. I was relieved by his kind treatment because I didn't want to think that Chris was a violent person. Violence made me feel truly uncomfortable at the time.

There was a cook who was my friend. He used to be a drummer in a band. He played in Mother's, a local bar, and was on the same stage as Twisted Sister. He quit playing in the band to go to culinary school. All of his fellow band mates were living with their parents at home, but he was independent. He had given up his life's dream of being a rock star, but he was proud to be on his own. This cook would always experiment with new items for the menu. He would ask me to taste what he made and tell him what I thought. I wasn't allowed to eat the expensive food, but on the pretense of trying a new recipe I could have whatever the cook prepared.

The dishwasher was from Haiti. I'd always get him carafes

full of Coca Cola from the bar because he wasn't allowed to go on the dining floor. Dishwashers weren't dressed appropriately enough to be seen by the customers, so I would get the refreshing beverages for him. I noticed the dishwasher never spoke English around Dan the manager. I remember seeing Dan with a mop in his hand telling the dishwasher to mop the floor. The dishwasher looked at him puzzled, pretending not to understand English. He never had to do the mopping after that.

For some reason, the managers once hired a fat and lazy bus boy named Stan. He liked to hang out at the bar and watch television while the rest of us toiled away. Shah wanted me to beat him up. He always tried to convince me to hurt him, yet Shah never wanted to do the roughing up himself, even though it was he who despised Stan. I didn't like him much either because he was lazy. But, worse of all, we had to share our tips with Stan, despite his poor performance. I never beat him up; we simply resorted to calling him names and such behind his back. He eventually got fired. Years later, when I was in the psych ward at Solomon Hospital, I was surprised to find Stan being treated for mental illness as well. It was a strange coincidence.

One of our many duties was to deliver the dirty tablecloths to the hotel laundry room. The cleaning people collected pornographic magazines in their room that were left behind by the hotel customers. Shah and I would sneak into the laundry room late at night and open the desk to look at the dirty pictures. Sometimes I would take them home, and I would always make sure that delivering laundry was my last task of the night. I would hide the magazines in my apron, so my mother wouldn't see them. Pornography is an extremely addictive animal, especially for a seventeen year old boy. It demeans sexuality for both men and women, but it seems that youths always find a way to get their hands on the stuff, no matter how careful adults hide it. Having X-rated magazines as a teenager was a huge deal. It made me feel more man than boy. Now I wish the industry did not exist, but it continues to thrive.

Yet, even with the magazines, or maybe because of the magazines, I was uncomfortable with sexual intimacy in the real world. One night I was delivering room service to the hotel. I knocked on a door and a man answered wearing a bathrobe. A could see a young lady lying under the covers in the bed behind him. He saw me look and smiled. "She's a whore I hired for the night," he explained. "Would you like a turn?" The young lady smiled at me with an inviting look. I uttered a hasty, nervous negative and made a hasty retreat.

One of the female cooks had a crush on me. I was seventeen and she was twenty three. Word got around that she liked me ... in a sexual way. At this point, I still had a hang up about sex. Sex, in my mind, was some mystical act that was the greatest thing possible. But I had a disconnection. As much as I desired it, the idea of actually doing it terrified me. I didn't fear the thought of it until the possibilities of doing it became real. The cook was good looking, but somehow, as much as I desired to have intercourse, I couldn't bring myself to do it. Instead, I ignored her. She got the message and lost interest. It would be a while before I understood intimacy.

At the end of my time at the Grayforest I again got lazy. When I worked with Freddie on Saturday mornings, he would punch in for me, and I would show up an hour late. The same pattern that happened at Vito's was repeated. I had started with enthusiasm, only to slack off later. The pattern would repeat again when I went to engineering school at Edwards Institute of Technology.

Memories are a precious commodity. My heart is warmed when I think about my experiences at Vito's and Grayforest. I still wonder what happened to Shah. Maybe he will read this book and contact me. He was a good friend, and will always be dear to me.

WRESTLING

In the ninth grade, I had the junior varsity wrestling coach, Mr. F, for biology. Two of my good friends, Joe and Howard, had already joined the team. At the end of the year, Coach F asked my biology class what extracurricular we planned to join during high school. By having every student, one by one, state their future plans, he compelled the students to get involved. His sly tactic worked on me. I didn't want to answer, so I told him that I planned on joining the wrestling team. "Oh, you'll have fun," he said with a big genuine smile.

The next year, I kept my commitment and joined the team. Joe and Howard, who knew how physically grueling practices were, encouraged me to get into shape. We began training during our summer break. I jogged a little and lifted weights, but I would eventually find out that it was not enough. The season began with captain's practice. Due to specific rules regarding summer practice, the captain's practice was held without the coach's supervision. It was voluntary and was conducted by the team's captains, Harold and Arthur. The practice consisted of running a mile and a half over hilly terrain. It was a tough going and I consistently finished last. And because I was so short, I always walked around on my toes to make myself slightly taller. I did this so often, it became a routine practice. Unfortunately, running this way also led to excruciating pains in my calf muscles. Somehow, I made it through the captain's practice alive and almost unscathed

When regular practice began, the team was divided between

varsity and junior varsity. We did the warm-up exercises together and worked out together at the conclusion of practice. But when we learned how to wrestle, we were separated. The JV was full of beginners who needed to learn the basics, while the varsity team had been wrestling for years. Being so small, I wrestled in the lowest weight class, ninety-eight pounds … even though I only weighed ninety.

I didn't have a difficult time sparring my first year. I trained with two other beginners named Sam and Joel. The three of us practiced new moves as we learned them. Joel was a muscular guy who was born without legs. He had stumps with a couple of toes and, despite having no legs, weighed nearly as much as me. He was outgoing and made friends quickly. Sam suffered from Down syndrome. I can't help but look back and admire the determination of these two young men. I would crush them repeatedly during practice, but that proved useless when it came time to contend with opponents who were not held back by a disability.

I remember watching Joel wrestle in the freshman tournament. As a sophomore, I worked the score table, so I was able to witness Joel's very first match. The kid he wrestled must have weighed only sixty pounds. He was thin as a rail. The match began with both wrestlers in the standing position. Joel maneuvered around the mat like a spider in the center of the web. If his opponent was quick enough, he could easily spin around and score a takedown; I executed this move dozens of time on Joel, so I knew he just couldn't combat it. But if Joel could capture his foe in his muscular grasp, he might achieve victory. His grip was like a vice and his opponent didn't appear that strong. The match began, and it looked like a spider was trying to capture a fly. Joel, unable to move quickly, looked on as his much smaller foe maneuvered around. Joel made his move, reaching out his arm and grabbing the other wrestler's arm. The other wrestler jerked back with all the strength he could muster. The small kid went to the mat like a felled tree. Joel pounced, covering his foe and locking his two hands in a move called a cradle: one hand around the neck and the other around a leg. The small kid couldn't break Joel's steel grip. Joel got a pin in the first round. I was proud of him; he had overcome so much

John Kaniecki

to earn that victory. Life is just like that; victory is measured by what you are. For some, a little task is a great accomplishment; I learned that fighting my mental illness.

Joel's family came to every match. He was adopted as a child, and his father was also in a wheel chair. My mother encouraged me by attending every match, both home and away. My father, however, never came. Mom was generous with her time and volunteered as the secretary of the wrestling team. She kept notes at the meetings and typed them up. It was a lot of work. We had a raffle that year to help supplement the expenses of the team. We got a book of twenty tickets to sell for a dollar per ticket. I was too lazy to go out and sell the tickets, so my mother bought them all. It was a good investment; she won the grand prize. She was able to talk the store into giving her a computer instead of the TV, so we were one of the first people in town to get a home computer. To this day, I don't know if the contest was fair or if my mother was rewarded for her hard work as team secretary.

As the season progressed, the pain in my calves continued to hurt tremendously, because I was still running incorrectly. Day after day, the pain got worse and worse. Finally they hurt too much to bear. I was in tears when I went to Coach S, the head coach, and told him my legs hurt. Following his advice, I saw a medical doctor, and, instead of practicing, I sat in a whirlpool stretching my legs, per medical advice. I would draw letters with my toes, stretching and strengthening my muscles. This helped remove the pain. After only a week one of the coaches told me I should toughen up. This comment stuck with me. I remember feeling like a wimp. I went back to practice immediately, despite the pain.

I had to wrestle Sam before the regular JV match. It was a practice match, so the coaches were keeping score. Before the match, Sam boasted out loud, "I'm gonna pin you, Myron." Even Sam used the old moniker that I hated so much. The gym was full of people, and, of course, all the cheers and support were for my opponent. They desperately wanted Sam to win. However, I promptly pinned Sam in about 30 seconds. I vividly recall the cry of anguish as I turned Sam to his back to pin him. After the match, Coach F came up to me and said, "You did what you had to do, Killer."

Killer was an accurate adjective to describe me. I was brought up to believe in America; in my eyes the United States was something unto God that could do no wrong. As we learned the country's history, I defended the United States' policies in every single matter, without exception. Not only did I defend the use of atomic weapons on Japan, but I was also in favor of using nuclear weapons against the Soviet Union if they were to invade Western Europe. I subscribed to the theory of Better Dead than Red. I knew nothing of being red or of communism, but since my country objected to that group, I simply fell in line. As we studied the Vietnam War, I defended the policy of killing babies. Whatever it takes to win was my philosophy. I was a child reared in a society that mocked and hated me. I was only a teenager, and I believed everything I was taught without daring to question it. I can forgive soldiers who go to war at age nineteen and twenty. I could have easily taken that route. It is the generals, the weapons makers, the politicians, and the bankers that I blame for the evils. There comes a point where one should learn better. I am glad my eyes were opened.

The day after the match, some kids hassled me for not letting Sam win. Thankfully, Joe defended me. "It would have been twice as bad to lose to a retard!" he repeated somewhat insensitively. If I had lost, I would have become the laughing stock of the school. However, if I could go back and do it over, I would wrestle to a draw or have won by one point.

I only won two matches that year, not counting the one with Sam. The first was at a tournament in New York State. It was a close match against another inexperienced wrestler. We were both awkward on the mat, not knowing what we were doing. I was able to eke out a one-point victory. The other was a home match where I actually pinned my opponent. I had been taken down and was struggling underneath my foe. It seemed like I was going to lose yet again, but somehow I kicked my legs in a move called a sit-out and my opponent dropped to my shoulder. With my arms I grabbed my foe's leg and rolled my opponent over in a move called a Peterson. When I was on top, I executed a Half Nelson and turned my opponent over. The coaches and my teammates were screaming in encouragement for me to lock my hands. I thought it was illegal to lock hands around the head. But since an arm was in the grip, it was legal. Oh well, I pinned him anyway, and it felt amazing. Everybody was happy for me. Wrestling is a true one-on-one event. You walk out there and there's nobody to blame except yourself for a bad performance.

I did get teased for losing so many matches. I especially remember one instance after gym class ended, when we were waiting for the bell to ring so that we could leave for the next class. Coach S heard the taunts. It was a kid named Steven, a little guy around my size. Coach got right in this kid's face and started chewing him out; he defended me. "I don't see you out there," he screamed. He kept at it until the bell rang and then a little after the bell rang for good measure. Steven looked like he wanted to disappear. I felt good that somebody cared enough to stick up for me. Overall, wrestling was a great experience for me.

After the first season, my friend Vinnie and I joined a gym called Racquetball Twenty Three. They, of course, specialized in racquetball, but they had Nautilus equipment and free weights. It was much nicer than the small weight room the high school offered. Every day after school, Vinnie and I would walk a mile to go workout.

Vinnie was a tall skinny person, so he wanted to beef up with some muscle. Fortunately, the staff was excellent. Specifically, a guy named FG who knew all about weight lifting. We were taught the correct way to lift, how to properly use the weights and how to train on certain days, so we could focus on different parts of the body. One day we would focus on shoulders, chest and triceps; the next day we would focus on the back and biceps. Vinnie and I pushed each other, and we worked hard. Other patrons heaped up the encouragement as well. We made a lot of friends and had good healthy fun. Many nights we'd come home exhausted, but it wasn't in vain. Between growing and weight lifting I gained twenty-five pounds of muscle in about eight months. I was ready for my junior year. My weight class jumped from ninety-eight pounds to one hundred and fifteen.

My first match was against a freshman with a big mouth who was working out in the weight room. It was just before the wrestling season was about to begin. We got to talk, and he claimed he could out-wrestle me. I, of course, insisted that he couldn't. To settle the matter, we rolled out the mats and started wrestling. I definitely beat him, though he didn't want to admit it. The most important thing, however, was that I was getting a little fire inside me started. I had that fighting spirit; it was something I had lacked. I began gaining confidence and belief in myself. My self-esteem rose.

My second match was against another freshman named Jordan. He had a little wrestling experience, but he wasn't a lifer. Some of the better wrestlers had been wrestling since the first grade or before. He was one weight class below me, weighing in at one hundred eight pounds. Since Jordan and I had close weights, we had a wrestling match to determine who was better. The winner would get preference in making matches, which meant more chances to wrestle at tournaments. I dominated. I don't believe he scored any points. In the third period, I pinned him. I firmly believe Jordan was intimidated because I was an upper classman. Later matches would prove that we were even in talent. Later on in the locker room, Jordan claimed that I never pinned him. I didn't argue; it didn't matter to me.

As my relationship with Jordan developed, he grew a solid dislike for me. I really don't blame him; I wasn't the nicest person in the world. I was emotionally immature. I also didn't understand many things about the social world. People take that knowledge for granted, but, truth is, I never had a good example to follow. Be that as it may, Jordan challenged me several times to fist fights. I refused; I had had enough violence as a kid. I truly didn't believe in violence anymore. It never solved problems for me, and just made matters worse. But there was a positive aspect to this animosity. Jordan was my only sparring partner. When we practiced, we went at each other with vicious competitiveness. All the other wrestlers would take it easy during practice, but not Jordan and I. Many were the times we would continue the battle beyond the blowing of the whistle. As a result, we both improved as wrestlers.

The struggle had made me better and my performance on the

mat proved it. I had ten victories that year and only two losses. I developed a style that I repeated match after match. A typical match would begin with me shooting a single leg to my opponent's left leg. From there, I would secure my position and then reach over and pull in the adversary's other leg, which would cause him to fall down. This would result in a takedown, scoring two points. Then I would use a Half Nelson for the pin. I won six matches in this exact manner, pinning my opponent in the first round in each case.

Early in the year we had a scrimmage with two teams. I practiced all evening with two competitors, one from each of the two teams. One I beat easily, the other beat me repeatedly. Later on, during the season we had a duel match against the same two teams. My first match was against the tougher opponent, the one who handled me so easily. I wrestled the best match of my life. I had full control of the contest. Every move I made was successful. I bullied the other wrestler, but the climax was when I performed a textbook Jap Whizzer. This move is like a headlock, except you lock your hand around the opponent's arm. Then you fall down, bringing your opponent with you. As I fell, I rotated my body, putting myself on top as we collided with the mat. The move was risky because it often leads to disastrous results. But this time it resulted in a beautiful pin! Coach J found me after the match and said, "I'm so glad you beat that kid." Perhaps Coach J observed that my opponent was a little too cocky. I still think back on that win with pride. My hard work had paid off in a big way.

The only bad thing was that I was exhausted. I had very little time until my second match began. The lower weights wrestled first. I went out there and wrestled the worst match of my life. I was promptly pinned. The junior varsity team was concerned because we were unbeaten. A pin scores six points for the team, the highest total. Fortunately the rest of the guys picked up the slack. At the end of the night we were still unbeaten. Coach F gave me words of encouragement, "You did good tonight. You won one." I felt better. The junior varsity team went undefeated that year.

Sometimes, in practice, I wrestled with Don, the varsity wrestler at one hundred eight pounds. He had been wrestling all his life. He even went away to wrestling camp in the summer. He was both the district and regional champion. He had even advanced a few rounds in the state finals. Of course, Don always beat me. He would establish hand control, grabbing my hands so I couldn't move. At times, he would actually have both of my hands behind my back, holding both of them with one of his powerful hands. While I was defenseless, he would crossface or, in plain language, he had one hand across my face and gripped his other arm above the elbow. At that point, I could do very little, no matter how much I struggled. I always fought so Don couldn't gain control of my hands but, try as I might, he was always successful. But I would have my moment. One practice, I successfully executed a Pancake, lifting him up as he was attempting a takedown. After lifting him up, I used my arm and swung it across my body, hitting his face, and knocking him down on his back. I had Don pinned. His head and arm were in my grasp. He jumped and twisted like a fish out of water. It was sweet satisfaction. Even though it was only practice, it felt like the Olympic Games to me.

The biggest match of the year for the junior varsity team was against Saint Benedict's Prep. The match was to be held in Newark. Not only were they a good team, but they were also black. We white folks had a message to send. Though it wasn't said in such explicit words, it was the impression the coaches sent. We worked out extra hard the week before the match. Since their mascot was The Bees, we would make buzzing noises to pump us up. The crowd jammed the bleachers for that match. I pinned my opponent in the first round, using my typical strategy. When the referee blew that whistle and slammed his hand down at the moment of the pin, adrenaline pumped through my veins and the hair stood on my back. It's a feeling like no other. I've been on both ends; I have also felt the shame of the other side.

Wrestling wasn't always a pleasure. One day Coach J was bragging about how good a wrestler he had been. He was talking about going to the state tournament and winning matches in college. He concluded by boasting that, "the cream rises to the top."

Unfortunately, I sometimes speak without thinking and this was one of those occasions. After his comment, I spoke out loudly enough for the coach and the whole team to hear. "So does the shit," I muttered. He stared at me, surprised and a little offended. He sentenced me to a Goon Squad, a penalty that involved extra workouts after practice. A common Goon Squad infraction would be drinking water after practice, which was forbidden. We could only spit, in order to keep our weight down. Sometimes somebody would cheat. If they got caught it was an automatic Goon Squad.

I ran the hall for about twenty minutes as Coach F supervised. Then I jumped rope until I was at the point of total exhaustion. Finally Coach F said that if I could jump rope ten successive times, I was finished with the punishment. Try as I might, I couldn't muster the energy. Fortunately, he exhibited mercy, and told me I was through. It was my only experience with Goon Squad. One time was enough to keep me in line.

One senior on the team was Moe, a big guy and a good athlete. He had gotten a scholarship to play baseball at some college. He was a catcher. The only thing was that he needed to keep his weight down. So Moe joined the team in his senior year. Moe was a big shot at school. He was always very nice to me, which was unusual. Most cool kids didn't like me at all. In fact, almost everybody didn't like me at all. One day Coach J decided to deflate Moe's ego. Coach J began to wrestle with Moe as the entire JV team watched on. Coach J was clearly the superior wrestler and could do any move at will. Coach J was on top of Moe who was lying on his stomach. Coach then pulled Moe's leg up, bending it so his heel was by his rear. Then Coach J pulled the poor kids underwear out. Next, he captured Moe's toe in the stretched-out Fruit of the Looms. Moe was so helpless he couldn't get up and move. He rolled on the mat, to the left and then to the right. Of course the whole team burst out in laughter, all except Moe that is. Moe was released and, to his credit, graciously accepted the fact that he was the brunt of the joke.

At the conclusion of the season, we had a fancy team banquet. We even dressed up in suits and ties. I was rewarded the trophy for the most improved wrestler on the Junior Varsity team. Even Jordan, who still didn't like me, offered his congratulations. I would later go on to wrestle at Edwards Institute of Technology. However, the only success we had as a team was getting served at the bar after the matches, despite the fact that we were mostly underage.

One day, years later, while I was attending the center for people with mental illnesses in Pequannock, I ran into Coach S at a candy shop downtown. "How are things going?" he asked.

"I don't think you've heard," I said, clearly distraught. "I went crazy." He looked at me for a second, a little confused. Then he smiled and repeated, "Yeah...but how are things going?"

I thought and reflected a little before answering, "Fine." I discovered I was really multi-dimensional. I was never state champion. I was never a varsity wrestler, but that really didn't matter. It was a good experience. Wrestling was vehicle to achieve self-improvement. Self-improvement is as worthwhile as victory.

The Porcelain God

It was near the end of our senior year when Jess decided to have a party. I was one of his closest friends, so he confided in me about his secret intentions. While his parents were gone, he would have a bash for the entire senior class. Our town, for some reason, didn't interact that well socially. There were too many cliques that bred isolation. To fight that, the party would be for all the classmates; everyone was welcome.

Jess had grown up to be a very personable young man. The ladies definitely found him charming. Unfortunately, none of his charisma ever rubbed off on me. Jess had also mastered the art of lying. Our group of friends, who had seen Jess in action, referred to it as bullshitting. Jess would take the truth and exaggerate like a cowboy telling tall tales. Often there was no basis in reality at all. Yet, many were the times when Jess would tell us something so preposterous that we dismissed it as fantasy, only to discover there was some measure of truth in his tale. Whatever you'd like to call it, Jess was an expert.

The word of Jess' party spread around town like a wildfire. Perhaps his parents knew but didn't let on. I doubt this because they gave Jess a strong warning not to have anybody over. However, the news of the party was such common knowledge that one of Jess' neighbors heard about it from a bank teller.

Since Jess and I were such close friends, I was the first person to show up. Somehow Jess, only seventeen-years-old, had managed to buy two kegs of beer, and I had brought a half-gallon glass container from which to drink. I had lived a very restricted life and was aching to let loose. I no longer wanted to mortgage the present for the future; I wanted to live life and enjoy the moment. I was to heading into an unknown territory with grave consequences because I had little experience with alcohol.

The party was finished almost before it started. Only a half of a dozen people had arrived when the police showed up. We hadn't even started drinking yet. Two cops pulled up and said, "We hear you're having a party." As I said, the word had gotten around. Jess talked to them briefly. He must have worked his bullshitting magic because they left. Once they were out of sight, we got the word from Jess, "The party is on."

I had no idea how to handle my liquor, being totally naive in the finer points of drinking. It was only my second party of this nature. At the first party, one of the frequent drinkers came up to me and shook my hand. Then, in a kind welcome, he said, "I'm so glad you finally joined us." I was in shock for two reasons. First of all, I didn't know this person had the slightest bit of interest in me. Secondly, I didn't realize that I was actually welcome.

As soon as the cops left, I began drinking the amber liquid, both too fast and too often. I was soon at that stage commonly referred to as buzzed. I was trying to figure out why the room was spinning when the stripper showed up. This was Jess' only chance to have a party, and he planned to make it a memorable event. This included hiring a professional stripper.

Roger, a classmate of ours, quickly befriended the stripper. He was friendly with everybody and had charisma like Jess. Years later, I would reflect on how Roger was nice to almost everyone, and I would come to greatly appreciate that quality in him. He escorted the stripper upstairs, so she could prepare for her act. I got the sense that the stripper was intimidated by the unruly nature of the crowd. I think our lack of age and maturity didn't sit well either. We all gathered by the stairs, and she undressed for us in a tantalizing manner. She would sway and swing her body and, every so often, take off another piece of clothing. She removed everything except her fancy underwear. She had promised Jess that she would strip naked, but she stopped short of that. It didn't matter; we were all satisfied with the act. But to our disappointment, the stripper didn't hang around. She quickly got dressed and left.

I continued guzzling beer after the show. I was timid, even when drunk, and didn't talk to many people. Yet, people started to notice that I was drinking out of control. One guy, Ben, told me, "You'll be praying to the porcelain god before the night is over." I later learned that he meant I would be puking my guts into the toilet bowl, appearing to worship the porcelain commode.

On top of the two kegs, Jess had purchased a hundred White Castle burgers. When he started heating them up, the aroma filled the entire house. "We want Rat Burgers," a chant started. Rat Burgers was the nickname for the White Castle food. I quickly gobbled down my share, and then promptly threw up on the carpet. Ben was only partially correct. I did vomit; I just couldn't make it to the toilet bowl in time.

The party eventually thinned out, but I hung around. A couple of classmates, a young man and woman, showed up late and snorted a few lines of cocaine. I was shocked to see the drug use. I had only heard of people using drugs, but never had I seen it. If only the night had ended there.

I was drunk, sick, and lying in a bed when a couple more guys showed up. They were partiers who drank every weekend. One of them was still angry with me because, at the one other party I attended, I had called his friend, Carlo, a liar. At one point in the night he had said the cops were outside. Being drunk, I blurted, "Liar!" out loud for all to hear.

The anger on Carlo's face was evident to everyone. He was a big tough guy. The crowd who knew Carlo well began to chant, "Head butt, head butt," over and over. Soon everyone at the party was egging Carlo on with the chant, hoping for a fight. Thankfully, Carlo just walked away. He had the right to be angry with me. Either way, I was lucky I didn't get beaten up.

Now Carlo's friend wanted me to apologize for the comment. Unfortunately, I was stupid and refused to budge. I was clearly in the wrong when I called Carlo a liar. He had been telling the truth; the cops were right outside. But still, I adamantly refused to recant my words. Instead, in my drunken stupor, I began to tell Carlo's friend about my family life. For a little while, he listened intently to what I was saying. He actually sympathized with me.

It was no secret that I was abnormal. I didn't fit in with many people, and I was always tense and nervous. I couldn't just let go and relax. I was always so serious about everything, while at the same time caring for nothing. I explained my problems to this total stranger. It was the first time I had talked to anyone about it. I never even discussed these things with my closest friends. I guess the alcohol had loosened my tongue.

Even though I was pouring my heart out, Carlo's friend got so serious in his demand; he wanted me to apologize. He started tormenting me by slowly pouring beer on my head. I was drunk and dizzy and really just wanted to go to sleep, but he wouldn't leave me alone. I suddenly got angry and a fight ensued. I threw a couple of punches, then tried to throw a headlock, a move I had learned on the wrestling team. However, I was too drunk and too out of practice to succeed. All I managed to accomplish was to twist around blindly. My foe picked me up and promptly put my head through the wall. By the grace of God my head went perfectly through the sheet rock. A few inches either to the left or the right, and my head would have been flattened on a beam. I could have gotten seriously hurt, even killed.

At this point, the fight ended. I pulled my head out of the wall and asked the other guy if my punches had even hurt. When he replied that he was okay, I got angry. I had wanted to inflict pain. I relented, however, and hurriedly wrote a note to Carlo, apologizing for calling him a liar. I made Carlo's friend write a note saying he would never bother me again. He wrote the note, except he included a disclaimer: he would never beat me up again, unless I deserved it.

Jess, who hadn't been around for the incident, came downstairs and made a note of the crazy surroundings. He was angrier than I had ever seen him before. The house was a wreck. His parents would definitely find out about the night's events. He wasn't supposed to have anyone over, let alone throw a party. I alone had puked on the good rug, and my head had destroyed the wall. Jess' parents would be home in only two days.

He started making frantic phone calls. He claimed he had an emergency as he talked to carpenters, begging them to help. Then we rented a rug cleaner, which actually worked well enough to erase one of my contributions to the mess. Then a carpenter showed up. He worked quickly and repaired the wall. Miraculously, he had paint that was an exact match and the damage was repaired. We hoped and prayed Jess' parents wouldn't notice anything. If there is one thing I did right in this mess, it was that I didn't abandon Jess in his hour of need. Instead, I helped clean up and even paid for all the work that was done.

I had to call the Grayforest because I was supposed to bus tables that morning. When my boss asked why I couldn't work, he wasn't prepared for my answer: "I got my head put through a wall." I guess he never heard that excuse before. He needed no further explanation.

The following Monday I was the talk of the school. I saw Carlo that day. I felt compelled to apologize for calling him a liar, but I didn't. He made no mention of the incident, as if he was unaware of the night's events. That was a possibility. Years later, after the mental illness set in, certain events tormented me. I was manic and, for some reason, I was wracked with guilt for calling Carlo a liar. I wrote a note apologizing for my offense. I told him I was very drunk at the time and was going through a lot of difficulties, so I was truly sorry. I concluded the letter by wishing him a nice life. I never got a response, and I don't even know if he even got the letter.

My brother Bert was tempted to retaliate by beating on the guy that put my head through the wall. I guess he felt compelled by his duty as the big brother. I was glad he didn't act on his impulses because the whole situation could have escalated into more violence.

I honestly can't recall the guy's name. After the fight ended and things calmed down I told him, "One day I'm going to buy a shot gun and blow your head off." When I told him this he looked at me funny. I think he dismissed my comment as drunken gibberish. Perhaps he heard that I had gone crazy and has wondered if I would fulfill my threat.

Intelligence can be more correctly described as book smarts. I may have been intelligent back then, but I lacked wisdom. In reality, I was very stupid about so many things. You would think that, after this incident, I would have given up alcohol. Instead, my problem only got worse. The shiny apple was still very tempting. I had bitten in deep and had tasted the rottenness of the worms and maggots. As a fool, I had more hard lessons to learn.

I was hollow and aching. I felt alone and unloved. I needed a diversion and I needed something to kill the pain. For now, alcohol was that something. Eventually the love of God would fill the void. But I had to hit rock bottom first.

THE SUMMER OF '69... IN '85

Graduation from Pequannock Township High School was a rewarding experience. The entire graduating class had gathered for one final celebration. The student body was dressed in their gowns and robes. It was both absurd and profound at the same moment. My robe had a yellow stole, indicating that I was graduating with honors. I was fairly high in the class ranking; my grade point average had put me in the top twenty percent. But weirdly enough, I really didn't care too much about it. In fact, I didn't care about anything at all; that was my problem. Still, I hoped things would get better.

My mindset at the time was mostly, "Goodbye and good riddance." I was full of joy that I was through with the high school ordeal. I had little affection for my classmates, and I imagined the feeling was mutual.

My yearbook entry fictitiously listed me as captain of the yachting team. I had put it down as a joke. We had no such organization. The personal statement that accompanied my picture was a misquote of a Grateful Dead song. It read, "To which of you to gain me, tell/will risk uncertain pain in hell?/I will forgive you/if you do not take the chance." The correct lyrics were, "I will not forgive you." It was a foreshadowing of what was to come.

My favorite quote from one of my classmates was, "Go ahead and die, see if I care." To me, the quote was wonderful. These were words of defiance, not submission. I asked a nice friend from my English class to sign my yearbook. Her note read, "Good luck becoming totally heartless." When I read her comment, it struck me right in the heart. Not with a deep pain, but with a twinge of truth and realization. Her observation was accurate; like the tin man in the Wizard of Oz, I had no heart.

After graduation, I took the summer off before going to college. I perceived the world as a cruel place where only the strong survived, so I started to train for combat. It was my theory that I should get as physically fit as possible. This way, nobody would push me around anymore. I began a grueling and extensive workout routine. My music blasted on the radio as I did endless push-ups, sit-ups, and other calisthenics. It was in the middle of one such workout that my friend Stan called.

Stan was a friend of mine from history class. We shared hardcore right wing political views. We didn't know each other well, but we got along just fine. He had called to invite me to a party with his good friend Murray. The three of us cliqued and a friendship began. Together we attended all the little get-togethers our classmates had to celebrate graduation. We had a great time.

Stan had a summer job working as a landscaper; he mowed lawns in the morning. Murray worked as a lifeguard. When they weren't working, which was most of the time, they hung out at the town's local beach PV Park. This was a man-made lake, complete with imported sand. Stan and Murray invited me to join them there. I decided to take them up on the offer; it seemed better than training for war.

Stan and Murray were not the only ones who went to the beach frequently. All of the teens from our high school gathered there as well. The beach was exclusive, allowing only people living in Pequannock to get a membership. Stan and Murray's friends were mostly underclassmen, still toiling away in high school. I sat in with the group as we tanned ourselves, lying in the hot sun. After a couple of weeks, I had a couple of dozen new friends. My plans of training for war were gone. I felt as if I belonged somewhere.

The best thing was that I could be myself, and I was appreciated for it. The beach crowd accepted me with all my quirks and faults. I had one joke that I would repeat over and over. I would tell everybody that I hadn't eaten for five days; I usually said this as we waited patiently to get some food from the truck that was permanently parked at the beach. I also carried around a large glass bottle of Perrier water. It became my trademark. Most of the crowd was into pop music, but I was a huge Neil Young fan. I would talk about him all the time, and when I spoke the folk star's last name, I would lower my voice and almost sing it.

We always had a radio at the beach. Music, particularly rock and roll, is very much ingrained into American youth. The songs gave us meaning and defined us. That summer Bryan Adams had his hit song, "The Summer of 69." We weren't stupid though, we realized Bryan Adams was far too young to be in a rock band and have a girlfriend in the summer of 1969. Therefore the song was a charade; it couldn't have been about his life. But we loved it anyway. It was our theme song. We were also drawn to Dire Strait's song "Money For Nothing." The introduction of the song is Sting singing the line talking about how he wants his MTV. The guys on the beach used that line as our code for wanting sex. We would repeat the line, laughing and singing. The girls always wanted to know what was up, but we never told them. In hindsight they probably knew, but at the time I was very naive and thought they would never understand.

I still preferred Neil Young to the more popular singers, but he didn't get much airtime. Every night before I went to sleep, I would sit in the room downstairs and play his albums on the turntable. I bought them all and loved each one. I would listen intently, hanging on every word. His songs spoke to me. From Neil, I learned to love the Natives of this country, especially due to the song "As Long as We Can Sail Away." It's about the Native Americans fleeing down a river to go to some unknown land. I wanted to leave my life and go to someplace new. I listened to his music at night, eventually falling asleep. To me, Neil became something larger than life. He wasn't a messiah, but was more than human; somewhere between man and a god. Everything about the summer was great, but the best moment of it all was when I met Kate.

I remember the first day I saw her. She put her towel next to mine. Her white bikini showcased her extraordinarily sexy body, and golden blonde hair perfectly framed her pretty face. I admit it;

I got a little excited, so I had to turn over and lie on my stomach to avoid embarrassment. Kate saw my natural male reaction, and smiled a little wicked grin. I was in love. Lou Reed's song "Walk on the Wild Side" was playing on the radio. I'll never forget. I don't think Kate had ever heard the song before because when Lou sang the line about being calm when giving oral sex. Kate smiled again with a little laugh.

Meanwhile Murray, Stan and I became inseparable. I was beginning to lose my inferiority complex. I was breaking out of my shell and learning to relax. Miraculously, my love life manifested in the wonderful rose named Kate. She had actually taken a liking to me. It was hard to believe that this beautiful girl was interested in me. I can think of no better ego boost than that.

Later in the summer, Jess told me that he was also attracted to Kate. She worked part time at a bakery, and he had met her there. This was very bad news to me because Jess was much better with the ladies than I was. I was an amateur with next to no experience, while he was an expert. When Jess found out I liked Kate, he nobly backed down and didn't interfere. Jess was a true friend, and soon I had a date with Kate. I took her to a small party. We kissed good night … and then kissed a little more. I can still smell the scent of her perfume and taste the fruity flavor of her lip gloss. It was my first real kiss.

It wasn't long before Kate and I became an item. Stan was dating a girl named Maud, and Murray was dating a girl named Candy. All three of us had somebody special in our lives; it was fantastic. Kate and I weren't technically boyfriend and girlfriend; we were just dating. She was very clear about that aspect of our relationship. She had just ended a long relationship and didn't want to make a commitment. I was just happy to be involved with such a pretty girl.

One night Stan, Victor and I were leaning back sitting on the hoods of our cars, starring up into the starry sky. As we talked about the future and the fine summer we were all having the stars took on a new light. Suddenly, I had hope, and for the first time I had a reason for living. As I stared into heaven, heaven returned the favor and entered into my heart.

On one of our dates I took Kate to Friendly's, a local restaurant. As we ate our dinners and enjoyed some ice cream, we talked. All I could talk about was my desire to sleep with her, but she wasn't up on the idea. In retrospect, I am disappointed by her reaction, or lack thereof. Kate was a Christian, and my talk was more than unwholesome. She should have slapped me in the face and walked out the door. If I ever had a daughter, and someone spoke to her as I spoke to Kate, I would expect her to react as such. Instead she compromised and let my foolishness go on. I wish she was stronger; it would have been a good example for me.

One night I was at Kate's house, just hanging out. Her dad had a friend over, and he noticed that my break light was broken on my car. The next day I was driving home and, all of a sudden, I saw a police car behind me with its lights flashing red. I pulled over, wondering what I had done. As he approached, I recognized him as the same man that had just pointed out my broken light. He gave me a ticket. I always wondered if Kate's father was trying to send a message. In reflection I don't think so.

The night before I left for school, Kate got permission from her usually-strict parents to stay out an extra hour. We went to a movie. I can't recall the film at all I was only concentrating on Kate. After the movie, we bought a tub of popcorn and took it to my car. Kate took exception to the radio station I had on. We had always argued over music. As the fight progressed, we began to playfully toss popcorn at one another. Soon the car was littered with fluffy kernels, like snow covering the ground. We laughed until we ached. As we drove home, I stopped at a red light. I leaned in to kiss Kate, but she said stopped me saying "Why do you always want to kiss me?" This, of course, upset me.

Next we went to Burger King and ordered a couple of burgers from the drive-thru. As we sat alone parked in the parking lot, Kate elaborated on her comment. It wasn't meant to be a denial. Instead, she had the desire for me to do other things to her, to move beyond kissing. Then she said that she wanted to do the very thing I had been begging for all summer. She didn't want to disappoint me. Pleasantly surprised, I considered my options. I had no condom, and I had no place to take her. But most importantly, there was this nagging thought in the back of my mind. I still thought of sex in connection with love and love in connection with marriage. Though I very much wanted to have intercourse, I decided against it. I looked Kate in the eye and said, "You'll never disappoint me," and I drove her home.

I wasn't ready for sex. I didn't receive physical love at home, like hugs or kisses. Looking back, I am proud of my decision; I know I did the right thing. I'm sure Kate was surprised, if not shocked, especially after I pestered her so much about it. I suppose maybe she was disappointed.

After I went away to Edwards Tech, Kate and I decided not to see each other anymore. The truth is, she found it too hard to have a relationship while I was away, so she ended it. When she broke it to me, I gave her the impression that I didn't care the slightest bit about her when inside I was ready to cry. My cold exterior was a result of both pride and insecurity. I did love her. Not as a man loves his wife, but as a friend and companion. Kate was a very nice person and she treated me well.

A couple of years later, I would drop by Kate's house with flowers. He father answered the door surprised. He told me Kate was away at college. Her first semester had been rough. She got very ill, and as a result, had poor grades. I told him I was receiving treatment in a psychiatric hospital and was home for a weekend. I also told him I had become a Christian. "That's all that matters" he told me. I handed him the flowers and asked him to keep them for Kate. I don't know what happened to her because her family moved out of town. I often wonder how she's doing.

After that summer, my life would never be the same. I had experienced a lot of pain and confusion up to that point. Now I had experienced both compassion and love. These diametric forces would tear my mind apart. Just like Bryan Adams sang about the some lasting forever. That summer did last forever. That summer is as eternal as the stars in heaven.

Sticky

A name is a very important thing; names have meanings. John means God's grace. Up until this point in my life, I had two nicknames John John and Myron, and I never cared for either of them. At Edwards Tech I received a new title, Sticky.

My second trip to Edwards was the day freshmen were to get acquainted with the campus. The entire freshman class gathered in the dining hall. When our names were called, we were directed to the upperclassmen that would accompany us for the day. These upperclassmen were all members of fraternities and sororities. Unbeknownst to us neophytes, the recruitment or rush of the freshmen had begun. The fraternity members were alert for prospects that could potentially join their clubs.

The Alpha Beta Gamma Fraternity supervised my group. They were the so-called jocks of the campus, and they had a reputation for being obnoxious bullies. They weren't serious athletes, like you would find at other universities. Edwards Tech is a division three school, so sports were, at best, an afterthought. Athletics weren't the center of campus life; they were far on the periphery. The central focus of Edwards was engineering. So a fraternity that prided itself on being the tough guys in a school, where none of that ilk really existed, was somewhat of a joke.

Being primarily an engineering school, Edwards attracted more nerds than jocks. In high school, I had a couple of friends, but I was not popular. There was a longing and emptiness in me. Later I would discover that this resulted from not having a relationship with God. For the moment, however, I only knew I needed something better. I was not satisfied with the tame life of studying. All of these people were strangers and nobody knew me. I could begin a new life without stigma. I was not Myron but, once again, John; at least for the time being.

That first day, I met two other incoming freshmen: Larry and Alex. They too were assigned to the Alpha Fraternity group. Later, they would be pledged and become brothers of mine at the Phi Alpha Beta Fraternity. Trying to make a good impression on them, I revealed that I had a bottle of Jamaican rum in my car. Larry and I drank it, while Alex abstained. Alex never had a drink of alcohol for as long as I knew him. He resisted tremendous peer pressure, and I admired him for that. Larry and I searched all over the campus for a soda machine, so we could mix Coke with the rum. The three of us had a good night, and we became quick friends. Alex and Larry must have become even closer, because they selected each other to be roommates for the semester.

The next time I visited Edwards Tech, it was to pick up my computer. I wore my gray Pequannock wrestling shirt. I thought it would be impressive. I was trying to assume a new image: I was still unsure of what exactly it was that I was trying to achieve though. I met Al, another freshman who also wrestled in high school. We had a common ground. We started to talk and exchanged phone numbers. He suggested that we put each other's name down as roommates, which we did. "You'll never know who you'll get," Al said with caution. Before school started, I decided to drive up to Oldtown, New York to visit his house. I met his parents and we attended a Foreigner and Joe Walsh concert. I recall Foreigner performing their hit song "Juke Box Hero." During the song, a huge inflatable jukebox was blown up. In all honesty, it looked pretty lame. Al met a girl during the concert; she had hitchhiked down from Woodstock. He held the girl on top of his shoulders the entire concert. Afterwards, they entered the fun house, only to exit about two minutes later. After she left, Al started bragging about having sex with her. What kind of sex was that? I couldn't help but wonder about the brevity.

That night, Al and I both slept on his bed. "I guess I'm going to find out if you're gay soon enough," he said strangely, instead of "good night." Al could say the stupidest things.

We ended up living in room 305 of the Thomas Hall Dorm. All five floors were exclusively for freshman. Al's father was an alumnus of the school so, on moving day, his family was able to park on the grass right in front of the dorm, while my parents and I parked quite a distance away. By the time I got to our room, Al had already claimed the lower bunk for himself, which didn't bother me. Besides the bunk bed, the only other pieces of furniture in the room were two desks with chairs.

Barny was a senior who lived on our side of the third floor as the resident assistant, orRA. He was the authority in our hall and represented the school. On the first night, he sat us down and explained the rules. Of course, alcohol was not permitted, and it would be confiscated. Barny also stressed the importance of studying and warned us about drinking the punch at fraternity parties. The punch tasted good, but it had a high concentration of alcohol. Sitting among my fellow students, I realized I had a new opportunity in life, a chance to start over. This time, instead of going in blind, I had a little insight into what I wanted. I wanted friends; that was for sure.

Our dorm room was across the Hudson River from Manhattan, and we had a fantastic view. But more important than anything else, it was the first time I was on my own. I was exhilarated by the freedom. I had a deep desire to do well in school and, for the first time in my life, I applied myself to something. I read the textbook assignments, did all my homework, went to every class and studied for the tests. It was a successful formula. Some of the other students failed to make the adjustment, while some were just plain lazy and slept late. Others spent valuable time just talking or shooting the breeze. Others tried, but couldn't handle the difficult curriculum demands at Edwards Tech.

I decided to join the soccer team, even though I hadn't played organized soccer since sixth grade. I wasn't very good and, in order to make the varsity soccer team, I was required to run a certain distance in a given time. I never met the qualifications, so I didn't play in the games. But I was very friendly and outgoing with the soccer team, and I was able to make a lot of friends. Al was even more outgoing and attracted an even larger group of friends. We both liked liquor, and we partied together. The main difference was that I studied, and he didn't. By the end of the first semester, Al had almost failed out of school, while I missed a perfect semester by getting just one B. However, it's only fair to say Al eventually graduated from Edwards, while I did not.

The weekend after I broke up with Kate, there was a hurricane that hit the New York City area, so we did what any college kids would do. We had a hurricane party in our room. We knew that Barny would realize what we were doing, so we bribed him with a small bottle of rum. He was glad to get the liquor; his classes were cancelled too. But, most importantly, he allowed our party to proceed.

We really got blitzed drinking rum and vodka. I played Neil Young's song, "Like a Hurricane" over and over. I played it loud, it had a double significance that day: there was a hurricane going on outside and, on top of that, the song is about a man getting rejected by a woman, just like Kate had rejected me. Neil compared a woman's rejection to being blown away by a hurricane. Those words reached into my soul; I could experience the meaning with significance. I still felt, in my heart, that if I could just find a woman to love me, all my other problems would vanish.

One night Al and I went to a Phi Alpha Beta party, and we promptly got drunk. All the fraternities had parties to attract freshmen. They were recruiting the males and romancing the females. Phi Alpha Beta was a fraternity that occupied the brownstones in Hoboken. They were isolated from the other frats by quite a distance. The two brownstones were equipped with a bar room. Al and I were drinking beer after beer from the keg. His drinking practice only encouraged my drinking but, in truth, my newfound habit didn't need much encouraging. Drinking, especially drinking to get drunk, was a convenient escape for me. I promptly vomited on the bar. Not wanting to make a bad impression, but also being stupid drunk, I took off my shirt and cleaned the bar with it. Later in the week, a Phi Alpha brother returned it to me washed.

There was little enforcement of underage drinking at Edwards

Tech. As an eighteen-year-old freshman, I had no problem gaining access to alcohol. In fact, most of the time the booze was free. Things have changed at Edwards. In fact, I understand the policy is now quite strict. This is excellent because drinking is the beginning of a downward slide. That was my personal experience. Maybe if the rules had been stricter in my time, things would have been different.

As I said earlier, Al and I had many friends. I was, perhaps, one of the most popular freshmen on campus. I was trying to open my life up to others. I tried to get beyond the façade people wear in order to reveal my true inner being. I wanted meaningful friendships, not just acquaintances. I had a deep yearning to be loved and to belong. I didn't shy away from topics that used to make me cringe. That is why I found myself one night talking about masturbation with my friends. The word sticky was somehow mentioned, and my friends laughed mockingly. My new nickname was born.

One day I even told Al I had a wet dream about Kate. He turned around and broke my confidence by telling some other friends. They had a great big laugh at my expense. Sam, another friend of ours, was there when Al mocked me about the dream. He said he thought it was cool to share deeper feelings with others. Sam appreciated that I wasn't being superficial, but I still decided to never open up with Al concerning deeper things after that.

I tried to keep up with Al over the years. He was a dear friend, and we shared many wonderful experiences. He once told me, when he thought of his years at Edwards Tech, I would immediately come to mind. He became a successful engineer. He was instrumental in the effort to clean up ground zero after the attack of September 11th. He worked long hours, seven days a week, to complete the task. When I found out that the Environmental Protection Agency had lied about the dangers of breathing the air, I felt anger at the injustice. I contacted Al to ask about his health, and he was fine. He gets his lungs tested every two years as a precaution, but, as of date, he has had no problems.

Even though I was teased at times, I was still making friends and developing relationships. I didn't really know who I was at that point in life. I was transforming and growing, trying to find a meaning and an identity. I knew that I was starting to like people, and it seemed that people were starting to like me. My shyness and inhibitions were disappearing. I was gaining confidence and self-esteem. It was true that alcohol was a crutch I leaned up, but there was more to it; I was beginning to believe in myself.

ROCKY MOUNTAIN HIGH

It was my first semester break as a college student. I was a pledge of the Phi Alpha Beta Fraternity, and my priorities had already shifted from academics to the frat. Being a pledge was very demanding, perhaps more difficult than any course. However, it offered the sweet attraction of belonging to something bigger than myself. That, in and of itself, was a compelling force, very similar to the feeling of patriotism. If I needed somebody to talk to or hang out with, there was always a friend available.

Brandon was my big brother in the fraternity, the older member assigned to guide me through the pledging process. During the break, some of the brothers were planning a skiing excursion to Colorado. A bonus included in the package was that we wouldn't have to pay a lot of money for a hotel; instead we would stay for free. The plan was to stay with Ronnie, a fraternity alumnus: a perk of being a part of a brotherhood. We would be sleeping on the floor, but that didn't faze us in the slightest bit. Despite the fact that I had only skied once, I decided to go along.

The plane ride was unremarkable, except for the stewardess hitting on Mick. He was a good looking guy, and always did well with the ladies. The brothers would often bow down to him in mocking reverence, in awe of his powerful attraction. Love God was his assumed title. Yet there was a distance in Mick, as if he were lost. I had brought some weights from my house and moved them into the basement of the fraternity. Mick and I would work out down there together. He wasn't a happy guy, and neither was

I. Our misery fed one another's bitterness. I would complain that I didn't know what I wanted from my life while Mick, ready to graduate, didn't feel great about the prospects of his future. We were two lost ships at sea. We couldn't see the light from shore, but we found comfort in the lights of each other. At this point in my life, I was seriously contemplating joining the marines.

The first night in Denver, we all packed tight in a car and rode to a Chinese restaurant. Conversation drifted from one topic to another and, at one point, Ronnie gave us a warning. The alcohol was going to affect us more because the higher altitude had less oxygen. Maybe I should have listened. We all ordered fancy cocktails, which turned out to be the size of large soup bowls. To exacerbate matters even more, I ordered a second enormous drink. Thankfully, I didn't have time to finish. We were all so drunk, that we didn't even leave enough money for the bill. The proprietor came running out after us as we were entering the car. I paid with traveler checks, and he demanded the identification number from my driver's license. I got concerned because I was drinking alcohol while I was underage, but, thankfully, nobody cared.

The ride back to Ronnie's place was a blur. It was a miracle I didn't vomit then and there. After stumbling into the house, I dropped on the couch like a fallen soldier. Somebody suggested that if I drank some water, it would make things better. I was far too intoxicated to know who was making the suggestion or to understand the logic behind it, but anything would have been better than what I was going through. I drank some water from the bathroom faucet. That's when everything came up. I was praying to the porcelain god once again. I crawled from the bathroom to my place on the floor. It was there that I chose to lay still with my eyes closed, wondering once again why the world was spinning like a top.

A significant thing happened as I lied there in my misery. Two of my brothers, Fred and Harry, snorted some cocaine and began a vigorous conversation. I have never used cocaine in my entire life, but, at that point, I had been around many people who had. One common side effect of getting high on cocaine is excessive talking. Fred had never met Harry before the trip, and now Fred wanted to get acquainted. Harry seemed to be especially concerned about the fraternity.

They began discussing Work Week, a euphemism for Hell Week. Harry mentioned the fact that I was present, and that Work Week was perhaps the most highly regarded secret in the fraternity. Fred noted that I was unconscious and not to worry. I felt the urge to tell them I was still awake, but I was too drunk to do anything but listen. He began discussing the biggest secret of all, the pledge final exam. The whole thing was a farce; there was no pledge final exam. The test would be the theme of Work Week. We would be required to memorize fact after fact in order to pass. When it was time to take the test, the questions would be so incredibly difficult that nobody could ever pass. Everyone would fail. Then we would be told we couldn't become members: no brotherhood for us. The whole concept was, at the moment of rejection, we would realize how much the fraternity meant to us.

Skiing in Colorado was phenomenal. The first time I went down the hill, I fell every ten feet, despite the fact that I was on the easiest hill. It was only my second time on skis. I felt like getting on a plane and going home early; I was so frustrated. Yet, I persevered and made it through the whole week. My skiing progressed nicely, improving every day, if not every hour. At the end of the trip, I could glide down the beginner's slope without falling, and I even dared to venture on a few of the more difficult hills.

But the greatest part of the trip was the Rocky Mountain High. The ski slopes were hours from Denver, where we slept on Ronnie's apartment floor. We had to navigate over curvy roads, winding up and down steep mountains. At times, the roads were narrow, and I could look down into what seemed like chasms without bottoms. The combination of snow, trees and mountains were exhilarating. I had never been touched by God's creation so deeply. It truly moved my soul. There was a popular song on the radio at that time called, "Life in a Northern Town" by Dream Academy. It played frequently as we drove, at least six times a day. Anytime I hear that song, I am transformed and taken away to that Rocky Mountain High. It was my first glimpse into eternity.

COMMUNISM AND MY EVIL ESSAY

My first semester at Edwards Tech was a success, academically. I received an A in every subject, except for the B in Political Science. If I had earned a perfect 4.0 or straight A's, I may have tried to repeat the accomplishment the next semester. However, tainted by a B, I gave up caring about class. I was happy with my grades, but there was no fulfillment in it. My soul was still aching and empty, and my academic accomplishments didn't help relieve that pain.

My second semester changed my life. One of our professors had gotten pregnant and was unable to teach the subsequent class. We instead had a replacement professor named Ted Jones. He couldn't have been more than thirty, and he had long blonde hair that flowed past his shoulders. But his most distinctive and unusual quality was that he was a communist. I had never met a real communist before. Edwards Tech, like most engineering schools, was conservative in nature, so it always puzzled me that Mr. Jones was even hired. He definitely didn't fit into the big picture that Edwards was trying to achieve. Mr. Jones's Political Science class made prospective engineers think and challenge authority. However, I believe Edwards' philosophy was to create engineers who would fall into line and use their talents for whatever purpose the state desired.

I say this for a couple of reasons. First of all, the majority of the class load was dedicated to engineering. We only had one humanities course a semester. If one learned the formulas and knew how to apply them, they would do well on the tests. The exams seldom asked challenging questions that would require thinking outside the box. There were no ethics classes, nor were there classes on the environment or anything aesthetic.

Furthermore, the classes were separated. Freshmen would only have freshmen in their classes; sophomores would only have sophomores, etc. While this may have been necessary for the engineering classes, it was not for humanities. Why were humanities courses divided according to our class? I personally believe that Edwards wanted to promote a hierarchy. A freshman was below a sophomore, who was below a junior, who was below a senior. In this way, the engineer-to-be was kept in his place. Yet, there was the promise that if you kept going in the system, you would one day have your turn to be superior. The fraternities and sororities taught this concept as well. One had to begin as a lowly pledge. A pledge was subservient to the establishment. Yet if the pledges behaved and did everything that was required of them, they would one day belong.

Thus, an engineer was being taught to do as he was told, not to challenge the system. The worst thing that could happen for a company making weapons is for an engineer to think creatively and say, "What is what I am designing going to be used for?" If this occurred, then there would be fewer weapons designers. The ideal engineer to be produced would be one that was intelligent enough to handle many complicated and difficult problems, yet they should fall in line and be obedient without questioning authority.

In his political science class, Mr. Jones proselytized. He tried his best to convert us to his great cause. I believe he was more concerned with making us Red than in educating us. All his teaching had a slant, and it was not in the least bit subliminal. While it was true that he welcomed debate on the issues, he was not so opened-minded when it came to grading. We discovered that it was impossible to get an A if you did not endorse the communist ideology. The best grade possible without regurgitating his propaganda was a B.

My friends and I liked Mr. Jones as a person. He would argue that the government spent a fortune on weapons to the detriment of the poor of our nation, while we often explained that, since we were all going to be engineers, we would directly and personally benefit from weapons production. After all, we would be the ones building and designing the implements of war. Therefore, in a practical sense, war was a good thing for us. He really couldn't argue against our selfish motives.

We even invited Mr. Jones to our fraternity house for dinner. It was Phi Alpha Beta policy to have prominent people visit us as guests. We usually invited professors. We would dress up in suits, taking the formal dinner seriously. There was an upper classman named Kurt who also had Mr. Jones. Kurt and was quite the reactionary conservative. I felt like Mr. Jones had his eye on Kurt. If the revolution had ever come, I'm sure Kurt would have been first on the list to be killed, provided he didn't kill Mr. Jones first.

At this point in my life, I was still lost. I didn't take anything seriously. I lacked direction and meaning and had no purpose in life. So it came to pass that we had a test in Political Science. I decided to do something daring. The test was in the form of an essay. In my paper, I admitted that capitalism was indeed doomed to be defeated. I really didn't believe this, but I wrote it anyway. Furthermore, I conceded that there was nothing to stop the red tide. I was sure that as Mr. Jones read the paper, he would feel a sense of accomplishment for converting me to his way of thinking. My conclusion stated that, while we capitalists still had the upper hand, we might as well have our fun in the world.

I wasn't quite prepared for Mr. Jones's reaction. The next day he devoted the entire class to rebuking my essay's conclusion. This was serious stuff he said. Destruction, devastation, and the killing of civilians was not his idea of fun. I don't know if the rebuke affected me greatly at the time, but I got the point. If nothing more, it began a maturation process. I began to consider things beyond my own selfish sphere.

Later in the semester, at Mr. Jones's invitation, we attended a protest in New York City, focusing on the chaos in Nicaragua and El Salvador. Earlier, Mr. Jones had stormed a courtroom and got himself arrested in an act of civil disobedience. I wasn't really convinced about the politics involved. I just wanted to attend a protest to see what it was like.

I marched around with Mr. Jones and two of my fraternity brothers. Dick, another brother in my class, was torn about whether to attend or not. On the one hand, he wanted to get on Mr. Jones's good side, so he could get a better grade in the class. But he was also cautious, and for good reason. As we marched around in a circle, Mr. Jones pointed out a group of photographers. They weren't the press; they were the FBI. The government liked to get pictures of protesters to see if there were any faces that popped up too often. These people would be considered agitators and would warrant further investigation. I remember us chanting so loudly that Mr. Jones's voice was hoarse from yelling and he could only speak in a whisper. But it was a loud whisper.

At the end of the year Mr. Jones had a party at his house in Brooklyn. It was full of strange people. He felt big and proud when he pulled out one lousy marijuana cigarette at the party. It turned out to be a dull night.

When I became a Christian, Mr. Jones and I had a long talk. He used to be a believer in God, but he had abandoned the faith. I believe he had a genuine concern for people in general. I think he lost his faith in God because of the hypocrisy that is so prevalent in the Christian world. Although I don't consider people who kill in God's name the least bit Christian, Mr. Jones and I did try to find common ground. He pointed out how the Communists and the Catholics worked together in El Salvador to combat the death squads.

Later on as the years passed, I would think about Ted Jones. I wrote a song about him called, "I Will Raise My Voice." It was published as a poem in The Struggle, which is a communist magazine. It was my first publication, and it holds a special place in my heart.

I have since tried to find out how Ted is doing, but my efforts have been fruitless. It's next to impossible to track a person with the last name of Jones, despite modern technological advances. I wonder if he's still radical, or if he's become a too cynical. I'd like to talk to him. I have definitely moved to the left, politically, since those days, although it's in my own unique Christian way.

Mr. Jones was both smart and devoted, a man on a mission. He helped me become aware that every drop of rain contributes to the flood.

YANG AND YING

The concept of the Ying and the Yang comes from the Eastern Asian religions. My interpretation of it is personal and may not be accurate. The symbol is a circle with half being white and the other half being black. Yet in the white half there is a small black circle, and in the black half there is a small white circle. The idea is that every good has its opposite evil, yet neither the good nor evil are absolute. Dick was my other half in the Ying and the Yang.

Dick had become my friend during freshman year. My roommate Al was very outgoing and had collected quite a following of people. They would sit together as a unit in lecture and go to lunch at the cafeteria in mass. Among his gaggle of friends was Dick. He was in my Political Science class as well as being my partner in chemistry lab. When we all pledged the Phi Alpha Beta Fraternity, the bonds of friendship were strengthened. Al became pledge president while Dick was the treasurer.

I recall Dick getting into trouble before we became close friends. There were a number of people at Edwards who lacked social skills. Even though I wasn't a prime example of charisma myself, I was more socially developed than the majority. We referred to these people as nerds. We also knew an odd girl who liked to date nerds. We appropriately labeled her The Nerd Girl. I can't remember the details, but Dick did something very offensive to her. It was serious enough that the dean got involved and suspension from school was discussed. Dick liked to say that he was on "double secret probation." This sounded like something dreadful to me. But it was just a joke, a line taken out of the movie Animal House. Dick was almost black-balled from the frat due to his rude and offensive behavior, but he hung on and prevailed. Being black-balled meant being expelled from the fraternity, and it was called that because the brothers actually held a vote using white and black balls. Some of them did drop black balls. However, a pledge was only dismissed if he received two consecutive black balls, or if he got a black ball on the final vote. I believe he apologized to The Nerd Girl, and we all put the incident behind us. She faded into obscurity as one of the many freshmen that dropped out of school.

During my first semester, we had a problem with the Alpha Beta Gamma Fraternity, or Gams. Rush is the recruitment time period for the fraternities. Brothers from all the frats descend like locusts unto the freshman dorms. They wear their letters and knock on all the doors in search of prospective members. They also had parties called Smokers, designed just for the freshman. The competition was very serious. Every frat wants to recruit the best guys. Therefore, most of my friends who pledged the Phi Alpha Beta Fraternity also got invitations to join the Gams. When we pledged, Phi Alpha Beta was a proverbial slap in the face to the Gams, as we all rejected them.

The Gams were considered the jock house. The truth is that many athletes were not even in the Gams Fraternity. Jocks often had the mentality that they were superior. My freshman year only two freshmen pledged their house; though they got a good number of sophomores. It was a dismal recruiting class. In anger, some Gams broke into our fraternity house while we were playing a football game against them. All our brothers were at the football game, which we won by the way. They stole two paddles: making a paddle out of wood, without tools, is a pledge tradition. Because of the extensive time involved in making them and their symbolic nature, they were quite precious.

We, of course, were furious. In retaliation, Dick, Al, Sam, and another guy named Roland, who was a fellow pledge, decided to take action. They actually kidnapped the Gams' pledge president, a guy named Byron. They took a plastic pumpkin and put it over his head, then walked him down to the Hudson River. There, at the bank of the river, they told him, "The bottom line is the river's cold and we want our paddles back."

When I heard about what had happened, I was pretty upset. Byron was actually one of our friends. In truth, his pledging a different fraternity ruined our friendship. This paddle episode was the beginning of a division brought on by the rivalry of the two fraternities. Furthermore, it wasn't Byron's fault that the paddles were stolen; he had nothing to do with it. Worst of all, it was just a nasty thing to do to someone. Unfortunately, a couple of nights later, the Gams retaliated. I heard my roommate Al's voice cry out in distress, "John, wake up. It's the Gams."

I woke to see the room crowded with people. They whisked my roommate Al away and told me to stay on the bed. Foolishly, I jumped down in a vain effort to prevent them from taking my friend. There were at least twenty guys. I started shoving and pushing them around in desperation, but I was eventually thrown to the ground. I locked my legs in a figure four around the bedpost, so they couldn't drag me away. After a long struggle, I was overcome. They carried me into the hall, wearing only my underpants. I noticed they had put tape over everyone's peephole. However, the door across the hall was open. Saul, the room's occupant, was watching what was going on. The Gams slammed his door shut. But to his credit, Saul reopened his door to observe. He wasn't scared, but he didn't help. Perhaps he thought it was some frat thing, being done all in fun.

They flung a pillowcase over my head and carried me to their frat house. I had a decent sense of direction, even though I couldn't see. They took pictures of me in my underpants with the pillowcase draped over my head. The click of the camera and buzz of the flash were distinct. Somewhere along the line, they tied my hands behind my back. I got angry and started to resist, but it was futile. I heard the mocking laughter of my captors. After half an hour of humiliation, they put me on the Zeta Omicron Fraternity doorstep. It took about five minutes to free myself from my bonds. I took off the pillowcase and started back to my dorm. The sun had just begun to rise.

I was angry and distraught, while walking across campus in my underwear. The experience was humiliating, and I felt powerless. I was even more upset because I had disapproved of Byron's capture in the first place. First, I wept a little. Then my anger rose, and I became determined to pound on Byron for revenge. When I arrived at my dormitory, I realized I didn't have my key. In frustration, I punched the glass door. Even though the glass had a metal weave in it, I busted through it with my fist. I marched straight to Byron's room with fire in my veins. Finding no Byron, I ripped up his Alpha Beta Gamma pledge book instead. Eventually the paddles were returned, and we all made up. But the deep resentment fueled a competition between the two houses. Phi Alpha Beta would rise in popularity and even challenge the Gams in athletics. All the fraternities participated in sports against one another. The Gams prided themselves in being the best, but Phi Alpha Beta would always give them a run for their money.

The second semester of my freshman year, I got to know Dick better. I left the third floor and moved to the first floor to live with Sam. Sam had suggested that I change and come live with him. Al was quite upset with the move, but I told him we would still be friends. Al had the habit of playing talk radio all night and I used that as an excuse for my departure. I am very prone to follow a suggestion. I guess it was just time for a change.

Dick also lived on the first floor with another pledge brother, and, like I mentioned earlier, he was the treasurer for our pledge class. He would collect money from the pledges from time to time to support some efforts. Usually, it was just money to buy a keg, even though we were under the legal drinking age. Somehow he was never asked to reimburse the brothers. I guess it was a lack of communication, so Dick would just use the money to buy pizza. I always ate the pizza, so I guess I was just as guilty of stealing as he was. Dick would make sure that every pledge would give their dollar. He was diligent in that aspect of his duties. I guess that way we could get mushrooms on the pizza instead of eating it plain.

That year after Work Week we were officially initiated into the Phi Alpha Beta fraternity. Now that we had more time on our hands, some brothers and I joined the junior varsity lacrosse team. We wound up only playing two games, both against Kean

University. Our mascot was a duck, and we played like ducks. During the second game, Al was playing defense. A player on the opposing team gave him a cheap shot from behind. Al turned around and smashed his stick over the offender's head, bending his stick in the process. The other team rushed out onto the field. I also rushed out to Al's aid. Unfortunately, I was the only one on our team to take action. One of the players on the other team said something offensive to me. As if I was back on the elementary playground, I took off my helmet and stuck my stick in his face.

He got angry and charged me. He was taller than me, but that didn't matter. Since I was a wrestler, I knew exactly what to do. I took the rushing man's momentum and used it to throw him to the ground. The move was similar to a head lock where I used my hip as a pivot. He went flying through the air, his aggression working against him. After throwing him on the ground, I landed on top of him in full control. I grabbed his face mask and began twisting his head. I taunted my opponent repeatedly saying "Don't mess with us." Eventually, I relented and calmed down. Al and I were ejected from the game.

A fellow teammate said that Dick was distraught about the whole thing. Another teammate and fellow Phi Alpha Beta named Gerald said Dick wanted to go out and help us. I recall the coach had yelled, forbidding us from running onto the field. I had ignored him; I guess everybody else listened. After the brawl, the coach only had these words for me, "Next time, keep your helmet on."

The next year Sam, Dick, and I were rush chairmen, and we had the largest pledge class in our frat's history, or at least recent known history. It was Dick's job to divide the brothers into different groups that visited dorms, recruiting freshman. Each member of the fraternity had to participate every day for the month and a half of rush. Reflecting back on this requirement, I am upset by the lack of the zeal for evangelism in some churches. If a frat can put this much effort into recruitment, why can't a church dedicate this much passion into evangelism? Members of our fraternity spent an hour and a half a day, five days a week persuading freshmen to consider our fraternity. This was in addition to attending smokers and parties. However, there were a couple of the guys in the frat we thought of as "undesirable." In our opinion, they weren't as cool as the rest. Because of this, along with the memory of our stolen paddles, Dick invented a security team made up of the "undesirables." This meant that people we didn't want representing our frat would stay back and "protect" the house. The truth was, Dick didn't want these guys creating a negative impression on prospective pledges. I thought Dick was cruel in this practice, but I didn't voice my objection; maybe because I thought it effective.

The day pre-freshmen came to campus to experience a day at Edwards Tech was huge for fraternities. It was our chance to get a jump on influencing the freshmen to pledge. Dick and I had a plan to throw paint on the Alpha Beta Gamma wall, but that morning I was losing my nerve. Deep down, I was still adverse to breaking rules. Dick chided me for being all talk and no action. So at 4 a.m., we grabbed two cans of black paint and stealthily walked to frat row, where the Gams had a nicely painted wall bearing their letters. As I threw paint, my lips trembled from the dual emotions of anger and hatred. It was a bizarre moment for me. I definitely did not feel satisfied. After our deed was done, we fled the scene. I carried my paint can over a hundred yards until I realized I should probably drop the evidence. Everybody was happy that somebody had defaced the Gams' wall; they were commonly disliked for their arrogance. Yet, when we told a couple of our brothers what we did, they got upset. After that we kept quiet.

If it weren't for Dick, I probably wouldn't have broken so many rules. He was Ying and I was Yang. Or I was Yang and he was Ying. Either way it doesn't matter.

First Tokes and Suicide Jumpers

Honesty is a sacred virtue that I ascribed to. But the truth is, I was lied to. I was taught that America was a virtuous country that was perfect in every way. I was taught that salvation came by works and adherence to the Roman Catholic Church. It was implied that adults were all-knowing and knew exactly how to live properly. As a child, I simply had to follow the path set before me, and all would be well. There were other lies I was exposed to as well, lies that were cleverly hidden in advertising and movies. These lies lead to anorexia, suicidal thoughts, and mental illness, among other things. These lies eventually all collapsed one by one, shattering the illusion, leaving me empty and aching.

In high school I was strictly against drug use, but, to be honest, hallucinogenic drugs like LSD always interested me. Since I was not in the drug crowd or the party crowd, I never actually had an opportunity to experiment with them. I recall an episode when I was a senior in high school. I was hanging out with six classmates who started smoking a joint of marijuana. I refused to participate and stayed in the car, being quite the prude.

One thing I had learned was that no matter what, drugs were bad. There were no positive aspects to narcotics. It was a rule written in stone, like God endorsing America, the Pope being infallible, and grown-ups knowing better. Furthermore, the use of drugs was a quick one-way ticket to being a failure in life. This clearly appeared to be true in my high school. As I mentioned before, the people who were heavy into drugs were labeled Burnouts. They were low achievers, both scholastically and athletically. They were the true definition of losers.

Things changed when I went to Edwards Institute of Technology. I was introduced to a new world, where people who were bright and successful were also very much involved with drugs. Drugs, I discovered, were not an instant recipe for disaster. Instead, it seemed on par with drinking alcohol; not worse, just different.

Let me address this point very clearly. The use of alcohol is legal in most parts of the United States. I knew teachers and other responsible adults who drank alcohol. These role models were a functioning part of society. Therefore, the message given is that drinking alcohol is okay, even normal. Furthermore, alcohol is a symbol of adult status. Adults drink; therefore if I drink, I am more like an adult. The government cannot condemn drinking alcohol like it does other drugs because it's legal.

I would estimate that over thirty percent of the students of Edwards Tech used illegal drugs at least once a month, and this guess could very well be too low. I knew people who received excellent grades, were star athletes, or held high positions and used illegal narcotics. This discovery shattered my opinion that drugs were a diabolical evil. In fact, when I was around drug users, they all seemed to be having such a wonderful time. No one had told me drugs were fun; instead I was taught they would only bring agony. I was starting to question the absolutes that I thought I believed in. Reality was crumbling; there was nothing left that was sacred.

The Phi Alpha Beta fraternity held their first annual scavenger hunt as part of our pledging process. We went into Manhattan and had a wild time. Our first task in the scavenger hunt was to get a menu from Windows of the World, the restaurant on top of the World Trade Center. One of our pledge brothers had worn his suit. He looked like a cheap pimp. I said he looked "Cheesy" and a nickname was born. My roommate Sam claimed he came up with the nickname, but I disagree. Even with his "Cheesy" appearance, he successfully stole the menu.

The second item was to get chopsticks from a famous Chinese restaurant. Thankfully, we had been given some money for expenses. I was hungry and jokingly said that I'd go eat dinner and take the chopsticks. Everybody thought it was a great idea, and I got a free meal. Win-win!

We also had to buy a product from some sex store. I was amazed at all the accessories, everything from whips, chains, dildos, and things too obscene to mention. We bought a toy resembling a giant male sex organ.

The most difficult thing to obtain was the hat of the Trump Tower doorman. One brother, Vince, was athletic and planned to grab the hat and run. I was directly involved in this caper as well. My part was to "accidentally" get in front of the doorman once the hat was stolen. Vince grabbed the hat and bolted down the street. I casually walked right in front of the shocked doorman, giving just enough time to aid the getaway. Unfortunately, we all got scattered in the process. Cheesy was in a panic and thought the entire New York Police Department was after us. They, of course, were not.

The last item we had to scavenge was a dime bag ($10 worth) of marijuana. We decided that Washington Square Park was the best place to buy it. That night, however, the park was full of cops. It wasn't hard to pick out the drug dealers, so we singled one out and told him we wanted to buy some pot. He walked with us and kept whispering, "keep on walking." Finally, we reached a secluded spot away from the cops and the exchange was made. Ten dollars for a small bag of weed.

Marijuana seemed to be decriminalized in Manhattan, as far as I could tell. People smoked it openly on the streets, and it was a simple matter to buy it. A person walking through Washington Square Park would get offered weed at least four or five times in only one block. Usually the cops didn't mind, but sometimes they caused trouble for consumers. Once, my friend Sam was buying drugs in the city. The money was exchanged and the drugs given. All of a sudden, a cop appeared out of nowhere. Sam, being street savvy, quickly swallowed the small bag. With no evidence, there was no crime.

I was in the habit of drinking on Friday and Saturday nights. Even though I was three years shy of the legal drinking limit, I never had a problem getting alcohol. In fact, I did 99 percent of my drinking before the legal age limit.

After the scavenger hunt, a group of us went down to one of the freshman dorms to see one of our fellow pledges. His room was different, because he had built a loft, creating a big area to hang out. We took out the dime bag from Washington Square Park. Someone produced a large green bong, a device that allows the smoke to pass through water when you inhale. This way the harshness to the throat is minimized. The bong was passed around, each person inhaling the green smoke.

I had been at other marijuana parties and had always declined. When the bong came to me, to everyone's surprise, I placed my lips on it and inhaled deeply. Hot air filled my lungs. I felt a sudden daze and began to cough uncontrollably. The whole room was staring at me in shock and surprise. This was completely out of character. A few people were concerned about my coughing, but the general reaction was hysterical laughing.

I sat basking in my high, while the rest of my pals finished up the pot. Some people say they don't get high the first time they smoke pot, and it takes a little while to feel its effects. I got high. It was on the same level as being drunk, just faster. I was light headed and felt euphoric. The experience was both pleasant and relaxing.

My head was still buzzing when we left the party. Sam, my new roommate, escorted me down to our room on the first floor. Walking through the hallway, we spotted some young ladies. With no inhibitions, I called out to them. Sam, embarrassed, initially told me to stop, but when they started to come, he began to beckon them as well. We actually talked to them and arranged a meeting at The Point later, a nice, elevated spot overlooking the Hudson River and the Manhattan skyline.

I was flying high. The drugs were lifting us up, and so were the thoughts of the babes we would soon be meeting. I took a shower, which was unusual. The water flowed and flowed, soothing my scattered thoughts. I got dressed up as slick as I could manage, and, in eager anticipation, the two of us walked up to The Point.

As fate would have it, we weren't the only ones up there that night. Sam and I had hopes for a romantic interlude, but some upperclassmen, whom we had never seen before, were killing the mood. There were two guys and a girl, and one guy was distraught. "I've had enough. I'm going to end it all," he yelled threateningly. He had one foot on the wrong side of the protective chain. He was starting down at a hundred foot drop. There were tall trees growing up from below that may have slowed his plummet, but he would have most likely died.

I was still stoned, and couldn't grasp the reality of what was going on. "Go ahead and jump," I said, laughing. Everyone looked at me in shock and horror.

Sam tried to inform me of the levity of the situation. "John, I think he's serious." His voice was a stern sobering whisper.

"Go ahead and jump," I repeated, still oblivious to reality. The guy threatening to kill himself, of course, didn't like my attitude, but it was a perfect example of reverse psychology, though purely by accident. He stared at me and stepped back from the edge, embracing his friends who were trying to save him. Strangely, he began singing a song from an educational cartoon I had watched as a child. "Today I have become a bill," he sang weeping.

As soon as he started singing reality began to dawn on me. This person wanted to kill himself, and I was coaxing him on. I felt a wave of guilt and began to apologize profusely. Meanwhile, the chicks had split. It must have become too weird for them. It was a long and strange day that I'll never forget.

WORK WEEK

Spring break of my freshman year was designated for Work Week. As the time approached, the hazing dished out to the pledges increased. During dinner, a computer was programmed to dial the freshman numbers over and over. It was a rule that a pledge must run to the phone to answer it, no matter what. During dinner, we would barely get a bite in before having to run up two stories to see who was on the phone. It was almost always "brother modem" calling.

Why would someone allow themselves to be subject to such abuse? After all, it wasn't like we were drafted into the armed forces; we volunteered for this. At this point, we had invested too much into the fraternity to turn back. During the rush period, all the fraternities denied hazing. At first, the whole thing was like one endless party. Slowly, after time, the hazing grew and grew. This was especially true after the end of the first semester.

A lot of freshman decided that Edwards wasn't their kind of school and dropped out. Those who decided to tough it out were those who did better academically. Thus, they were committed not only to the fraternity, but to the school. Work Week was the climax of pledging process, where the antagonism and friendship between the brothers and pledges really manifested itself.

In the days leading up to Work Week, we were led to believe it consisted of working on the house and partying. The pledges were encouraged to bring an ample amount of alcohol and drugs, so that they could properly live it up. This was outright deceit. The pledges did very little partying, while the brothers partied constantly. In fact, to rub it in, the brothers would drink the alcohol or smoke the marijuana in front of the pledge that provided it. It was like a bully rubbing a person's face in the mud.

On the last, faithful day, all the pledges gathered in the front room of the fraternity house. The front room was the TV room, which was the size of an average dining room. We handed in the wooden paddles that we had spent so much time constructing. Next, we were forced to surrender all jewelry and watches, including our pledge pins. As pledges, we had to wear our pins at all times. We even put them on our towels, so we would have them when we showered. Pledging was a serious thing.

After giving up our stuff, we all moved into the dining room. We had a wonderful meal of lasagna, with brownies for desert. The brothers were as nice as could be, but something was up. A careful eye would reveal that they were wearing sweats and running sneakers. Furthermore, they were encouraging us to stuff ourselves, while they were eating very little.

After dining, we were ushered back to the front room. Then the music started. It was a song by Madonna called "Into the Groove." That entire week, this song was blasted on repeat, without stopping. We were instructed to get in order from the smallest to the tallest. I was second in line, being the second shortest pledge. That's when we started to run. All brothers and pledges participated, without exception.

Before leaving, one of the seniors told me that he wouldn't be attending Work Week. Seniors were allowed to skip Work Week. However, when he made this statement I almost said, "Good, because I hate your guts." Fortunately, I was wise enough to hold my tongue. It was nothing but a lie. That was the nature of Work Week, to get you to believe something that wasn't true. It was the same brother who announced on the eve of Work Week what he had learned in psychology class: "The more an individual was hazed the stronger his/her loyalty to the group."

After running, I was ushered downstairs to the slop sink. It hadn't been cleaned for months because the drainage system had backed up. The odor was foul and mold was floating in stagnate water. I was handed a paper cup with a hole in the bottom and was promptly told to bail out the sink and clean it.

The music was still blaring at full volume, the same stupid Madonna song over and over. All the while, the brothers were drilling us with questions. They asked me, "What do you think of the music?" When I started to reply they interjected, "No, you can't hear the music; you're working too hard." So every time they asked us what we thought of the music we screamed, "I can't hear the music, I'm working too hard."

We were forced to run everywhere. When we weren't actually running, we had to jog in place. Every time we entered through the door we had to scream, "Rah, rah, rah, Phi Alpha Beta, pledge so and so, speaking." Multiple brothers would constantly ask us questions. If we didn't immediately answer the question we would be asked, "Are you hesitating?" The proper pledge reply to that being "I hesitate to articulate for fear of deviating from the true path of rectitude." Those words are still crystal clear in my head.

The first night the pledges were in for a surprise. After a day of exhausting cleaning and running, we were led back into the front room. We were told that we had to sleep there, but there were stipulations. We couldn't move any of the furniture to make room, so we all scurried to find a place for the night's rest. Many of my pledge brothers twisted and contorted to fit. I found a good spot where my legs were fully extended, though I was half under a table. The next morning we woke to Madonna's voice and a banging at the door. The pledges jumped up to g about the business of being abused.

Most of Work Week was a blur. I recall running with cinderblocks on the second day. I ran from the top floor of one brownstone to the top floor of another with heavy blocks heaped on my shoulders. The buildings each had three floors. All the while, every stereo was blasting our Work Week song, and I had to answer the thousands of questions tossed at me.

After lunch, all the pledges gathered in the front room again. A brother entered and barked out my name, "Pledge Kaniecki!" I dutifully went forward. He handed me a green toothbrush and said, "You are shit, the sacred holder of the ignominious toothbrush.

In order to secure a cleaner flush, I go forth with my brush."

I was immediately sent to a bathroom and made good use of my brush on the dirty commodes. I cleaned a lot of toilet bowls that week, and I took strong offense when my cleaning was interrupted by a brother needing to relieve himself.

Out of everything that was done to us, the most degrading thing of all occurred in the back yard. I was wearing my toothbrush like a necklace. "What's that?" yelled one of the more obnoxious brothers.

"I am shit," I began reciting my personal mantra.

"Well, is he shit?" asked the brother, referring to my good friend Al.

I wanted to scream obscenities at the brother. I was so close to doing so that the words formed in my mouth before I forced them down. Instead, I meekly responded, "He's shit."

"How dare you call your pledge brother shit," screamed the brother. Something snapped inside my head when I called him shit. It was the first time I had ever been broken. I had surrendered my will, so to say. I shouldn't have said anything negative about my fellow pledge. The brother yelled at me, but the damage had been done.

One good aspect of Work Week was the unification. All the pledges were equal. We referred to each other as "pledge brothers," definitely not the forbidden word, "pledge." The brothers liked to ask us if we wanted a drink. We were all hot and sweaty, so it was obvious that we did. However, the correct response was, "Not unless all my pledge brothers get one." Then, each pledge would receive one, tiny drink.

We also talked about love. When asked, "What do you think about Work Week?" we responded with a rousing yell, "We love Work Week, brother so and so." Also, we were asked what we thought about brothers and pledge brothers. We hollered our love at the top of our lungs.

When we couldn't answer a question, we had to run and ask our fellow pledges for the correct answer. The brothers kept emphasizing the final exam that needed to be passed to become a brother. We were told that no pledge of our fraternity chapter had ever failed the test. The brothers stressed that they didn't want this record broken. In fact, all of the abuse was justified because it was preparation for the intense exam. By forcing us to run around and asking endless questions, we were just getting ready. Of course, I already knew it was all a lie. There was no final.

My friend Sam became The Joker. He had a Work Week mantra, too. His speech was "I am The Joker, I am here to entertain you. Would you like to hear one joke or two?" Then, the brother would expect a joke. They would do their best to resist laughing and demand that Sam come up with a funnier joke. During our breaks, we would try to help him learn new jokes.

One day the pledge master put me in the basement and told me to paint numbers on cinderblocks. As I went about my task, I started feeling extremely happy. I felt good about the fraternity. I felt good about my many friends. I felt good about finally belonging somewhere. So I painted a smiley face on one of the cinderblocks. When the pledge master Arthur came down to check on my progress, he saw the smiley face and flew into a rage. He probably thought I wasn't taking things seriously. As punishment, I was forced to carry the cinderblock wherever I went. I did this for several hours. When it was time to run to lunch, there I was, hauling my smiley-faced cinderblock. One of the older brothers intervened and took the stone away from me. He thought the pledge master had gone too far.

At the end of every day, we were asked, "What do you want from Phi Alpha Beta?" Different pledges would be called on, and no matter what answer we gave, it was criticized. We didn't learn the correct response until the end of Work Week.

We learned another saying during our trial. The brothers would ask, "Do you know what time it is?" Our response was to be, "Due to the fact that my chronometer is not in exact synchronization with the Cesium sixty-nine atom, I cannot ascertain the correct time. However, governed by the laws of probability and statistics, I may venture to state a guess what the correct time is, brother so and so. May I see your watch please?"

It took me an extremely long time to learn that saying. It was introduced by the brothers one time. From then on, we relied on fellow pledge brothers to help us out. One of the brothers spent a lot time teaching me the saying. It literally took hours for me to learn; so long, he suspected I was trying to play stupid.

A remarkable thing did happen during Work Week. The pledges rebelled in a significant manner. After being released to "shit, shower and shave," we gathered around and started talking. The focus of our discussion was on the pledge final. Though I insisted it was a lie, a good portion of the pledges didn't believe me. Still, we all agreed that the abuse wasn't in any way preparing us to take the final, so we decided, as a group, not to answer as prescribed.

When we arrived, well over a half hour late, there was a palpable tension in the air. It only increased as some of the pledges refused to answer questions. We were eventually ushered into the front room to discuss the matter alone. At that time, we decided to go along with the brothers. I particularly spoke in defense of the older brothers, saying we should trust them. I knew for certain that the final was a fake. Fortunately for me, the brothers heard me defending them, because they had a listening device in the room. After the rebellion, I received less hazing than my fellow pledges.

Somehow our unique uprising was labeled the Quiche Eaters Rebellion. In reflection, I am very proud of our little act of sedition. We were willing to stick together and take a chance on losing something we all desired. So much so that it empowered us. We gave the brothers a clear message that they did not hold all the cards.

During all of Work Week, we were forbidden from drinking alcohol or using drugs. However, a day came when I was in the basement cleaning commodes under the supervision of Brother Benjamin. When I lifted the toilet seat, I found a large bottle of Coors Beer floating in toilet water. "Drink it," he said. I told him that it was forbidden for pledges to drink beer. Benjamin responded by saying that I should trust him. I relented, twisting off the cap, and gulped down a good portion of the amber liquid.

I went upstairs and it was pandemonium. Some of the pledges were drinking from big bottles of beer. Others, adhering to the rules, refused. Eventually the brothers persuaded the refusing pledges to drink. Finally, a party broke out! The beer flowed and the distinctly recognizable sent of marijuana filled the house. We all congregated in our dining room, where all the tables and benches were cleared. The revelry of beer drinking continued until everyone was smashed.

The pledges were divided into two teams. We were told that the floor was dirty, and each team was given a mop without handles. Then the pledges had a contest. On our hands and knees, we scrubbed the floor one-by-one in haste. One team finished ahead of the other, and then we were once more rushed into the front room. It was the first real happy moment that we had experienced that week.

Arnold came by on the final day of Work Week. I didn't know that it was the final day, because the pledges were kept in the dark about such matters. The fact that we were finally cleaning the front room should have been a clue. Arnold pointed out a framed document that hung on the wall. It was the fraternity's charter, the thing that made us what we are. I was told to clean the wall where the charter hung. I got some paper towels and scrubbed and scrubbed. Forty-five minutes had passed. Yet, no matter how much I cleaned the paper towels continued to get dirty. It was my desire to make the wall perfectly clean. One of the other brothers came in and told me to stop. Apparently, Arnold was finally satisfied.

Why did I feel the need to scrub the wall until it was perfectly clean? The charter that hung there was a tangible representation of the abstract fraternity. I was brainwashed. I was dedicated to all my brothers in a bond of love. I was a member of something that was bigger than myself. I had finally found a place where I belonged, or at least, so I thought. Arnold's psychological lesson was apparently correct, the greater the hazing the more loyalty one feels.

On the final day of Work Week, we all lined up in front of the Phi Alpha Beta house, wearing our finest clothes. There was a slight drizzle, so we were let inside. By tradition they usually kept the pledges standing outside for a good while. We were called in alphabetical order. When my turn came, I was ushered into a small room. I was given a paper, which I presumed to be the pledge final. The questions were impossibly hard and obscure. After several minutes, I was told that my time had expired. I was taken to another room with several brothers. Brandon, my big brother, was there. He told me the bad news; I was the only pledge to ever to fail the final. With pure disgust, I was told to get my disgraceful butt out of the fraternity. Playing along with the game, I exited the room. It was all just another head-trip. When a pledge is told he has failed the final, everything he worked so hard for was made vain. At that moment, the pledge was supposed to realize how much the fraternity meant to him.

After I was told the pledge final was a ruse, I hugged one of the brothers. In my heart, I had realized I had discovered a form of love. At that moment, with the torturous week vibrant in my mind, I understood that this was not the true love that I was searching for, yet realized that it was better than any love I had felt before that.

Work Week worked wonders for me personally. It was one of the greatest achievements of my life to become a Frat Brother. I finally felt a sense of completeness, and I now had an identity. I began to see other people as creatures like me, with wants and needs. My compassion extended beyond the fraternity into all society.

Did Work Week hurt me psychologically? Absolutely. Without a doubt. But, I still insist it was not the root cause of my mental illness; rather it only exasperated it. After all, as far as I know, I was the only one from the fraternity to wind up in a psychiatric hospital.

SOME STONED CATS

It was a Saturday night and a group of us had gathered in my dorm room to party. The night's entertainment was a bag of marijuana and a pipe. For some reason that I cannot recall, there was some catnip in the room. Catnip is something given to cats which felines greatly enjoy. In the stupidity of our high, we put catnip in the pipe and smoked it. After amusing ourselves, we exited the room meowing like cats. The resident assistant down the hall watched us. We looked and acted like fools, but because we were stoned, we didn't really care.

The next week we gathered in my dorm room to get stoned again. There was no pot this time, so instead, we smoked some catnip. We did not get high.

Then someone made a clever observation the catnip looked exactly like marijuana. It was green and had similar texture. The only problem was that half of the catnip was a grayish color. Soon, we were busy separating the green from the gray. In the end, we had a nice pile of green catnip.

We took a walk down the hall to Little Dude's room. He was a big pot smoker and did a little dealing as well. He took a small piece of bud from his marijuana supply and mixed it with the catnip. Then, he smoked some of his grass and blew the smoke into the plastic bag to create the proper smell.

With the fake pot in hand, I went up to the third floor and found some guys named Felix and Walter. I handed Walter the bag for him to examine. The deal was for ten dollars.

Walter took the bag and carefully examined it. He opened the bag and smelled it, inhaling a deep breath. I was certain my deception would be discovered, and I'd be in deep trouble.

Instead of an angry scowl, I was met with a genuine smile. "Good stuff," Walter declared. It was all I could do to keep from laughing. We took the ten dollars and went back to Little Dude's room. We used the money to buy the real stuff.

In the morning, my conscience got the best of me. I visited my old roommate Al on the third floor. When I told him the story he was shocked. "People get killed for what you did," he warned me.

I later apologized to Walter. He said "Don't worry about it. We all got high anyway." I still felt really bad, but not bad enough to give back the ten dollars. Instead, I drank to cover my guilt.

At this point, I was suffering from some very serious psychological issues that I was unable to deal with. Instead of facing the pain and turmoil head on, I took the path to oblivion, paved with marijuana and booze.

ARTY AT THE PARTY

Appearances can be deceiving. People often put on a front. Arthur fit the category of winner in every worldly criterion, but underneath it all he was not well.

I recall going to a fraternity party my freshman year. It was something called a "Y Be Normal?" party. Standing next to me was a strange looking man with and bow tie and a suit jacket. He had a pair of thick black glasses with masking tape around the bridge. He portrayed the classic, stereotypical look of a nerd. As we shook hands, he said, "Arty, Rush Chairman, damn glad to meet you." This was an exact line taken from the movie Animal House. It took a while for me to understand that he was trying to be funny, but I'm not one to catch on to things that quickly.

Arty had heaps of confidence. He could talk to strangers easily, and he had a fun wit about him. He had a talent of making awkward people feel comfortable. He was also a big partier and was responsible for making the punch. He would mix delicious concoctions of juices and hard liquor. Every time, he managed to make it a different color. Arty would sample the vodka, rum, and Ever Clear liquor as he created the punch. As a result, he was always drunk before the party began.

He had good grades, was confident, had fun, had a good girlfriend, was a nice person, and was always the life of the party. In every way, he fit the label of a happy person. There was no reason to suspect the darker side that lurked inside him.

One day Arty confided in me. "Stick" he said abbreviating

my Sticky nickname, "I'm gonna go down to the river. I want to throw myself in, but I haven't got the courage. A lot of times I walk the bad neighborhoods of Hoboken hoping someone will kill me." The confession shocked me.

I too had some pretty solid social credentials at the time, at least to the outward eye. But I was also miserable. I would never have dreamed that Arty had wanted to die, but I was young and naive. I have learned the façade is the rule, not the exception. We deceive others by making them think we are something we are not.

I loved Arty and still do. I heard he had replaced drinking with overeating and obsessive work habits. I hope one day he conquers his demons. Arty, my hand is always extended to you.

A WITNESS IN DAYTONA BEACH

It was the summer of 1986. I had completed my freshman year at Edwards Institute of Technology. I was caught up in the fast lifestyle and the fellowship I had found in the fraternity. It was nice to have so many friends, especially after having so few in high school.

That summer my friend Freddie and I flew down to Daytona Beach, Florida. We had been friends since fourth grade. I still recall the day I met him. Some of us kids were horsing around, and I was pinned under some other kid when Freddie came by. He accidentally stepped on my face. I was incensed, and when I got up, I chased him with the intentions of pounding on him. His mother, Karen, a rather short but wide woman, worked at the school. Freddie ran to his mother, and I chased him around her legs, making circles until we got tired. Then, we became friends.

On that trip, Freddie was deeply obsessed with meeting girls. We were both socially awkward, even though we had improved in that area over the last year. There we were, walking on the boardwalk, searching for girls, when we were suddenly interrupted.

We were approached by three kids, each about our age. They walked right up to us and announced that they had just finished praying to God. As a result of their uplifting experience, they were directed by God to come and talk to us. They came out on the boardwalk and the Holy Spirit told them to talk to us. One guy said that only a year ago, on the very same boardwalk, he had gotten down on his knees and accepted Jesus as his savior.

We hadn't talked to anybody else on the trip, except a few women who gave us the cold shoulder, so the distraction was welcome. Also, I had a genuine interest in God. Brad, the leader of the small group, said that we were in the middle of sin city. I laughed, because I'd been to 42nd Street in Manhattan, New York, which was full of whores, sex shops, bars, drugs, and more. This was nothing.

After some conversation, the question was asked, "Are you saved?"

I thought about my Roman Catholic upbringing. In particular, I recalled a sermon about gaining access to heaven through works. It went like this:

There was a woman who was very rich and very greedy. She lived her whole life selfishly not caring about anyone but herself. Then one day there was a poor beggar. In a moment of compassion, the woman gave the poor man an onion. The woman eventually died. Unfortunately for her, she went straight down into the depths of Hell. There were flames burning hot, tormenting her. Then in the midst of her agony, an onion was extended down to her attached to a rope. The woman grabbed the onion and was pulled up out of Hell. She, then, spent her eternity in holy bliss."

Brad looked at me with a straight face and said, "I never read that in the Bible." In hindsight, I don't know how he didn't laugh hysterically at my gross ignorance.

I had the urge to accept Jesus. I was standing there by the ocean and thought of getting baptized, but I didn't. Freddie was completely unaffected by the night's events, and we never talked about it again.

That night, I realized that I didn't even know what the Bible said. This was the book I professed to believe in, but I didn't have a clue about what it meant. When I returned from Florida, I moved into the fraternity house. The brother who moved out conveniently left his Bible behind. I started reading it, beginning with the book of Mathew. I was impressed.

A couple of years later, I shared this story with Ernest Powers, the minister of the Manhattan Church of Christ. He said "You probably wouldn't agree with their doctrine, but look how God used them to help you."

Those three individuals changed my life. They were bold and confessed Jesus as Lord. They were a link in the chain, a very obvious and necessary link. To all you witnesses, thank you from the bottom of my circumcised heart.

SLIPPING INTO THE ABYSS

After surviving Work Week my freshman year, I fell into a deep depression. I would lie in bed and mourn over people who were less fortunate, even though I really had no interaction with the people I was mourning. It was just general blues over the state of the world. My friends began to notice after a week or so. Finally Dick spoke up, "You ain't doing no good to anybody by just complaining and lying in your bed all day." I realized he was right, and forced myself to get up. I finished the semester with only one A, a C, and a slew of B's. My grade point average had plummeted, but it was still a respectable showing.

One day, Sam and I decided to take off to Rhode Island on a motorcycle. Sam had borrowed the motorcycle from a friend, but unbeknownst to me, it was taken without permission. In Rhode Island, we visited Sam's friend who was in the navy. We did some heavy drinking, and one night we got drunk enough to take a ride with a complete stranger. We somehow wound up in a random churchyard, both passed out on the wet grass. When we sobered up enough to walk, we had a seven-mile trek in front of us. How Sam managed to find the way back, I'll never know.

During this time, I was attempting to escape my problems by drinking and using drugs. I saw how it was a detriment in my life. My grades had certainly suffered, and my physical condition had deteriorated. In the midst the partying, I began doing sit ups and pushups to get back into shape. When I got back to Hoboken, I took a course called Dynamics. It was a difficult course, but I was taking it to get ahead. My mind was still partially focused on engineering school. I had started running seven miles a day, but each evening I would get a four pack of wine coolers and drink them on the fraternity steps.

Without a doubt, I was having a problem dealing with reality. In a lot of ways, the fraternity had helped me. It taught me to get past being so self-centered. It had instructed me that I was part of a whole, and that sacrifice for the group was essential. Most importantly, it stressed a brotherly kind of love. However, most of the members really didn't live up to these ideals. Looking back, all this was preparing me for my acceptance of Christianity.

During my first semester as a sophomore, I was rush chairman along with Dick and Sam. As far as academics, I took two additional courses. One was Psychology, which was supposed to be taken senior year. The other was Biology, simply to enjoy it and learn. My peers thought I was crazy. Sophomore year was supposed to be the hardest year at Edwards Tech, and here I was taking two extra courses. Dynamics turned out easier than I thought. I initially studied hard and was acing my tests. However, I slacked off in the end and wound up getting a B. Still, it was better than the majority of the class.

I was definitely brainwashed at that time. I began recruiting freshman early before the rush period, trying to get them interested in the fraternity. I made a whole host of friends and lived a wild and reckless life. I was the life of the party. There was a girl Anne, who I met walking my dog. I invited her to come to a party we were throwing that night. We started dancing and soon we were off on a walk. I took her to a secluded area near The Point. We started kissing and caressing under the night sky. We returned to my room in the fraternity to have sex. It turned out to be an unrewarding experience. I remember being engaged in the act and feeling zero pleasure, constantly wondering when the good part would start. I couldn't climax and the interaction went on for hours.

Anne and I did begin a brief relationship. I still connected sex and love, so I felt a permanent connection with her. We had a few more nights together, and it seemed like we were an item. Our fellow students on campus even started speaking of us as a couple. However, Anne decided to sleep with some freshman. When I found out, I told her we were through. I had unrealistic expectations about forming a lasting relationship with a girl I had sex with the day I met her. Anne stayed with that guy for a while, but a few months later, she came back asking for another chance. I refused.

I was so busy partying, I didn't have any time to pay attention to my studies, but somehow I managed to pass all my classes. The fraternities' rush was successful. We got a record number pledges, which we considered high quality. You would think this accomplishment would have been more satisfying. It did feel good, but I was still unfulfilled.

After rush, I became a changed person. The partying transformed into drinking alone. The change was dramatic and everybody noticed. I became self-reflective and contemplated the bigger things in life. My new philosophy questioned the significance of engineering school. Did it matter if I got a B or C in circuits in the grand scheme of things? My friend Dick listened to my new line of thinking. We discussed it and came to the same conclusion. In the big picture, much of what we now held so important was meaningless. This led to both apathy and laziness.

After the first semester of sophomore year, I was in a deep sea of depression. I wasn't suicidal yet; I would later dive much deeper into the water, where my only focus was how I was going to kill myself. Even still, the foul mood prevented me from attending classes, and I was always sleeping late. As a result, my mother took notice and was extremely alarmed.

Here is where life played a cruel trick on me. With the urging of my mom, I went to see my doctor about my abnormal behavior. When I arrived for my appointment, my regular doctor wasn't in the office. Instead, there was a substitute doctor who was just out of medical school. He didn't diagnose depression. It was his opinion that I had low blood sugar. As a result, I began taking a regiment of fruit drinks. If I had been correctly diagnosed, I feel like I could have avoided mountains of trouble. I was acutely aware that I was having difficulty; I would have been open to medical treatment.

In spite of my depression, I finished my sophomore year.

The chronic drinking continued; it helped me get through daily life. I was miserable, to put it bluntly. Worst of all, I didn't know why I was so down. My life was a deep darkness, and I was slipping into the abyss.

How I Became a Christian

My roots began in the Roman Catholic Church. It was there that I got a good Christian base. I now realize that the Catholic Church does not follow the teachings of the Bible. It promotes the worship of Mary and creates a hierarchy of believers in which the priest outranks the ordinary churchgoer. The bishop outranks the priest, the bishop is below the cardinals, and everyone bows before the Pope. I now believe this ideology is wrong. The Pope is a man just like me, not God's representative on Earth, but the Catholic Church, despite all of its shortcomings, introduced me to Jesus.

In the Catholic Church the Bible is not the primary focus. My education came from Sunday services and something called CCD, the Catholic equivalent of Bible school. We were taught religion, but, to be honest, I don't recall much of what was taught. I remember pitching dimes with a classmate outside the school building. The person who threw the dime closest to the wall collected both. Usually we broke even. We did this until a nun caught us and scolded us harshly.

Confirmation was when I became an official member of the church. We were forced to memorize a bunch of prayers, and every time we recited the prayer correctly, it was checked off of a list. The Our Father, The Hail Mary, The Act of Contrition and The Beatitudes are the ones I vividly recall, but there are many more I have forgotten. I found the nuns and priests to be cold, stern, and borderline cruel. One day we were singing in the Church. I was an awful singer and probably still am. My friends, annoyed by my terrible voice, ran from our pew holding their hands to their ears. It was funny to me, but the nun was upset and cracked down on us like a Nazi. No fun allowed in Church: that was the message. I guess they never read about joy in the book of Philippians.

The Catholic Church has some peculiar rituals. Upon entering the sanctuary, you are supposed to dip your hand into a basin of holy water. After wetting the right hand with holy water, you then make the sign of the cross. This water is supposed to be holy. Churches actually sell holy water at inflated prices. The water is holy because a priest blessed it. I think this is garbage, but at the time I was exposed to it I was a small child and very gullible.

After applying the holy water, you bow down before the altar. The idea is that Christ's presence dwells there. The actual church building itself is supposed to be holy as well. In order to show reverence, one must never talk above a whisper.

As a child, I went through all the motions. Confirmation was the last sacrament before becoming a full member of the Catholic faith. It was a big deal. We practiced for months, learning how to sing the songs and recite the prayers. We also rehearsed the ceremony over and over. We memorized when to stand, when to kneel, when to sit, when to come up front and so on. I almost didn't get confirmed, because I got in a fistfight with a friend, but I was there for the big night. In many ways, it felt like a marriage ceremony. Our families came dressed up in their finest clothes. It was so important that the Bishop himself came out decked out in his funky robes and humungous hat, looking like the Pope, except his pointed hat was a little smaller.

I recall the week after confirmation. I came to the realization that Jesus was something very profound. I concluded that in Jesus, there was eternal life. I also realized that if I truly believed in Jesus, I would go on the mountains and shout for joy for the whole world to believe, too, but since I rarely talked about or even thought about Jesus, I believed it meant I didn't even believe in Him. I wept bitterly all night long

Despite my doubts and disbelief, I was dragged to Church every Sunday morning. My mother was, and still is, habitually late for everything, especially Church. One Sunday, walking in late as usual, the priest stopped his sermon as we tried to find a seat. He made some hostile comments about arriving to church on time. He never mentioned us by name, but it was obvious whom he was talking about. That was the last time we attended Church.

My cousin Judy was an early, more positive, Christian influence in my life. She was confident and cool. I looked up to her. Judy would say, "John, you have got to read the book of Revelation with me. There's some wild stuff in it." I had never heard of the book of Revelation until then. I was looking forward to reading it with her. Unfortunately Judy had heart surgery and died soon after. I never read the book of Revelation with her as we intended; instead I went to her funeral and heard the 23rd Psalm, but, somehow, because of Judy, I started seeing the Bible in a favorable light.

Fast forward to age seventeen. I, like any other teenager, was dealing with the difficulties of leaving childhood behind and becoming an adult. One night I decided that I would read the Bible. My parents had a Catholic Bible that I snuck out of the living room. For some reason, I was embarrassed to let anyone know I was reading the Good Book. Without a proper Christian education, I was lost in the difficult content. I didn't even know there was a New Testament and an Old Testament. I just opened it to the middle and began reading. Being a Catholic Bible, it included the Apocrypha, which the majority of Christians don't recognize as divine scripture. I ended up reading a story about believers leaving food before an idol, convinced that the idol would actually eat the food. The hero of the story then had the grounds raked. The next morning the food was gone, but there were footprints leading to a secret passage where the priest's family was munching on the goodies. After reading that, I came to the opinion that the Bible was nonsense. If only I had turned to the book of Matthew.

Two years later, my sophomore year at Edwards Tech, I was in front of my fraternity house. We were horsing around, throwing a football around. Our neighbor, Moses, was sitting and watching us play. I tossed the football in his direction, and soon Moses and I were playing catch. We started talking, and I asked him where he went to Church. I believe the Spirit of God compelled me to ask him that question.

Soon after that, Moses invited me to a Bible study in Hoboken. I figured I would give it a shot. I showed up a little bit late one Thursday night, just after the regular meeting. I was almost forced into a more private Bible study. I was curious about the Bible, so I gave no objection. The additional Bible study was great; it taught how the Bible was the Word of God.

That was the last Bible study I would attend for a good while. Unbeknownst to me, the group was known as the International Church of Christ, the ICOC, which was widely considered to be a cult. Allegedly, they were heavy into controlling people and manipulation. Moses soon quit that organization. I believe that if I had gotten involved with the ICOC, I would have categorically rejected Christianity. But praise God; He knows what He's doing.

Life progressed and my mood grew foul. I was entering the world of bipolar disorder. I was going through a mild, but very real depression. To fit my grumpy composure, I had my head shaved into a Mohawk. The day after the new hairdo, I walked into my differential equations class. The whole class was silently staring at me in shock. The professor broke the ice with a joke about my hair. We all laughed and life continued normally.

Apparently, my Mohawk turned off the people from the International Church of Christ. "John seemed like such a nice person," they told Moses. "What happened to him?" God had kept these false prophets out of my life at a very delicate time.

Around this time, I was having sex with a girl named Gina. She was screwed up just like me. I believed in romantic love. My belief was that I would one day find my "true love," who would love me for who I was and everything in life would then become wonderful. This was not that relationship. We didn't talk on the phone or go out on dates. We just hooked up several times.

Despite the delusion of my "true love" philosophy, our relationship was shallow and physical. I did care for her, but not that much. One night she was chasing me around at one of our fraternity parties. We ventured down to the basement where I had my weight set, the laundry machines and our marijuana garden. We had sex.

Afterward, Gina was despondent. "Sticky," she said. Even she called me by my nickname. "Sticky, what's it all about?" Deep inside, I knew the answer. The answer was Jesus. I wanted to tell her that, but deep in my heart I still didn't believe. My answer was silence.

I had hit bottom. I gave up alcohol, drugs, partying and my wild ways. I kept tabs of how many days I remained alcohol free. Every day, I would announce the total. When I reached two weeks, a fraternity brother, whom we called Salty, cursed me out. He didn't give a damn how many days I had stopped drinking. I must have hit a sensitive point with him.

I was on a quest for God. There was a small library in our fraternity with a Hare Krishna book. I read about how some prophet would go about talking to animals. I dismissed it as fantasy. My Catholic teachings were pointing me to Jesus.

My depression was beginning to lift. I was on the upswing, and I changed my behavior for good. I am certainly still a sinner and have done bad things, but my true motivation in life is to follow God's teachings.

With absolute perfect timing, Moses came back into my life. "Are you still interested in God?" he asked.

Yes. Indeed, I was.

We began having Bible studies. Although he was no longer with the ICOC, he still loosely followed their Bible study method. The studies really didn't focus around Jesus, but we discussed belief, faith, and obedience. The lessons supplemented my continuing private Bible studies. Moses also opened his life and shared it with me. I asked him hard, personal questions and he always gave me honest answers.

I started to attend the Manhattan Church of Christ and group Bible studies. I met a host of new friends. Good, honest, nice, decent people. Frank, Patty, Gene, Kimberly, Ophelia, Leslie, Ray, and Emmanuelle among others. I started feeling a connection, but unlike my fraternity brothers who talked about love, these people were for real. In the frat there was plenty of selfishness and sin. My new Christian friends seemed to strive for a higher state of being. They were sincere in their devotion. I remember Miss Kitty. She would give me a grand kiss every time she saw me. Love like this was the rule, not the exception.

I announced to Moses and everybody that I was going to take a cross-country trip, hitchhiking. That week Moses had two Bible studies in one week. When we read Acts chapter two, I realized I had crucified Jesus Christ. I loved Jesus and just like those who heard the message on Pentecost two thousand years ago, I was cut to the heart. Scripture teaches that non-believers are to be baptized in water by immersion. On that night, as Moses and I drove to our friend Gail's apartment in Union City, I prayed to God to not to let me die before I was baptized. When we arrived, the bathtub was already full of water, and I was dunked. I was born again!

Baptism was only the beginning. I was still a sinner, but I was a sinner with a covenant relationship with God. Just like the blood of lamb marked and protected believers during Passover, I too was marked and protected by the blood of the Lamb.

Ever since that day, I have been walking the straight and narrow. I drank alcohol a few more times and used drugs only once. I went crazy numerous times and had my ups and downs. I continued to sin somewhat but my whole perspective on life had changed. Life was no longer about pleasing John but about pleasing God.

Moses was the man who led me to Christ. He was the one who taught me the gospel, and I am indebted to him, but there are so many more who have loved me. I owe these people too.

Finally, let me say I have never made a better decision in my entire life.

ON THE WAY TO PITTSBURGH

In 1987, I was twenty years old and hitchhiking across the good old US of A. My concerned parents provided me with an Ameripass. With this wonderful pass I could ride the Greyhound bus as much as I wanted for an entire month. I had some urge just to go where I could go, simply to explore.

The night before my departure, Moses drove me from the Manhattan Church of Christ and dropped me off at Roger's house. Roger was the Vice President of Edwards Tech in charge of development. We had traveled together before and had grown close because of it. I had represented the student body and I spoke to alumni about the school.

Roger was concerned about my safety on the trip. After all, I had no set plans. The only plan I had was to go with the flow. I quoted the Bible, saying "the Lord's eye was on the sparrow and that he watches over me." This did nothing to settle Roger's concerns. In the morning he was to drop me off at the Port Authority bus station in New York City to begin my journey.

However, my wanderlust got the better of me. After about an hour of rest in the room provided for me, I got my pack and sneaked out of the house. I must have disturbed Roger's family, because as I was walking the street, his daughter drove up. She coaxed me into the car and said, "My dad is very worried about you. He loves you like a son." She took me to the Path Train. Arriving on the Manhattan side at 33rd Street, I took a short cab to the Port Authority.

When I was walking to my bus to Philadelphia, a beggar approached me. After I gave him a dollar, he began to follow me. Another beggar came up to me and asked for a dollar, so I gave him a dollar, too. At that point, the first beggar got angry. "That should be my dollar," he said.

I ran through the bus station so I could catch my bus ride to Philadelphia. To my dismay, the first beggar ran along with me. I needed to get rid of him. After looking around, I found a police officer. "This man is harassing me," I told the cop.

"Why are you bothering me? Just punch him in the face," the cop said. I had thought that police were supposed to help people, but apparently this cop didn't follow the same code. The beggar did not follow me on the bus, so it was a great relief when I was finally seated.

I recall getting to Philadelphia. The reality of my excitement for adventure began to soak in. It was early in the morning long before sunrise. I wasn't tired in the least bit despite not getting any sleep. I wandered away from the bus station into a park. I took a short walk after the long drive. In the park was a small building not much larger than a closet, covered with windows. Inside, a police officer monitored the park.

A man was nearby in the otherwise empty park, so I called him over. As we began to converse, I pulled out my Bible, hoping to enlighten him the same way I had been. Retrospectively, I was zealous to the faith to the point of obsession. When the man saw the Bible, he stood and walked away without a word. With no one else to talk to, I stood and went back to the bus station.

My plan was to go on to Pittsburgh. I would have hitchhiked west, but it was illegal to do so in Pennsylvania. I considered it my Christian duty to obey the law, so I used my pass and boarded the Greyhound Bus once more. On the way to Pittsburgh, I sat next to a young man around my age named Phnom. Actually, he was two years younger at eighteen. He sat next to the window and I set on the aisle.

To look at the man you would not have been impressed. He didn't have fancy clothes, was of Asian descent, and his mouth was deformed with a bulge caused by protruding teeth.

"Why are you going to Pittsburgh?" he asked.

"Going to see America," I said. "I want to get to Alaska, God willing." That was my standard answer to the frequently asked question on the purpose of my cross-country journey. I never did make it to Alaska, but I traveled as far as Washington State.

"Why are you going to Pittsburgh?" I asked.

"I'm going to see a college," Phnom mumbled. His broken teeth severely hampered his talking. "I've been offered a full scholarship."

Full scholarships are given only to exceptional people. It cast Phnom in a new light, and I looked at him with different eyes. "That's great," I said. "How did you get that?"

Then Phnom told me his story.

Phnom was from Cambodia, which is the country west of Vietnam in South East Asia. The country was torn asunder during America's infamous conflict against the communists. It was bombed and occupied in a "secret war" that wasn't really a secret at all.

Unfortunately for Phnom, there was an awful despot in power called Pol Pot. This tyrant murdered millions of his own subjects. One of the many atrocities he committed was to execute as many intellectuals as possible, as being intelligent was a threat to his dictatorship. Somehow the mad man made a direct correlation between spectacles and intelligence, so everyone who wore glasses was promptly executed.

Things weren't much better for nonintellectuals either. Life for Phnom and his parents was a living hell. His entire family worked as slaves in the rice fields for twenty hours a day in hard physical labor. I am not exaggerating at all. They were never given any breaks and were treated harshly. Fortunately for them they escaped to Burma.

From Burma, Phnom and his family immigrated to the United States. There, for the first time in his life, Phnom attended school. Unfortunately, he could not speak English at all. He was used to working hard, however, and worked as hard at his scholastics as he did in the rice fields in Cambodia. Four years later, all his hard work paid off and he graduated as valedictorian of his class. Quite an accomplishment!

Phnom didn't talk to me much on the way to Pittsburgh, aside from telling me about his life. It wasn't that he didn't want to converse; his mouth being deformed as it was made it painful and difficult for him to speak. As a result, most of the time he listened to me and two old ladies sitting behind us.

I left one thing with Phnom that I hoped stuck with him. "Phnom, you were one of the fortunate ones to get out like you did. You have a responsibility to your people, to help them, too." I still wonder if my words had any impact on this capable young man.

PASS IT ON

When I hitchhiked cross-country, I was fortunate enough to pass through West Virginia. The state is a sight to behold. Its rolling hills are covered with lush green trees. Its majestic scenery is second only to Idaho, but a close second. However, I've been told that in winter the hills are barren and ugly because of the strip mining.

The people, like the scenery, are the nicest I've found anywhere. They are friendly and kind, even to strangers like me who talk funny. The West Virginia accent is thick like pea soup; it's halfway between talking and singing.

I walked a great deal in West Virginia, up and down hills, the roads curved with twists and bends. I walked through towns that took all of two minutes to traverse. There was no other place I visited where drivers were quicker to pick up a stranger like me.

It was a hot June day that found me with my thumb extended. A pickup truck slowed down and pulled over a short distance ahead of me. I clutched my orange backpack and trotted to the vehicle, then climbed into the back. Hitchhiking is an exhilarating experience. I compare it to fishing; you never know when you'll get a bite.

Sitting in the front was an old woman with two young boys. The woman slid open a small glass window in the back of the cab. "Hello," she said, after pulling back onto the highway.

"Hello and God bless you," I replied.

"Where are you going?"

"Alaska, God willing."

"Where are you from?"

"I'm from New Jersey, which is close to New York City."

We continued to talk as we drove. Soon the woman pulled the truck over. "John," she said, "now that we know you are no threat to us, you can ride with us in the front."

With a smile, I jumped out of the back and entered the cab. I sat in the middle with the woman on my left and the two boys on my right.

We drove a little while longer, when the tone of conversation got serious. "You see these two boys?" she said, motioning with her hand towards the youngsters. "Their parents just died. My husband and I took them in, but the farm burned down and we've got nothing left. Then my husband died, too."

The news hit me like a wave pounding on a beach. I sat silently stunned.

Then the woman pulled into the drive-thru of a Roy Rogers restaurant and ordered three sandwiches. When she picked them up from the window, she handed one to each boy and the last one to me. I was surprised.

"John," she said. Whenever she spoke my name, it was as if she was talking to an intimate friend. "I don't have enough money to buy more. I know you don't have much money, but I want you to eat, so I gave you my sandwich."

I ate the sandwich with a thankful heart as we drove on. Soon, she pulled over to an exit. "Boys, do you want to take John farther?" she asked.

"Yes!" the two boys cried.

"John" said the woman once more. "This is our exit but it's not a good place to hitch another ride. So we're going to take you to the next one. You'll be able to get a ride there much easier."

I gave my sincere thanks and we drove on. West Virginia exits are not like the ones in New Jersey, where there are exits every couple of miles. This kind woman drove me over twenty miles to the next exit.

I exited the truck and stood by the driver's side window to say good bye to this generous soul, but the woman who had already provided me with so much gave me even more.

"John," she said. "I know you're searching for the words to thank me. Just take the love I've given you and pass it on. If you do, one day, it'll go all around the world and will return to you."

Then, she drove me away. I can't remember her name but I'll never forget her.

FROM TEXAS TO TULSA

On my cross-country trip in 1987, I wound up in Nashville, Tennessee. There, I stayed with a friend of my mother's. I gave her a call from a payphone when I got off the Greyhound Bus. I was waiting on the corner for her to pick me up, when a young man approached me with a smile. We had a quick conversation as I waited. I told him I was a member of the Church of Christ. The stranger told me that he used to be in the Church of Christ, but that he switched. In the true Christian Spirit, he offered to put me up for the night. Normally, I would have accepted, but since my ride was already coming, I had to decline. Something about the man made me a little leery, and there was no sense taking chances.

The woman picked me up, and I had my first real sleep in a week. I took short catnaps on the buses, so sleeping in a bed was a luxury. In the morning, she took me to all the landmarks and major sightseeing areas. Soon after, I was on the bus again, to Texas. I slept through the entire night as the bus traveled across the entire width of Arkansas. I had heard good things about Arkansas from my friend Moses who had traveled there before. One night he had needed a place to sleep, so he knocked on the door of a house to ask permission to camp on their lawn. They wouldn't let him sleep outside; however, they invited him inside to sleep on one of their beds.

My next stop was Dallas, Texas. When we arrived at the bus station, I stepped off the bus with my pack and began to explore the city. I had found a park and was strolling through when I spotted an elderly man sitting on a bench. Intrigued and excited with the prospect of interacting with someone new, I sat next to him on the bench and began to speak about Jesus. He told me that he was a Christian and that he knew all about Jesus. He seemed angry and disturbed about our conversation, and left me feeling troubled.

After this, I boarded a public bus to further explore the parts of the city that I would take me time to walk. The broad windows of the bus gave me an excellent view of the surroundings. I sat in the front seat, right by the bus driver, and I struck up a conversation with him. I stayed on the bus for two circuits around Dallas, but I didn't see anything impressive, to my disappointment. The bus driver informed me about the legality of hitchhiking in Texas when I asked, as every state has their own unique regulations on the matter. Hitchhiking was indeed legal in Texas, but only on the entrance ramps of the highways. It was illegal on the highway itself. The driver said that if I did hitchhike on the highway, however, I would most likely get a ride in a matter of minutes. The bus driver went out of his way to drop me right in front of the entrance to the highway.

My goal was to hitch a ride going south and check out El Paso. There I was standing on the side of the entrance ramp, with my thumb extended. As a Christian, I was not going to violate the law. It would be miserable to get arrested or in trouble over something so trivial. I waited, thumb extended, as driver after driver passed me without stopping. Some would approach, see me, then grin and extend their own thumb to mock my efforts as they passed. This happened car after car. I was far from West Virginia.

Disgusted with the attitude of the passing drivers and disheartened, I sat on my day-glow orange pack right there on the side of the ramp. The pack was lying on the dirt next to the highway. After sitting for about a minute, I felt an itch on my back. Alarmed, I stood up to see a whole host of ants climbing over my knapsack.

As a child, one of my fascinations was ants. I would read books about the different kind of ants, from the benign to the dreaded army ant. The ones crawling on my pack and me were fire ants. I know from the books I read as a child that these ants were quite deadly. They would swarm over a victim and then when a signal was given, they would bite and sting in unison. Some people were allergic to the sting and would perish as a result of the ant's bite. I wasn't going to find out if I was allergic. I put my bag on the concrete and began the long process of killing the ants. An hour later my sack was purged of the offenders.

I managed to get a ride that day. I had given up on going down to El Paso. The ride I received was just local. The man who picked me up was very nice and gave me a yellow hat to wear to help protect me from the strong summer sun. As the day dwindled into night, my adventure with the ants came to the forefront of my mind. For safety's sake, I decided not to sleep in my tent that night. Instead I paid the thirty dollars for a room in a cheap motel. It was the only time on my month-long trip that I paid for lodging. Every other time I slept on the bus or in my tent.

The next morning, I was hitchhiking once more. It was Sunday morning, the Lord's day. A man had picked me up. I asked him if he knew where a Church of Christ might be. The man happened to be a brother in the faith, but a delinquent one. He had fallen away and he told me he wanted to get back into the Church. He knew where the church was and he dropped me off. The man would not join me, despite my encouragement.

The church building was quite large. It reminded me of the high school I attended in Pompton Plains. The people were nice and friendly, but not very concerned with me. They had a strange Bible study that I attended. I found it strange because they contradicted what the Scriptures taught. After the service, I asked a man if I could get a ride into town. He said no. Then, later in the parking lot, I asked the same man if I could have a ride. His answer had not changed. I was hitchhiking by the side of the road once more. The man who had refused to give me a ride drove by my extended thumb in a pick-up truck, which upset me greatly. Even if he thought I was up to no good, I could have sat in the back and he would be safe and secure in the cab.

After eating an ice cream sundae at a store near the church, a Methodist picked me up. He had a six-inch-tall statue of Jesus on the dashboard. He told me how he had accepted Jesus into his heart on his birthday, so he could always remember the exact date of his salvation. I tried to discuss the doctrine of baptism with him, but his beliefs were different than mine, so it was futile. The man was kind enough to go out of his way to drop me off right in front of the bus station.

I caught the next bus going north. I wanted to get out of Texas in the worst way. On the bus, I sat next to a young lady who was a school teacher. As usual, I began a conversation with her. She spent her summer vacation visiting friends she knew from college. She would spend a week with each comrade, and then take the bus to the next location. Our conversation progressed, as it almost always did with me, to discussing all the Scriptures dealing with baptism. At the time, that was the part of the Bible in which I was most comfortable in my knowledge. In the course of our discussion, however, the woman became flustered and fearful. When I thought about it afterwards, I realized that my preaching amounted to saying that she wasn't a believer. I offered to put my arm around her to comfort her. It was partially my fault she felt this way, and I wanted to remedy it. She refused the gesture, saying, "I don't even know you."

Another woman three seats back butted her opinion in. Soon, the lady sitting behind me was debating the Scriptures with me as well. The woman next to me accused me of manipulating the conversation. I hadn't seen it that way; I thought of it more like guiding. I say this because I have had dozens of conversations, and this was the only one that progressed into a discussion on baptism. When the bus stopped, a man announced to me that he was on the bus to ride it and that he didn't want to hear any more talk about the Bible. I was so fed up with the discussion that I got off the bus. It was the middle of the night when we had stopped in Tulsa, Oklahoma, but that didn't stop me from wandering through town.

As I was walking the empty streets, I came across a large building that was connected to a Baptist church. Hoping for some Christian compassion, I went to the door and rang the bell. After a few buzzes it was apparent that nobody was there. On the street, I approached a man in a pick-up truck who had stopped nearby. "Do you know where I could spend the night?" was my only introduction.

The man told me to get in. As he drove, he told me he worked part time for a place that took in people with no place to stay. He offered to buy me a drink at a bar, but I refused. I wanted only to go to sleep. Not much later, he pulled up to a two-story building. I thanked the man, then entered a room that was shared by several men. They were already asleep, so I unrolled my sleeping bag without a word and slept well for the first time since my night in Texas.

The shelter I was staying at was run by the Catholic Church and was meant for homeless people. As such, there was no fee to stay. I'm quite sure that they even fed the people, though I never ate any of their food. The people there were a unique bunch.

One friendly fellow was a cook who had run into a spell of bad luck, and wound up unemployed. Technically speaking, the man was handicapped because of his clubfoot. The small deformity could have been easily hidden and he could have passed as normal. The man had just been turned down for a cooking job. The interview, he said, had gone so well. Unfortunately, on the application he had written that he was handicapped. The man was in agony over his foolishness, blaming the rejection of employment on that one particular comment.

There was a woman with whom I got into a religious discussion. She told me about her church. There, they taught that by following Christ you would get quite wealthy. They misinterpreted the phrase in the Bible "riches in Christ" as to mean financial gain. I tried, in my foolishness and my zeal, to debate this issue. Of course, I got nowhere. She was quite convinced that she was on her way to millions and that I was stupid.

This stay in Tulsa was special in an unusual way. A volcano had recently erupted somewhere on Earth. As a result of the tons of dust thrown into the atmosphere, the sunsets were remarkably beautiful. Every evening in Tulsa, I would sit and watch the sky's performance of changing colors and drifting clouds.

A woman sat next to me each night. She was bizarre, and would remind me later on of people I'd encounter with mental illness. Even as inexperienced with psychological problems as I was at the time, I could tell this woman had one. She was quite out of her mind and would ramble on and on about nonsense. She had been employed in the childcare profession in the past, but at the time that I knew her, she couldn't find any steady work, so she was staying in the shelter. One night, she asked me not to tell anybody that she was enlightened. It was a very odd comment.

I had several encounters with the established clergy in Tulsa. One was with a Catholic priest. I began to show him the Scriptures, and how some teachings of the Catholic Church conflicted with the teachings of the Bible. To my surprise, he knew all of these contradictions and even more that I was previously unaware. He went on to explain that he had faith, and that it didn't matter that what he practiced violated the teachings of the Bible. We both became agitated and frustrated with the other. I was certainly not gentle and, looking back on it, perhaps I had an axe to grind. The priest, seeing my volatile mood, asked me where my peace was. I had no answer for him, so I left. As I started walking around Tulsa, remorse filled me. I had been needlessly cruel to the priest, and I felt even worse because the place I had stayed was financed by Catholics.

Another day I talked to a minister of a local church, which I believed to be Baptist. My favorite topic was, of course, baptism. The Church of Christ is big on that subject. The minister patiently and politely listened to me. We disagreed over what was meant in John chapter three when it says, "being born of water and the spirit." I contended that it referred to water baptism, and the minister said it referred to the physical birth of a child. To settle the disagreement, the minister took down a large and cumbersome book from a shelf, and then read a line of text out loud, a list of complicated words that I could not even guess the meaning. After his reading, I asked, "What did it say?"

He looked at me and said, "It says you're right."

Our conversation continued over baptism. He said he couldn't remember any scripture of Jesus baptizing people. I know now that it was His disciples that baptized people. When the conversation changed, he thought that I was questioning his calling as a minister. The pleasant conversation dissolved into an argument. He explained how as a child he was prophesied to become a minister, and that he began his illustrious career at the age of twelve.

After he calmed down, he said he had some business to conduct. He commended me for my zeal in approaching him. He prayed that I would be faithful in my walk with God. I left feeling good, as opposed to when I left the Catholic priest.

Elsewhere, I encountered a boxing gym. The name of it, if I recall correctly, was the Main Street Gym. The man at the door was busy working the passing pedestrians, trying to get people to join the gym. He stood at the door, and next to him was a clear sign saying, "Only boxers beyond this point." The fee for a month was thirty dollars, but I gave the man twenty to join up, and he was quite happy. I admitted to him I was lost. After explaining where I was staying, the happy fellow escorted me to my place.

The next day I came back for a workout. I had ideas of staying long term in Tulsa, as my stay thus far had been enjoyable, but I abandoned that plan a couple of days later. I recall a large, blonde-haired woman boxer who wanted to be the women's champion. The coach was also memorable. He kept complaining about a successful former boxer who had left him. He said that if he could only get the boy back, he would lead him to the championship.

The workout was quite grueling. He would take turns hitting the heavy bag, the speed bag, and using a medicine ball. I knew how to hit the bags from working out in Pompton Plains. The medicine ball was a unique exercise though. The coach would drop a large, heavy ball onto my stomach. Then I would toss it up into the air where the coach would catch it, only to drop it so that I could lift it again. The workouts were three minutes each, the length of one round in boxing. I would have liked to have gotten into it more, but it just didn't work out that way. I stopped going to the gym after a couple of days, after my motivation dropped.

It was a bright sunny day when I walked the main drag of Tulsa. I had never seen more good-looking young ladies. They were all slim, in good shape, and elegant. In the course of my wanderings, I encountered a man in a wheel chair panhandling.

He would smile and wave to everyone and give a quick thank you for some spare change. He was quite successful in his efforts. It is my practice to never give street people money since the instance in New York. Instead of giving him money, I bought the man a frozen fruit drink.

I struck up a conversation with him as he continued to beg. When he was finished for the day, he asked me to wheel him home. Unable to turn him down, I did as he asked, and we arrived in a complex where people stayed who needed some sort of assistance. After entering the man's room, the man, to my alarm, got out of his wheelchair and walked around. Hastily, he counted his money. Then, with urgency, he made a phone call. "I've got ten dollars, so go get some marijuana," the man blurted into the receiver. Realizing what was going on, I left, wanting no part in this.

Upon arriving back to the shelter, I quickly picked up my stuff and left Tulsa far behind. As I was leaving, a man was just dropping some grocery bags of food in front of the place. While walking down the road, the man with the clubfoot saw me go. He said goodbye, and I asked him to say goodbye to everybody for me. I left Tulsa a little wiser and a little more experienced in the ways of the world. Tulsa was far nicer than Texas. I think I'd like to return one day.

The Lord Is My Rest

I was hitchhiking leaving the twin cities of Lewistown and Clarkston on the border between Washington State and Idaho. The towns were named after the two famous explorers Lewis and Clark. I walked the path that these two pioneers had taken in their famous trek out west. I felt as if I was part of history. My path took me along the edge of the Clear Water River, traveling east through Idaho. I could hear the gentle rolling of the river over the rocks. It was fresh, clean, and vibrant.

I have never seen a more beautiful panorama. On my right hand side was the river. The water was crystal clear, true to the river's name. On the left were the gentle hills. They were full of trees, bushes, and grass. Above me, the heavens shined brighter than I had ever experienced. I saw a meteor soar across the heavens. I felt so special, like it was God's way of saying hello.

My habit while hitchhiking was to never stay idle, even in the beautiful summer nights. It was a labor of love to walk the roads of America.

As I was walking down the road a car veered to the right and slowed down. It was responding to my outstretched thumb, and I hurried with my knapsack to jump into the open door.

"May God bless you," I thanked the woman driving the car.

"Late at night, isn't it?" the elderly woman said.

"Yes, you see, I'm just traveling through this beautiful country of ours," I said to reduce any apprehension. There is always a risk when hitchhiking, to both the driver and hiker.

"You know why I picked you up?" the woman driving asked.
"No."

"When I came up to you, I saw not only your arms holding your knapsack, but also two arms extended out. They were the Lord's arms."

I sat in hushed wonder until miles down the road, when she had reached her destination and had to let me out. I thanked her heartily as we parted.

I walked and walked. I had so much energy. Little did I know that this great stamina was fueled, in part, by the manic depression. The mania was giving me energy, but no delusional thoughts had entered me yet. Finally, despite my increased endurance, I reached the point where I could physically walk no longer.

I looked to my right. The Clear Water River flowed next to me. I could have slept on its bank, but I would be exposed. Anyone driving by would see me. My only other option was to climb the hill to my left. With few options available, I resigned myself to sleeping on the ground under a tree.

When I reached the top, a park bench sat beneath a tree that couldn't be seen at all from the road. Grateful that the Lord had provided me with somewhere to rest, I rolled out my sleeping bag and settled down on the bench for a good night's sleep. The Lord is my rest.

DAMIAN

It was September of 1988. My third year began at Edwards Tech. We were in our recruitment phase, and the fraternity was in a buzz of activity.

I had picked up a new banner. No longer was I the dedicated Phi Alpha Beta, but the faithful Christian. I was baptized just two months before, and I had returned from my cross-country hitchhiking adventure. Instead of looking for pledges, I was seeking to save the lost.

I met a freshman named Matt in those first days and I invited him to explore New York City with me. That morning, at the appointed time instead of Matt alone, there was a whole flock of freshmen. Somebody in the frat had organized a day to New York City. I had intended to go to New York anyway, so I joined the crowd.

We crossed under the Hudson River through the Holland Tunnel and got off at the station close to Washington Square Park. As we walked through the park, we encountered a group of Amish people. True to character, they were preaching the Word of God. Their dress was unusual. The women had long dresses with bonnets, and the men had suits and hats. It looked like they were from another century. In a regular town, they would really stand out, but in a city like New York they were just one more oddity.

Intrigued, I engaged them in conversation. I recited to them every Bible verse that I knew on baptism. It's our belief that one becomes a Christian at baptism. Our belief was not to pray Jesus into our hearts but to be baptized for remission of sins.

I read from their Bible all the verses on baptism. The Church of Christ has the attitude that anyone not in the Church of Christ isn't really a Christian. So I viewed these people as lost, even though they were most likely well-informed, dedicated believers. The Amish group was very respectful. I recall one woman saying "He sure knows his Scriptures." That was not true; I knew very little about the Bible. During those long rides on the Greyhound bus, I began to read the Bible, starting at the beginning, Genesis chapter one, and I read up to second Samuel. Though this was quite impressive, the truth was that I hadn't read the majority of the Bible even once.

I was the only one in our group who was concerned with these awkward Amish. The rest of the group had left me behind. To make the best of the day, I began to wander around the city. I walked around Manhattan and greeted, without exception, each and every person with a pleasant hello. The responses were varied from looks of terror to an equal response. Yes, I was beginning to experience my mania, but I continued the practice of saying hello. It is not psychotic to be nice.

When I said hello to a thin, short, black man, he looked at me strangely. "Excuse me" he said, "Everybody's so cold and cruel, but you're open and friendly. What's different about you?"

It was the perfect invitation to talk about Jesus. In my zeal, I bombarded the man with the love of God message. After a brief sermon, the man said he was hungry, so I invited him to eat lunch with me.

As we walked to a diner, we chatted and got to know one another. His name was Damian. He had come to New York City a few years ago, attracted by the glitter and pizzazz. He sought to become a famous singer, but he was embraced with failure instead of success. He had too much pride to go back home defeated. He didn't have a place to live, since he couldn't find any work, and so he was one of the thousands of New York's homeless population.

We ate and talked. He was grateful for the meal. Damian told me that he was going into the subway, where it was warm, to sleep n a car. He hadn't slept well in a long time. His plan was to get on the train and just sleep as it went back and forth all over New York City.

My heart was full of compassion. I could not let this human being, whom my Father in heaven loved so much, sleep on a subway. A test I used to challenge myself when interacting with others was to imagine that the person was Jesus. If Jesus had no place to sleep, I would certainly help him. I had to help this man.

I had recently been to a Bible Study in which I had met a man named Eric, who was a solid guy and a brother in Christ, and who had converted from Judaism. He had given me his phone number and I had it on a card in my wallet. I gave him a quick call and said I had an emergency.

I hailed a cab and we drove to Eric's apartment building complex. I escorted Damian, who was now so tired he was straining to stay awake, past a curious doorman. We zoomed up the elevator and went in Eric's apartment.

Upon entering Eric's apartment, he looked surprised. Damian collapsed on the couch in exhaustion. I began to explain the situation to Eric when James, Eric's roommate, entered the room. He did not take kindly to the sight of Damian on the couch. "What's this piece of trash doing on my couch?" he asked. "I have company coming over."

It was as if George Foreman had crushed me with a punch. James was supposed to be a Christian, which I had known because of Eric, but he obviously lacked compassion. In my anguish, I fell down to the ground and I began to pray. James said, "Don't bother praying for him."

"I'm praying for you," I said in a cold voice.

Eric and James than had a quick debate over whether or not to call the minister of the Manhattan Church of Christ, a man named Ernest. It was Saturday night, and Ernest should have been busy working on Sunday's sermon, but motivated by the extreme nature of the circumstances, they decided to make the call. Eric handed the receiver to me after a brief conversation, and Ernest insisted that my actions were inappropriate.

Now unwelcome in Eric's apartment, I helped Damian to his feet. His starved, petite frame couldn't have weighed over a hundred pounds, so to an athlete such as myself, his weight was not much of a burden. Eric accompanied us to the elevator; he had a plan.

Eric was very active in volunteering and helping people, and as a result he knew of a shelter nearby. Eric, Damian, and I grabbed a cab and we assisted Damian into the shelter when we arrived.

The whole place was spooky to me. There were statues all over the place. One of the only ones I recognized was the Virgin Mary. I guessed the others were depictions of the Saints. Each statue had a cluster of lit candles. The room reeked of incense.

Eric hastily explained the situation to a kind man, who replied, "He can stay here if there is absolutely no other place he can go."

Eric was relieved, but I was freaked out by the whole situation. All the statues and incense was just too much for me. So I answered honestly, "There is a place he can stay."

We shuffled out of the shelter. We followed the same routine getting in yet another cab. I have never ridden in as many cabs in one night as I did that night. This time, the destination was to the Phi Alpha Beta fraternity.

Damian slept on the trip, oblivious to what was going on. Eric sat silently in contemplation. We stopped at a money machine at the main building at Edwards Tech and then entered the frat.

In the frat, things were going on as usual. There was a beer party in room eight on the first floor. The partiers stopped their revelry to gawk and stare as Eric and I walked up the stairs. I was carrying Damian on my shoulder. I climbed two flights of stairs to my room.

After a few minutes my roommate "Chowder Head" came in. I explained the situation. "This is my room too," he said, his voice strong and harsh. "And you can't bring somebody here if I don't want them here." But then, meekly and humbly, he added, "But I don't mind."

Satisfied with that answer, I eased Damian on the couch below my bed, and sat on the loft watching him.

In the morning, Damian used the bathroom, showered, and used my toothbrush. Then, the three of us went and caught the bus back to Manhattan to attend church. On the bus, we met Oliver, another man who attended the same church as us. Eric and Oliver talked over last night's events as Damian and I sat on the bus. In full hearing of Damian, Eric said, "He's just some bum who has nowhere to stay." This statement was accompanied by other derogatory comments. When we were alone at church, I rebuked them. It was incredibly rude to say such things in front of the poor man.

At the church, there was a clamor about the night's events. Word had somehow spread around. Most people were upset about me imposing on James in such a manner, while others were silent.

I sat next to Damian during the service, and when the collection plate came along I handed him a dollar to put in so he wouldn't feel so bad. Damian whispered to me, "I'd rather keep it." I nodded with understanding in reply. I believe gifts should be free without any strings attached.

After service, Damian went downstairs to wash and freshen up in the men's room. Ernest Powers, the minister, was very direct with me. "He can't stay here," Ernest said sternly. "It's against the city's zoning laws."

I promised him that I would escort Damian away. Downstairs, Damian was busy for quite a long time fixing his hair to make it perfect. He thanked me before he left, saying, "John, you've given me hope. I know now there are people who care."

In the church, I ran into my friend Eli. He was the only one who seemed happy about what I did. As we walked out of the church, we traveled the same way to the subway.

I spoke, "You know, Damian spent so long fixing himself up. You know what that means." I meant he was full of vain pride.

But, Eli, ever the visionary answered, "It means he's concerned how he looks to others."

"You're right, you're right," I said to Eli, happy to see the light.

At some point, friend Moses got an angry call from James, "Your disciple did something awful to me." Strangely, James thought I was Moses' disciple, because Moses helped bring me into the Church.

Moses answered him, "John's not my disciple and he does whatever he wants." James, Moses reported to me later, was quite disturbed by this answer and with what had occurred.

Meanwhile, back at the frat, I was drawing heat for the night's events. I was reprimanded and accused of a few different things, one of which being, "You brought a strange man here. It could have been dangerous."

There would have been no objection if Damian were some whore or slut who spent the night with me. When I explained the whole situation, especially emphasizing the part that I watched him all night as a precaution, the brothers were satisfied.

I wish I could give homes to everybody. It's sad that some have homes and yet so many don't. I never saw Damian again, but I've never forgotten him. I always hoped he would walk into the church. I wonder if he has forgotten me. Then again, it's not about me, it's about Jesus. "As you have done to the least of these, you have done unto me."

A MESSAGE FROM GOD

Things were spiraling down. I had long quit the alcohol and drugs. Unbeknownst to me, I was progressively deteriorating mentally. All the signs were there. I was functioning on less sleep, my thoughts were racing, and reality was slipping away. The first indicators of mental illness are almost impossible to catch until it's too late. How could I have known I was going insane? It's not sane to think you're going insane.

I have always communicated to doctors that I heard voices. Sometimes they come in audible forms. Sometimes I have conversations. Most of the time, they simply exist. It's like walking in daylight. The light is always present, but you aren't acutely aware that it's there. A lot of people in the hospital hear voices that tell them to do bad things, which often means trying to commit suicide or harming others. My voices have always been positive and wholesome. They never told me to do anything harmful to others or myself. They did, however, get me into trouble from time to time, as you shall soon read.

Imagine waking up one day and in your sleep you have done more than dream. Of all the people on this terrestrial ball, God has decided to give you a message for all humanity. What would you feel? Awe? Inadequacy? Joy? I know what it feels like; I've been there. Whether my message was real or just another delusion really doesn't matter.

I woke up and my heart was heavy. I had a message from God to deliver to the whole wide world. My method of getting

John Kaniecki

the news out was, in concept, simple; I'd just walk down to the United Nations, announce my intent, gather all the nation's leaders together, and tell them the message.

I was influenced by Hal Lindsey's book The Late Great Planet Earth. I read the entire book on a bus trip to the Jersey shore when I was around twelve years old. Even during that reading I saw myself as one of the two witnesses of Revelation in chapter eleven. In the book, the two prophets go to the U.N. and do their thing. It didn't matter to me that I was alone. I was undaunted. I would meet my partner somewhere along the way. When you're working for God and you are totally out of your mind, you really don't sweat the trivial details.

I rose from room thirteen in my frat and walked a block over to Washington Street. A quick bus ride on the Red Apple line, for which I paid one dollar, brought me to the Port Authority in New York City. From there I began to walk to the East Side to the United Nations.

Along the way, I had the deep desire to purge myself. "I must be free of all worldly lusts and desires," was the driving thought as I got closer to my destination. I stopped a man at random. I gave him all my cash and my bankcard. He was surprised to be given forty dollars. I told him my pin number so he could access my account and then I left him. I could imagine he thought I was a con man. After all, this was Manhattan. People just didn't give away money like that, but there were no strings attached in this deal.

On the way, I was very close to the U.N. when I passed a bookstore. A thought occurred to me; if I were going to deliver God's message, I would need a copy of God's word. I went in the bookstore and began to look through the Bibles.

Just one problem, however: I had given away all of my money. Approaching the first man I saw, I asked, "Can you buy me a Bible?"

The man was obviously a believer, but he said that he couldn't buy me one. He told me that if I wanted a Bible, they gave them out downtown at some location by City Hall. The denial didn't set me back. God would provide; I just needed to keep the faith and to believe.

I strode right up to the U.N. building. My path led me past a large stone monument, which quotes the book of Isaiah. Isaiah was a prophet who said, "They will beat their swords into plowshares and the spears into pruning hooks. Neither will they study war anymore." I thought that the time to fulfill this prophecy had arrived.

I went up to the gate and announced to the guard I had a message from God to give to the General Assembly of the United Nations. I expected to be ushered in immediately and taken right away to the Security Council, but no such thing occurred. The guard handled the whole situation coolly and cleverly. "Why don't you give your message to the State Department across the street?"

This seemed like a good idea to me, so I walked across the avenue and I entered the State Department Office. "Yes, can I help you?" asked a man dressed sharply in a suit.

"I have a message from God" I said matter-of-factly.

The man's eyes lit up. He got on the phone. Suddenly in just a few seconds the room was swarming with State Department people. There were around a dozen of them. They were all dressed identically, like pristine clones. These men (they were all men) gazed upon me with glee in their eyes and smirks on their faces. I guess they had an interesting story to tell their wives over dinner that evening.

I was kind of disgusted at the mockery. This was getting me nowhere fast. I had a message from God to deliver and time was passing. Frustrated, I went back across the avenue to the same guardhouse at the United Nations. Again, I told the security guard, "I have a message from God."

He wasn't in such a good mood the second time around. "Well, you can't go in" the guard said. In confusion I sat down right near the entrance with my back against the black metal fence.

The security officer was disturbed. "What are you doing?" he demanded.

"I have a message from God and I'm going to sit here until the time is ready," I declared.

"Well, how long will that be?" he asked, upset.

"Forty days and forty nights," I said. Neither of us was

pleased.

So there I was in the middle of winter planning to stay out forty days and forty nights just like Jesus stayed fasting in the desert. I wasn't worried about eating or sleeping or showering. Instead, I was worried about how I was going to use a bathroom without abandoning my quest.

I was deep in thought when a Spanish man left the United Nations. "What are you doing?" he asked, concerned.

"I'm a Christian," I told him. "I have a message from God to deliver."

"I'm a Christian, too," he replied.

"Were you baptized?" Baptism is very important. You don't pray Jesus into your heart; no, you get baptized and your sins are washed away.

"Yes" said the man.

"Are you a diplomat?" I asked.

"No, I'm a cafeteria worker."

We exchanged our names.

The guard, who was still watching me, said, "John, can you just sit across the street?"

The cafeteria worker encouraged me to do this. He was a Christian, too, and would not betray me. I stood and walked across the avenue and sat down on the opposite corner, determined to stay forty days and forty nights.

After ten minutes, a cop came. He wasn't fooling around; he had his baton out ready to take a swing.

"What are you doing?" he demanded angrily. His demeanor was miles away from the guard who was pleasant in comparison.

"I have a message from God" I said. "I'm going to stay here for forty days and forty nights."

"Well if you don't get lost you're going to be telling your story in Bellevue," the cop said. Bellevue is the psychiatric hospital that serves New York City. It has a reputation of not being a pleasant place.

I rose once again and he started poking me lightly with his stick, jabbing my ribs but not harshly enough to hurt. At the same time, two Asian men in suits walked by, gawking at the scene. I decided to use this to my advantage.

"Police brutality in America!" I yelled as the two men stopped to get a good look at what was occurring.

The cop was defeated. It was either lock me up and fill out his paper work or do nothing. He couldn't smack me around with foreign diplomats present on the scene; it could have caused an international incident.

Something just told me to move on. So I turned my back on the cop and walked away.

As I was walking away I heard a man in a suit talking to a woman who was neatly dressed. "This stuff in Central America with the Communists is going to start World War Three. The world's only got a few months left."

"God will save us," I interjected.

"I'm not talking to you," he said in a condescending voice.

"Well, this is America," I informed him. "In America we have free speech."

Neither he nor the woman said anything after that and I walked away with no small amount of satisfaction.

I made it back to the Port Authority penniless. How was I to pay for my bus fare back to Hoboken? I began talking to a young man selling newspapers. "Where are you from?" I asked him.

"Hoboken" he answered.

"Hoboken" I echoed. "That's where I want to go, but I'm broke." Without too much thought, the youngster handed me a dollar. It was enough for me to make my way home again. I walked in to the Port Authority, walked up the escalator, got on the Red Apple, paid my dollar fare and I was on the way home.

A week before this adventure, I had confided in my mother that I was chosen as God's prophet. She believed for moment, but as my illness progressed, she saw not the hand of God, but the hand of mental illness.

What was my message from God? I didn't know the answer for many years. I thought it would have been some complex plan to bring peace on Earth. After careful contemplation, I realized that my message could be boiled down to one simple declaration. "JESUS IS LORD!" That is my message from God.

My Five Minutes in Heaven

I was sitting in room nine in my frat in early September 1988. I was reading the book of Revelation from the Bible. I had just returned from my hitchhiking and bus trip across the United States and I had never felt so free. I was just about to take my greatest journey ever, maybe even the greatest trip ever taken by man. I'd rank the trip to the moon second to my trip. I ascended to Heaven itself, if only for five minutes.

The translation that I had said, "Blessed are those who read aloud the words of the book." So I began to audibly read the book of Revelation. I read every verse of all 22 chapters. When I made a mistake in reading, like a mispronunciation, I reread the entire sentence.

When I had completed the reading, which took over an hour, I was exhausted. To relax, I put on a CD; it was The Who's Quadrophenia. I lay down on the couch and closed my eyes. The music soothed me. Soon, I was adrift in sweet sleep.

Some way, somehow, I was in Heaven. It was not a dream yet it was not like this physical earth. There before me was Jesus. Remarkable as it seems, I was not in awe before a Mighty God, but in sweet fellowship with a dear friend. Jesus had an acoustic guitar and was singing the song, "I'm One." This is a song on the album Quadrophenia.

After Jesus finished the song, the music ended, despite that on Earth, the CD was still playing. Jesus and I ran down a beach with the sea to our right. Sand and water were beneath my feet and I could feel the sand Jesus kicked up from running sprinkle over my legs.

After a short run, we had reached a grove of trees. Jesus put his hand in mine and we twirled around in a gleeful dance, twirling like a top. Every time our flinging legs got near to a tree they simply went through them as if they were not there.

Suddenly we were where I had first entered Heaven. This time, we were not alone; the devil had appeared. His skin color was gray, almost black, with a body like a troll. Upon his head were two stubs and his head and entire body were deformed, lanky, and skinny. He wore no clothes, but he wasn't naked as humans are naked.

At the moment, the full realization of what was occurring struck me. Up until this moment, I was in a haze. I recognized now that I was in Heaven and before me was Satan and my Lord Jesus Christ, God Himself. I fell prostrate and worshipped the Lamb of God.

I saw Satan. In his claw-like hands he clutched a flawed and muck-covered diamond. The Prince of Evil attempted to destroy the diamond, but his frantic efforts only took the rough off of the diamond, making it more glorious.

Suddenly, I woke on the couch, in room nine, in my fraternity, in Hoboken, on planet Earth. Unbeknownst to me, there was darkness just around the corner of my life. A few days later, I would be admitted into a psychiatric hospital called Saint Anna's in New Jersey.

THE BLUE CAB

My first episode of manic depression was devastating. I went to Saint Anna's hospital for sixty days, thirty of which I spent in the restrictive committed ward, and thirty in the voluntary ward. When I was released, I was a broken and crushed man. Emasculated would be an understatement. There is no greater humbling force than losing your mind.

After my release, I went to my parent's house in Pompton Plains where I grew up, but there were just too many bad memories. I needed space to breathe, and my childhood home was not the place for that. I fled to my fraternity house in Hoboken instead.

My frat brothers welcomed me. I was taking my medicine regularly, which prevented the mania. However, I felt the depression in great force. I was very depressed and spent most of my time sleeping. I was literally paralyzed by overwhelming feelings of despair. As I write this, I am married, working full time, and living independently; three blessings and three accomplishments. The Virginia Slims advertisement "you've come a long way, baby," plays in my head, and I can't help but think of how much it applies to me.

The frat is a great place to party, but an awful place for recovery. My old neighbor Moses, who was instrumental in my becoming a Christian, saw me struggling and made arrangements for me to move in with a mutual friend from the church, Oliver. All of us attended the Manhattan Church of Christ at that time. Relieved to have a quieter place to live, I packed my clothes, took my mattress, and moved in with Oliver.

The room at Oliver's was very small, which I shared with another member of the Church named Michael, who hailed from Ghana. Oliver gave me space, while at the same time he gently pushed me to find work.

I spent months lying in bed, unable to think about anything except how I was going to kill myself. As time passed, however, I made progress and I began to improve. I got a job at Gino's Pizzeria, which was owned by a nice man named Tony. A lot of people called him Gino, but this was not correct. Tony was a great guy, but I was an awful pizza maker. I couldn't even cut the slices on the pie straight. I would wind up with big slices and small slices. Whenever a fat person ordered a slice, I gave him a thin slice and a skinny person got a large slice. After a month of working there, I realized it was time to move on. Tony's wife wanted to fire me, but he resisted. I realized I had no future there, so I said goodbye to everyone and resigned. Tony, in his gracious style, told my friends "John retired from the pizza business."

The next week, I answered an advertisement in the paper. All that was required for the job was a driver's license, which I had. I called them up and landed a job as a cab driver for Mohica Cabs. All of the cabs were old police cars that had been sold in auctions, and so were all painted blue.

I worked long hours from six in the evening to six in the morning, but I only have good memories from my time driving cabs. Every day, I saw the sunrise and the sunset. There is nothing more beautiful than the sunrise and sunset over Manhattan. I worked six days a week, and only took Sundays off. Sometimes, other drivers at the company would work their twelve hour shift, fill in for an absent day driver, and then work their regular night shift right after. That's an amazing thirty-six straight hours. It was difficult for me to get to church after work Sunday morning, let alone continue working marathon hours.

The first day at work, I was trained in the basics of cab driving. I was shown how to fill in a log sheet and the basic rules. A livery cab licensed in Hoboken could only pick up passengers in Hoboken and not at the Path Station, and only cabs could pick up fares from the train station. However, if a person called from out of town for a ride from the company, then it was okay to pick them up. We would get calls to go to Jersey City and Newark Airport to pick up customers. I was told that if I dropped somebody off at the airport, I should act like I was picking somebody up. I had to hold up a sign saying I was "Mr. Jones' cab." Any person in the know needing a ride would catch on.

On the first day, the other drivers told me how to cheat the company. They told me to write down slightly less miles in the log than I traveled, and then when I picked up a fare from being hailed, do not to record it on the log. The miles would work out and no one would be the wiser.

Unlike some cabs, mine had no meter; a book predetermined every fee. It was a dollar and seventy-five cents to go anywhere in Hoboken, and the further the distance, the greater the fee became. For example, a trip to Newark Airport cost twenty-five dollars. The cab driver kept one half of the fares, and also all of our tips. However, we tipped the dispatcher ten dollars and paid to have the car filled with gasoline.

One time, a driver on a Sunday day shift claimed that I didn't fill the tank with gas. I was furious when they demanded I pay him ten dollars. I knew I filled the tank. I even asked the gas station attendant about it. All Mohica cabs went to the same gas station and were always filled up at the regular price. At the time, I believed that because I was white the Spanish majority looked down on me. It took many years to get over my anger on this one. It was so unfair and so obvious that the guy was cheating me.

I was not the best cab driver for Mohica, but I was certainly the most honest. At the Path station, you would get a fare, usually uptown or downtown. Once you got your first passenger, you would call out your destination, "uptown, uptown, uptown." People wanting to head uptown would enter your cab and you would get the full fare from each passenger. Since they would be all in the same vicinity when dropping them off, the miles would look as if only one trip was taken. All the other cabbies would cheat and put down one fare. I, however, would put down the two or three fares that I would receive. As a result of being honest, I always booked the highest amount of fares.

As a reward for bringing in the most money, I was considered for the position of dispatcher. The only reason I was not promoted was because I couldn't speak Spanish. Hoboken had a lot of people who could only speak Spanish, so it was a must for the position. However, all these cheating cab drivers out there stealing could have easily done better than me and become dispatcher. The dispatcher sits in a locked room, nice and safe. When you drive a cab, you have no idea who will hop in the cab next. It could be a nice person or a lunatic. The dispatcher also made more money. They had access to a close bathroom. The dispatcher is by far the better job in my opinion. In truth these drivers were only cheating themselves.

My first day as a cab driver, I drove someone from Hoboken to Manhattan. On the way back I passed by the Lincoln Center. The show must have just ended as hundreds of people walked by the streets. A group of well-dressed people entered in my cab when I was stopped in traffic. "Sorry, I can't drive you," I said. "I'm not allowed to pick up fares in New York."

But they couldn't speak English enough to understand me. The only thing I understood was the destination and their repeated laughing words of "blue cab, blue cab." Since they were only going a few blocks I drove them there. Then as they exited, I said, "No fare." I always try to be honest. The man in the back handed me a twenty and walked away. I radioed the dispatcher and asked him how much the fare was. He said two dollars. It was the best tip I ever had.

I liked to talk to people on my trips. I love people, and I found that talking increases your tips. I started reading a book about Wall Street and one on the Spanish language, which are two things that would be very useful for a cab driver in Hoboken.

There is one instance of driving cabs that stands out above the rest. I've picked up whores, drunks, cocaine snuffers, arrogant rich men, people in mourning, crazies, and more; and all this in just one month of work. Limited space prevents full explanations of these things. The story I want to tell most is about the ex-missionary.

I had a routine when I picked up a fare. First, I'd let the person settle down and relax. Then I'd ask "How are you tonight?"

or "How was your day?" Usually this would start a conversation, which usually led to better tips and made the ride more interesting.

I picked up a passenger at the Path station. He was going out of Hoboken, so it was a road job, and made it a longer trip with a higher fare. Somewhere in the conversation, I mentioned God's name. I was a baby Christian still high on the thrill of the newness of a relationship with God and it tended to slip out in conversations a lot.

"I see you believe in God," the man said flatly. "I don't believe in God anymore." I could feel both the anger and the pain in his quivering, anxious voice. I listened to his story without one word of interruption.

When the man was my age, his beliefs were strong and he was eager in the Christian faith. He was so dedicated that he became a missionary. With the best of intentions, he went to serve in a remote village in Africa. The people there were pagans, but they listened to the missionaries. However, the joys of conversion produced disaster in this African village.

The Christians taught the Bible to the people of the village. Using the scriptures in the books of Timothy and Titus regarding elders and deacons, they proclaimed that a man should have one wife. This village was far from Western influences and their custom was to have as many wives as they could afford. The large family lived together as one happy unit. The men that successfully converted to Christianity wanted to be obedient to the teaching of the missionaries and divorced all of their wives, except for their favorite one.

This was a disaster. The wives who had once had support from their husbands found themselves no longer married. Thrown out of their homes with their children, possessing no skills and no land to farm, they became destitute. Many had no options but to become prostitutes. The children became malnourished and many grew sickly, and some even perished.

As the missionary saw the fruits of his labor, his faith in Jesus died.

I answered the man with silence.

On nearing our destination, the passenger pointed to a sign.

It read "Do Not Enter." The sign he indicated should not have been facing the direction it was. As it lay it seemed that the sign was telling people not to enter the main highway instead of the driveway it was intended for.

I dropped the man off in deep thought. As I returned I pulled off the road by the sign facing the wrong way. I lifted the sign out of the ground and turned it the way it should be. We can only do what we can. It may be small but it's important.

I still have no answer for the man, except that Christianity is not unbending rules. God gave us a brain to think and a heart to care. The Scriptures used were taken out of context; small comfort to the women and children and the ex-missionary.

Recently, I was in Hoboken on the way to Manhattan, to the Port Authority at the World Trade Center. I traveled through the Path Station. I passed by the cabbies hanging out. "I used to drive a cab" I said to one Spanish man.

"I know," he said, "I remember you." This surprised me, as it has been over fifteen years and I only worked for one month.

My time in the blue cab was very enjoyable. I could have done it longer but I got sick again. In my delusional state, I remember my last day in the cab. We didn't get much business because it was a slow night. When I filled up at the end of the shift, I needed very little gas. I thought, "Why does the cab not run on love?" I think it did.

A Devil Named Doug

There is so much evil in this world. Just read history or watch the news and this fact will become apparent. Yet, whenever something bad happens to us, it's shocking. How could this happen? How could this happen to me?

I was hospitalized in Saint Anna's again. It was my second time in a psychiatric hospital. I was in the committed ward against my will. I had stopped taking my medicine. I had fled to the refuge of Oliver's place. There, my state of mind improved to where I was working full time driving the blue cab. My suicidal thoughts had passed away and my depression lifted. Foolishly, I quit taking my medicine. I was in denial about my situation.

A lot of my denial actually had to do with my strong religious beliefs. I had this notion that God could heal me, but in order for Him to do that, I had to show faith. To me, this meant stopping my medicine. If I had enough faith to quit the medicine, then God would heal me.

In hindsight, I should have seen the warning signals blazing fierce. When I initially started driving cabs it was exhausting. I would work my twelve-hour shift and then get some breakfast, and after that I was so tired I could do nothing but sleep. Once I stopped taking my pills, I had all this excess energy. I recall taking walks after work. I even skipped sleeping to travel into New York City. All the while, the idea of being a prophet crept back inside my brain.

My father's first heart attack brought me from Hoboken back

to my parent's house in Pompton Plains. Off of my medicine, the mania returned and one thing led to another until I was committed once more. I was not happy to have returned.

I was in the hospital just a few hours when I got a rather rude welcome. This tall man who was my age came up next to me. I was twenty years old at the time. The man was obviously angry and disturbed. He showed me his arm, which had the words "Fuck You" tattooed on it. Pointing to his tattoo, he demanded, "What does it say?"

"Fuck you," I replied. I really wasn't scared because I was so much out of reality.

The question was repeated by this angry young man. I answered the same way over and over again. Puzzled to why he didn't understand my answer, I thought the f looked like a p, so I answered, "puck you."

After this answer, the man seemed satisfied. That was how I met Doug.

About ten minutes later, it dawned on me. That man was trying to intimidate me. An irrational rage swelled up inside me, out of control.

I found where Doug was sitting in the other room. I grabbed the hair on top of Doug's scalp with my left hand and with my right I made a fist. I knew that you could kill a person if you hit him just right in the nose. Murder was my intent. I spoke to Doug. "Do you want to die?" I asked.

Doug didn't look so tough anymore. Quietly and weakly, he said, "Yes."

This really threw me out of whack. I was still big on the Christian thing, so I answered, "You'll die when God wants you to." The man next to Doug started to laugh. To relieve my anger, I began to punch the nearby window, but the window was made of thick plastic and didn't get damaged. I only succeeded in hurting my hand. A staff member was passing by and saw my inappropriate behaviors. For punishment, I was confined to my room for half an hour.

I was released from my exile to attend a group meeting. I was told how inappropriate my anger was. I don't think the staff knew the reason for my anger, but I thought they did at the time. Anyway, I humbled myself and apologized to Doug. Doug in turn said it takes a real man to admit that he was wrong and accepted my apology. This made Doug and me friends.

The hospital was full of unusual people, even considering it was a psychiatric hospital. There was a woman who recited the Catholic prayer called the "Hail Mary" all day. She'd just sit in a corner saying the prayer over and over again. When I apologized to Doug, I mentioned that I was mad at Doug for offending God. "That's right," this woman chimed in, but the psych tech quickly overruled her and I subsequently apologized.

Every time this woman started reciting the Hail Mary the staff went bonkers. "Stop it, stop it", they would scream and yell as they violently shook her. Though no longer a Roman Catholic and not big on the so-called mother of God, I still viewed this woman as Holy.

Another woman was very mysterious. She was short and thin and young. Her face was the palest white I'd ever seen. She would wander out of her room and walk around not speaking a word. Every now and then, she would reach out her hand and grab mine. When she did, the color would return to her face and she would seem to be normal, but the staff disapproved of this behavior. Doug commented to me once, "Somebody must have raped her." I think Doug was right, though I never knew for sure.

Also at the hospital, there was an interesting man about the same age as Doug and me whose name was Kurt. His hair was black and he aspired to be an actor. He had a portfolio of pictures and they made him look as handsome as a movie star. I thought he was really crazy in his hopes, but after seeing the pictures, I thought that maybe he could achieve his dream. Kurt had a bizarre religious side. He was a Roman Catholic, a Buddhist and a Muslim at the same time. I found this not only very strange, but impossible. This, combined with being out of my mind, I believed that Kurt was the Anti-Christ.

One day, I saw Kurt chanting in front of a plant. He offered to teach me how to chant but I quickly refused. I told him that the presence of the plant symbolized harmony with nature. He had never considered why he chanted to a plant, but my inference made sense to him. He thanked me for adding to his knowledge.

A person who was only briefly in the hospital was a seventeen-year-old boy who was a good lacrosse player and intended to go to Rutgers University. As I was a zealous Christian, I tried to convert him to the Christian cause. He refused my attempts to proselytize him. When I saw he became a disciple of Kurt's and began chanting in front of plants, I got quite upset and jealous.

Kurt told my why he was in the hospital. He had gotten tired of living. He took a whole bottle of pills to kill himself. He had expected the angels to descend and to carry him to God's right hand. When a couple of minutes had passed and none of the angels showed up, he got very worried and phoned for help.

I remember how Kurt's hopes were raised up so high. His doctor was going to let Kurt out of the hospital and allow him to go to Chicago in pursuit of his acting career, but they quickly dashed his hopes. The plan wasn't deemed wise by the majority of the staff, and they canceled it. I don't remember what happened to Kurt. We became pretty good friends, especially after I decided he wasn't the Anti-Christ. He was my roommate for a while, but one day he disappeared without explanation.

We had a fellow patient named Carol. She had been in the army. The experience had severely damaged her psychologically. She would talk and talk about the army, bragging how tough she was. One time at group therapy, Doug made this comment about the sessions. "Carol talks all the time and John adds a comment or two. This is bullshit." The staff didn't appreciate this analysis by Doug, but it was accurate.

Carol was extremely mean to me. I, however, refused to be like her. In fact, I went out of my way to be nice and ignored all of her insults. Doug and I used to hang out a lot. Doug started picking up my verbal expressions, subconsciously imitating me. This made us laugh. Carol got jealous of our closeness. "What are you, gay?" Carol asked me once, since Doug and I were so close. To be nice, I let her have Doug's company some of the time and the two of them paced the halls together.

One day after three weeks Carol came into my room. She

said to me, "If everyone in the world was like you, it would be a perfect place." She took off the golden crucifix that hung around her neck and gave it to me. An hour later, she angrily demanded I give it back and accused me of tricking her.

Doug and I would talk about a lot of things. Being locked up affords you lot of time and one of the best ways to fill it up is with conversation. It helps your sanity to talk. Strange as it seems, too much time on your hands is a very serious problem. Doug had worked for an electrician before entering the hospital. His job had been basically digging ditches to put the wire in. He spent five minutes explaining all he knew about electronics. I had a course in electricity, magnetism, and circuits at Edwards Tech. I began to explain to Doug about inductors and capacitors, but he became very confused. The talking helped pass some time.

Doug told me how he once got in trouble with the law. He had gone to a police station with a knife and began slashing tires on the police vehicles. He was promptly caught and tossed into a cell. Then, Doug somehow managed to find a way to light the jail on fire.

One of the nurses was very large. She was grossly fat and overweight, but apparently that was how Doug liked his woman, big and broad. "Ooh, look at her," he would say as the nurse walked by. I thought he was mocking her, but he was sincerely attracted. Doug told me about his masturbating in the bathroom. He had a slogan he'd repeat in laughter, "I don't care if I'm gonna die, I'm gonna see the doda fly."

A large blonde woman was the same age as us. She used to be thinner, but that was before she came to the hospital. She claimed that she when she was thin, she had been a model, and that she had a boyfriend in the mafia. I believed her because she said it so convincingly, in a matter-of-fact and not bragging way. The staff was always accusing her and Doug of having sex, but as far as I knew, that wasn't the case. That never stopped the accusations.

Another odd person I met at the hospital was a homeless man in his mid-thirties. He spent his time collecting shopping carts, but he didn't work for a supermarket. He insisted that this was his job, and was fiercely defensive against any suggestion that it wasn't. He had spent some time in Italy working in a pizza restaurant. While we were together, for the first time in my life, I spoke a different language. In what I believed was perfect Italian, I said, "It's no fun to be an illegal alien." My sudden outburst amazed this man. I wanted to continue speaking in tongues, but my friend told me to stop. I have no explanation as to how this happened.

The man then took me to a large map of the country on the wall. "John," he said "when you get in power, give me these towns." He pointed to some towns on the map and when I agreed to this he was ecstatically happy. I guess this man thought that I would be influential in the future.

Herbert was the oldest patient in the place. His hair was gray and he wore glasses. All morning, from the time he woke up, he would repeat over and over again, "When's breakfast? When's breakfast?" Finally, when breakfast would arrive, he would devour it faster than you would think humanly possible. Then, as soon as he was done eating, he would begin to say, "When's lunch?"

One night I couldn't sleep. I took out my toothbrush and cleaned the bathroom with it. I even scrubbed the toilet bowl. Sounds crazy, but that's why I was in the psychiatric hospital.

After my hospitalization in Saint Anna's I went on to Heaven House. Doug, meanwhile, was transferred to the state hospital called Bluerock. A year and a half later I was quite ill once again. After a brief stay at Saint Francis' in Hoboken, I wound up in Bluerock. While at Bluerock, I went to an Alcoholics Anonymous meeting. I had a problem with drinking and drugging. More importantly, the meeting was held outside of the ward, so it was a nice change of pace. At the meeting, I saw Doug.

Doug and I took on as if no time had passed. He had been at Bluerock since he was sent from Saint Anna's a year and a half ago. While at Bluerock, my friend had gotten really depressed and despondent. This was a common occurrence. It's hard to stay locked up in a hospital, especially for a long time. Doug had taken a razor blade and slashed his head. Fortunately, he barely missed a major artery. If he had known what he was doing, he would have died.

The idea of the doctors and administration was to keep me at

Bluerock until housing could be provided for me elsewhere. They wanted me to go to a group home, which, for those who don't know, is a place of transition from the hospital to regular society that exists outside of hospital property in a community with a group of staff to supervise the occupants and maintain strict rules and regulations. It wasn't like being free, but it was less restrictive than a hospital. The one thing that is most strictly-enforced is the taking of medicine. The hope is that a group home will not only help prevent patients from returning to a hospital, but also help mentally ill people transition back into society.

The details of this meant that I would have had to stay in Bluerock for over a year waiting for a spot to open. I convinced my mother to allow me to return to my parents' house. I still didn't like going to their home because of all of the bad memories, but almost anything was better than staying in Bluerock.

Part of my treatment was that I had to attend a day center. There, mentally ill people were supposed to be rehabilitated. The philosophy of the center was to keep us busy, but not to overwhelm us. We did stuff like make lunch, listen to music, keep a garden, do some factory work, and attend group therapy. Most of the time we just sat around and smoked cigarettes. I was happy to be among my peers and others like me. Not long after I started at the day center, Doug began to attend each day, to my delight.

Doug was staying in a group home a couple of blocks from the center with two young ladies, one of whom was named Beth. The house always had a staff on duty making sure everything was fine. As we hung out in the center, Doug told me some interesting stories.

One thing Doug explained was his prison experiences, where he had been at least once because of his incident at the police station. He said that in prison, blacks dominated the population. In order to survive, the whites and the Spanish teamed up to keep the balance of power.

I asked Doug if he ever got beat up in jail. He said that yes, it had happened. Then I asked if he had ever got beaten up real bad. He said he'd got beaten up so badly that he fell to the ground and couldn't even move. Then, with an evil glimmer of light in his eye, he said, "But I got in some good punches."

Doug said jail was really rough. One day, he and some of his friends beat up an older guy, which he believed was justified because their victim was in prison for raping babies. They had thrown their victim on the ground and kicked him, and laughed as they cracked his ribs.

Doug spoke about the prison for the criminally insane, or as he called it the "vroom room." This, I was told, is the most dangerous place in all of New Jersey. A huge muscular black man was an inmate at this prison, but he only had one arm. Rumor had it that the authorities had had one of his arms cut off so they could manage him. I guess that was better than killing the poor guy. One day Doug was in the bathroom urinating, when the black man grabbed him from behind with his single arm. Despite the man having only one arm, it was quite a struggle for Doug to get free. Once out of the grip, Doug promptly punched the man in his face as hard as he could, and then fled the bathroom to alert the guard outside. The guard shrugged his shoulder and did nothing at all.

Doug told me he used to like speed. He would shoot the methamphetamines into his blood stream with a needle. I asked Doug if he ever tried heroine. He said he did but he didn't like it much. All it did was make him sleepy.

Doug eventually got Beth from the group home to be his girlfriend. She was pretty, but not that pretty, in my opinion. Beth was from a rich family and she was real stuck up. At first Doug and she did not like each other at all, but Doug somehow won her over. Every night when the supervisor, who was supposed to be alert, fell asleep, Doug would sneak silently into Beth's room to have sex. How they never got caught, I will never know.

Doug and Beth's relationship seemed to be a serious thing. They even talked about marriage. My friend Betty, who also attended the day center, gave Doug an emerald ring, with the intention that this ring would be used as a wedding ring. Doug promptly took the ring to a pawnshop and used the money to buy liquor and get drunk.

Doug reminisced about a party he once went to. All night he was hitting on this girl. The girl's boyfriend, whom Doug describes as a "small jock," lured him outside on some pretense. The athlete struck Doug as hard as he could. Doug smiled and then proceeded to hand out a beating. Doug laughed and smiled as he recalled the events.

In high school, Doug had made a bazooka and shot a projectile through a huge glass window. "What did you use for gun powder?" I asked curiously.

"Gun powder," Doug answered simply, with a mischievous grin.

Doug always enjoyed getting a rush. He was prohibited from drinking soda with caffeine at the group home. Doug would go to Quick Check, which was close to the center and his home. There he would buy the big bottles of Coke and Pepsi. He would chug them down, drinking two or three in rapid succession, all for a little high.

Doug's drinking eventually did him in. A couple of the guys would sneak away from the center and go to drink at a bar on a regular basis. One time Doug got caught. I think they smelled the liquor on his breath. The penalty for this serious breach of rules was either getting expelled from the group home or to go to the hospital for one month for rehabilitation. The stupid counselor asked Doug, "If you were feeling weak, why didn't you talk to somebody about it?" He thought Doug had a moment of weakness that led to a relapse. Truth was, Doug drank whenever he had the money, not when he felt weak.

With no place to stay, I took Doug down the shore to where he grew up. He rented a room in a trailer from a friend of his. His friend was a really big drinker who got drunk every night. Doug found a job in a car wash, where he would wipe the car down after it came out of the wash. One day, they fired Doug, even though it's quite difficult to get fired from a car wash. I suspect Doug may have been stealing tips. However, the life in a trailer was better than Doug's former life, even with an alcoholic for a roommate. He used to live in a car, siphoning out gasoline from other cars. As a clinically mentally ill person, Doug received money for disability from the government.

Beth went to move in with Doug. I took her down to him myself. At the time, I wasn't aware of Beth's status. Though over twenty, and perhaps into her thirties, she couldn't make decisions on her own. She had a legal guardian, who I believe was her brother. He made the important decisions for her, though I'm still not clear about the details. Soon after Beth arrived, the two of them managed to get arrested. They had no money and tried to steal cigarettes. Doug was distracting the store clerk while Beth stuffed cartons of cigarettes into her purse. If she had stolen one quickly, she might have gotten away with it, but she had gotten greedy and tried to stuff in two. As it was, they got caught. Doug claims he could have split and let Beth take all of the blame, but even Doug wasn't that cold. He did the noble thing and admitted his part in it.

At this time the police in Pompton Plains called me to drop by the police station, which I did. There, an officer explained to me that Beth had problems and her family didn't want me to have anything to do with her. The officer recognized that I, too, had psychological problems. He was aware of Beth's past and our interaction at the center we attended together. The cop spoke to me for ten minutes and I listened, and he was very polite and respectful. Beth's brother called me afterward to give me the same message. I told him I was just Beth's friend. He said if I were her friend, I wouldn't have helped her leave like that. He wasn't nice or friendly, but he didn't threaten me.

Doug and Beth went to trial. I'm sure they were both equally guilty of the crime. Beth's family got her a high-priced lawyer. Doug, with no resources, had to manage with the public defender. Money talked and Beth walked; Doug went to jail and Beth was found innocent. The lawyer portrayed her as an innocent, young girl who was influenced by the criminal, Doug—so much for justice.

It was a couple of years later I got a surprise phone call. Doug called and said he was getting married. I drove down on the big day all dressed up in my suit. He had known his future wife for only two months before they decided to get engaged. She was a large woman and I recalled how much Doug adored large women. They were dating for one of the months and living together for the second month. They met, of all places, at church. Doug and the woman got married by the mayor in the girl's parents' house. I was the best man and I signed the marriage certificate.

John Kaniecki

The whole thing was suspicious to me. Doug needed a place
to stay and the woman desperately wanted to get married. I visited
them two months later. Doug was complaining that his mother-in-
law was treating him like a baby and wanted no alcohol in the house.
In order to drink, he needed to sneak his liquor in or drink outside.

I called a couple of months later and found out that Doug
was in prison. Doug had failed to show up for his community
service and violated his parole. His wife said he was in bad shape.
I called a couple of months after that and the marriage was over.
The angry tone of the bride did not encourage me to ask questions,
so I never did learn what happened to Doug, or their marriage.

Doug once told me he was going to get the "Fuck You" tattoo
off of his arm. Doug is the craziest person I have ever met and
coming from me, that's saying something.

CRAZY IN STYLE

Once more, I had to deal with the dreaded Doctor Rug at Saint Anna's hospital. At the end of a patient's thirty-day stay, according to law, a patient must be evaluated. The idea behind the law is to prevent somebody getting placed into a psychiatric hospital indefinitely. Thus, after thirty days, a second doctor must be consulted. I was ushered into a room where there was some foreign doctor, but only foreign in the sense that I never had seen her on the unit. We sat down and she asked me some questions. I was very zealous as a Christian in spreading God's word. She explored this avenue. I do not know the doctor's exact report of our interview, but I must have failed the audition because I wasn't released. I am certain my religious convictions didn't help the matter. In fact, it may have been the major reason for my transfer. Instead, I was to be shipped off to a long care hospital called Heaven's House.

I said goodbye to all and was escorted downstairs to an ambulance. I distinctly recall a police officer in attendance in addition to the ambulance personnel. This made me feel more like a criminal than a patient. I had written a poem about the police and I shared it with the cop. After reading it, he said that I should get it published. I don't have a copy of that poem any longer. The poem espoused a virtuous, idealistic notion of authority. I was extremely naïve in my youth.

I have not only come to question authority, but to see authority as the reason for the majority of the world's problems.

Doctor Rug, for example, was presented as somebody who was in charge of my psychological wellbeing, but he was negligent to the point of criminality. He had no personal interaction with my despite the fact that it was his job to do so. Yet when it came to my fate, Doctor Rug had tremendous influence, if he wasn't the one making the actual decisions. I came to realize that you cannot trust authority simply because they hold a position. I could not assume Doctor Rug was a good, caring doctor based solely on the fact that he was a doctor.

Heaven House had various wards depending on the patient's exact classification. There was a ward of those suffering from anorexia and I am certain there was one separate unit for those struggling with drug and alcohol addiction. There were wards for voluntary patients. The committed ward which I was sent to was called Edward's Hall, or Crazy Eddy's, as it was known as in the hospital.

I met a host of characters in Crazy Eddy's. There was one young man whose name was Craig. His glasses were very scratched up and when I asked why this was, he told me that he had been chased by the police in a car. Craig refused to pull over and led the police on a high-speed chase. He even slammed his car into the cop's car. Finally, once the police put Craig into custody, they rubbed his glasses on the ground. They were scratched so badly that the poor young man could barely see out of them. I guess you understand why my attitude towards the law has changed.

Craig was very uncertain about his future. The high-speed chase had occurred in Texas. If Craig was found not able to be on trial because of psychological reasons, he might get out. On the other hand, if he were deemed sane, then he would most likely go to prison. I shared a few wrestling moves, instructing my nervous friend, which he seemed to appreciate greatly. The funny thing about Craig was that he got released a long time before me. We exchanged phone numbers. A month or two after leaving Heaven House I got a phone call from him. It was a simple, yet shocking, message. "I don't think I'm Jesus anymore," he declared.

A remarkable thing about Craig was that I never saw him as a person with problems. We had spent a couple of weeks locked up together, we were in group therapy together, and we had talked privately as friends for hours, so when this Jesus comment came up, it was most unexpected. I guess I, too, have this undercurrent of abnormality that I can seem fine on the surface, but there is trouble in the deep waters.

One thing that all patients had to undergo was a brain scan. This was quite a disturbing event to me. I was ushered into a small room containing only a machine and a bed. At the door stood a couple of blue-shirted workers who were pretty heavily built; Heaven's House had the habit of hiring ex-marines. In the small confines of the room, I was instructed to lie down on the bed. When I complied, the attendant began to prick my head with tiny needles in various places. I really wanted to call the whole test to a halt, but I was under their power.

Edward's Hall was far larger then both units in Saint Anna's Hospital combined. There was a dining room and music room. The whole ward was built with the theory of small incremental rewards. Every day the doctor would conduct a mandatory meeting. At the meeting, he would go over some basic stuff, and then at the end of the meeting, he would announce promotions. The best promotion was to be allowed out of the ward for a short period of time. The more you progressed, the longer you could stay away from the ward.

There was one very disturbed young man. All of the patients shunned him, mostly because he evidently had serious problems. He would speak at inappropriate times and converse with an imaginary friend. I can understand why the patients didn't want to associate with him. The boy was plain weird. However, despite his urgent need for help, the head psychiatrist of the hall joined the hypocrisy and would harass the young man. When this young man sought privileges, he was constantly denied.

There was another short, chubby man who became my friend. He would constantly talk about his wife. I felt sorry for the man as he expressed his marital woes, how his wife would cheat on him and treat him terribly. Worst of all, she wouldn't even visit the poor man in the hospital. Then, after a couple of weeks, he informed me that his wife was an alien. Not only an alien, but the queen of the galaxy. I felt very sorry for the man. When I tried to persuade him that he was imagining things, he became quite irate.

Another man was a biker. He wore a leather jacket at all times and thought that he was tough. Aloof is a good way to describe him. He kept his distance, that's for sure. One time when I was speaking with him, I asked what his first move in a fight would be. I, of course, had to demonstrate the wild move that I had created, which seemed to scare the man, and he fled the room.

A volunteer preacher would come in to the chapel in the hospital once a week. With my encouragement, this biker fellow came for a visit. After a few minutes, however, he left babbling about the power of the "sons of Satan" that he had witnessed.

Heaven's House had quite an impressive campus. Inside, there was a poolroom, an arts and crafts room, and a gym with a full basketball court. Outside, there was a swimming pool and an area where the patients could hang out and smoke. An immense field of grass sat behind the building and it was still on Heaven House property, so it was quite all right for the patients to walk around the field. When taking a walk, one could almost forget they were confined to psychiatric hospital. Almost.

The food at Heaven's House was an utmost delight. Hospital food in general is not too appealing. At this hospital, however, the food not only excelled the quality served in other hospitals, but it rivaled fine restaurants. Best of all, you could eat all that you wanted. Of course, us patients were paying for these amenities in our enormous bills, but it was still pleasant to be pampered with the best.

After spending thirty days on Edward's Hall, I was transferred to another hall. I didn't want to sign myself in, so I was technically still committed. On this new hall, I had unlimited access to the hospital. That is, I could freely leave the dorm at any time, as long as it wasn't during group therapy or after hours. I made many friends among the patients.

There was this one woman who was extremely beautiful whom I will call Hannah. Not only was she physically beautiful with a fantastic body, but she had a very pleasant personality as well. Every night she would apply some green cream on her face for her skin, which made her look like a witch. Hannah's story was very tragic. She had an awful husband. When they were dating, the man threatened to commit suicide if Hannah didn't marry him. Once married, he abused her. The couple would watch pornographic movies and then he would demand such performances from his wife. All these things made Hannah a regular at Heaven House.

There was this woman who was a fantastic artist. I was very impressed when I saw her drawings. She became my friend and confided in me. She had declared herself a nymphomaniac. When she revealed her background to me, I didn't think she was troubled; she simply had sex with one man, and not too frequently. Unfortunately, she was very ugly, to say the least. She was extremely envious of this very attractive woman who was in rehab, who was blonde, well proportioned, and physically fit. In fact, she resembled a Barbie Doll. My artist friend once started to talk to her self-proclaimed nemesis and the two became fast friends.

I would try to evangelize all the patients. My ranting must have upset many of my fellows. One day, a man cried out to me, "Jesus be damned." I rose from my seat and went into the crowd where I had heard the voice come from. Everyone was silent looking me over. Nobody owned up to making the statement. I looked at one small man who said, "I didn't say it, he did." I went over to the man who made the offensive statement and simply shook his hand.

Of course, we had group therapy every single day. I really have no memories of the events, but I am confident that it occurred. The best help patients get in psychiatric hospitals is from other patients. Staff can be helpful, even crucial. They can offer insight and propose practical solutions. Still, there is no substitute for walking the walk. Staff, at best, are outsiders looking in. The only therapy I can recall was when we were playing Pictionary. I enjoyed this activity more than the other ones, because it was one of the only ones that put me at ease. A hospitalization for psychiatric reasons is pretty intense. In some way or another, you are always focusing on your problems. To get a time of release, to forget your difficulties, is refreshing.

My doctor kept on trying to change my medicine so that I wouldn't hear any voices. I always told him I heard voices. But like

I said before, unlike the majority of other mentally ill patients, my voices are pleasant. They are neither intrusive nor negative. When off of my medicine they do prompt me to do some outrageous things, but when taking my pills, I can function as a normal human being. Unfortunately, the doctor couldn't consider wellness and the voices coexisting, so I was put on a variety of medicines. This was a long, frustrating process.

I would call my friend Eli up every Thursday night. Eli was an evangelist at the Manhattan Church of Christ that I attended. It was sort of a ritual. I would go at the same time, around seven p.m. He would talk to me briefly for maybe a minute or two. To end the conversation he would always say a prayer. On the weekends at the end of my stay, I would get passes to leave the hospital. My mother would take me to Manhattan to visit the church. I was extremely sensitive when people would ask probing questions. Even for them to ask how I'd been was upsetting to me.

I had to go before the judge to see if I could get let out. I recall my father had hired a lawyer. The judge began asking questions in the case. My father volunteered some information that was negative about me. Both the lawyer and I looked at my dad as if he, too, was crazy. Afterwards, when the judge ruled against releasing me I confronted my dad. "Why did you open your mouth?" I asked. His reply was that he just wanted the judge to get all the information. I did not want to stay in the hospital; I wanted to get out. Even though it was one of the nicest ones I had been to, it was still incredibly confining.

The second time before the judge, my regular psychiatrist wasn't present. Another was standing in to do his duties. The substitute doctor claimed that I had tried to commit suicide. I outright denied this; I had contemplated suicide many times, but never had I attempted it. As a result, the poor psychiatrist went into the notes of the other doctor. It was a comical scene as he had this immense magnifying glass he would use to aid his reading. While he was searching his notes, he was oblivious to what was going on in the courtroom. He was still looking when the judge said that I could be released.

I went off like a rocket ship and quickly packed my things.

In fact, I had everything loaded in my parent's car already when the staff told me not to begin packing just yet. It would take some time to process the necessary paper work. I had written two books of poetry during my four month stay, one of which I had lent to a fellow patient who was in the rehab ward. I was so eager to leave that I didn't even both to retrieve my art. Sure, the place was the nicest hospital I had ever been in, but it was still a hospital.

This is how the world works: if you are poor and you do drugs you go to jail. If you are middle class and get caught doing the same crime, you go to a hospital. If you are rich and get caught doing drugs you go to an extremely nice hospital. Heaven's House was an extremely nice place, but I was glad to be gone.

TRINIDAD

Never has my insanity raged so fiercely as in my trip to Trinidad. If it was a pit bull growling at other times in my life, in Trinidad it was a dragon roaring. I traveled to Trinidad with a friend named Jammos. We were to stay by his mother's house and have a nice relaxing vacation—so much for our plans.

Jammos and I both attended the Manhattan Church of Christ. He lived uptown in the Bronx, an area of New York City that had a reputation of ill repute. It was rumored to be flustering with crime and criminals. It was with terror that I took the uptown train headed to visit my friend. I remember clutching my Bible out in the open, so others would associate me with Christianity, looking out the window. It gave me a sense of protection. As I gazed out the subway window, I saw whole neighborhoods that were dilapidated. My fright and anxiety only increased. However, my fears were alleviated when I arrived at Jammos' apartment in the Bronx. Psychiatric hospitals have reputations, too, as do their patients, just like neighborhoods. Do not judge us prematurely.

We found ourselves on a plane headed south to the Caribbean island. I recall Jammos and me going into the cockpit to get a tour. One of the pilots showed us how the controls of the jet plane worked. Jammos commented that it was just like a garbage truck. I found the comment demeaning and I was fairly embarrassed, but the pilot simply smiled and repeated Jammos' comparison.

All was well on the flight down. After touchdown we had to go through customs. I hadn't taken any medicine for a good month's time before my trip. In those days, it took a long time for the mania to surface if I neglected the pills, so when I left, all was fine. However, I was very talkative when I was dealing with the customs officer. I began to converse about New York City and the United States, and instead of searching through our bags, he simply engaged me in conversation. In a matter of minutes, Jammos and I were cleared to leave the airport. Jammos remarked that was the quickest he had ever gone through customs.

From the airport, we got a ride in a taxi. The driver was a Muslim. In addition to performing his official duty, he also exchanged our currency. He gave us a much better rate then the official conversion. While on that cab drive, my mania was kicking in. I declared that "The Holy Spirit" had descended upon the island of Trinidad. Jammos smiled as he heard this, not knowing its dramatic implications.

We arrived at Jammos' mother's place. It was in the middle of nowhere, and primitive compared to what I was used to in the States. It did have running water, but that was it. For drinking water, they had to use a huge barrel that caught the rain. For the toilet, there was an outhouse in the backyard. In order to shower or bathe, we had to walk down to the pipe down the street. I wore my bathing suit so I wouldn't be completely naked. The pipe was located right next to the open sewer that trickled waste along its way. The house itself was elevated on poles. Hosts of chickens lived on the property.

There and then I presented my hosts with the presents I had brought them. To Jammos' mother, I gave a nice crocheted blanket. To Norman, Jammos' brother, I brought a book of pictures of New York City. To Sally, Jammos' wife, I delivered a bottle of perfume. All in all, it must have seemed like it was going to be a pleasant stay.

I recall Norman hanging out with me. He had this short Rasta friend that came by. He wore camouflage pants and had a green army hat. He was very polite, but I had a feeling that he didn't trust me. My mind was starting to slip into delusion. I renamed Norman "No Man". Then, I came up with a saying, "They say that No Man would be raised from the dead." I would tell that to a lot of people all over the island. With the play on the words, I was prophesying that, in fact, Norman would be raised from the dead. I would sing a song with the lyrics, "No Man will be raised from the dead."

I found myself a nice piece of sugar cane. Sugar cane is long and could serve as a good staff if it was strong enough. One night, I was singing and carrying on, twirling my stick of sugar cane. I was right outside of the adjacent hut where Jammos and Sally stayed. My heart was in the right place, singing hymns and talking about God, but unfortunately, my brain was in the depths of insanity. I had transformed the words without realizing it, so they made no sense. When I was twirling the sugar cane stick, Sally came out and admonished me, "Stop swinging that stick, because you'll break the light." I laughed and continued assuring her it wouldn't happen. Less than a minute later, I shattered the bulb.

While I was in Trinidad, a very important event happened back in New York City. My friend Eli, the evangelist at the Manhattan Church of Christ, passed away. I remember hearing this and not believing it. The next day, I called the church and Gail, the secretary, answered the phone. I asked for Eli. She said "John, Eli's dead." The reality of the tragic incident sunk into my soul. Eli was very important to me. He was always nice to me and could relate to me. Losing him was traumatic. I cried for a long time and then gathered myself together.

I began taking long walks all over Trinidad. I would talk to the people and engage them in all sorts of conversation. There were particular areas where I was instructed not to venture into, which were designated as places occupied by bandits. What that meant, I really don't know. In my mania, I disregarded all caution.

On one such journey, I passed by a bar. They refused to let me enter. I'm not sure why, they just told me to pass on by. The next day, a man drove up to where I was staying. "Come for a ride," beckoned the driver. Without a care, I took my lunch—a piece of steak—and jumped in the car. I asked the driver if he would like a bite. He snatched my piece of steak and gobbled it down like a starved dog. We drove together to the bar that had prohibited my entry the day before. We went in and began to shoot a game of pool. We were playing eight ball. The rules of the game said that whoever sinks the black ball, or the eight ball, wins. As we progressed in the game, a man I didn't know approached our table. He picked up a ball and put it into the pocket. My friend started to snivel and meekly say, "Please leave us alone."

I wasn't going to stand for this, and progressed down a different path. "If that's how you want to play the game," I said loudly as I picked up the eight ball and slammed it into the pocket, "then I win." The man who interfered with our game looked at me quite nervously. I introduced myself to him. His name was, of all things, Leslie. From that time on, I was welcomed inside the bar.

I believe that the patrons in the bar were involved with dealing drugs, and not on a small level. It seemed that their whole lives were centered on the bar. Perhaps this wasn't accurate, but it was real in my delusional mind. There was this one guy who I began talking to. He was boasting about how he came from the South Bronx. I slapped the man right in the face. He was shocked and did not retaliate. I fled the bar. The occupants of the bar came to look for me. They found me at a graveyard singing to the tombstones. I was, of course, trying to raise the dead. My mania had progressed and I had the belief that Jesus' resurrection of the dead would come in stages. I was trying to start with Trinidad. When the posse from the bar saw me, they left me alone.

I remember singing a song. "The U.S. dollar is falling down, burning to the ground." This lyric reflected my attempt to destroy the value of the U.S. currency. I wasn't trying to do this for any malevolent reason. In fact, the opposite was true. I understood from reading the book of Revelation that the mark of the beast was coming. It was my strategy that if the dollar was destroyed, so would the world economic system. With these events, the world would have to barter. Thus, we would circumnavigate the deadly effects of the mark of the beast.

Another brilliant idea I had in Trinidad was to make the Amazon a world national park. All nations of the Earth would contribute to its upkeep. We would build giant tracks of monorails for tourists to take trips on. The natives of the area would maintain these mechanisms. Unfortunately, nobody listened to my plan.

Years later, my mother's friend's son worked for a United States senator. I wrote a nice letter to him regarding my idea of a world national park. I was informed it was hand delivered to the senator. In a few weeks I got a reply from the senator. It was a form letter dealing with some totally unrelated topic. They weren't listening before and they aren't listening now.

While in Trinidad, I began to lay the ground works for the millennial kingdom. I do not believe the Bible teaches a rapture where Christians will be taken away from a tribulation. Rather, I understand scripture to teach a thousand-year period where Jesus will rule from Heaven through his Church. As such, I created the E.N.D., an acronym for Earth's New Dynasty. The origin of this began in Trinidad in scribbles on pieces of paper and written on the wall of my room. The plan had become quite sophisticated. It is basically an egalitarian system. There are twelve major kingdoms and various bases of powers. These institutions are designed with overlapping jurisdictions. That way if a despot develops, there is another recourse for justice. I have recruited a lot of people for positions in the E.N.D. However I think most think I am simply joking. In fact, the E.N.D. got off to a rousing start in Trinidad. At the beginning, I took the perfume I bought for Sally, had Jammos kneel before me, then I anointed his head with the ointment and proclaimed him king of the world.

As I began raising a ruckus over the island, the authorities got concerned. I was an American and I found out that brought certain privileges. Technically, I hadn't done anything illegal. I remember going out at night and armed soldiers with machine guns would be all over the place. At one such gathering of soldiers, I asked one if he would like it if I drew his portrait. He said yes. I proceed to get to work on my sketch. After a while, one of the soldiers got angry and said "Why does he look like a monkey?" I replied, "Because I can't draw."

The authorities of Trinidad sent a fellow American to straighten me out. He came up to me one night and said "My name is Bob Jones, the crazy American from the Teke. I am sure you heard of me." I responded that I never did. He took me around in his car. Wherever we went, he would repeat his mantra. After the speech, every single listener said they had never heard of him before, which infuriated the man. While trying to talk sense into my brain, he told me his story. He was an orphan who had gone into the marines at age seventeen. After Vietnam, he made money off of a television station he purchased and fled to Trinidad to reside.

We were hanging out in a bar when Bob began to tell the bartender how much the Trinidadian people hated Americans. His source of inspiration for the ill feelings was the history of the U.S. oil companies and how badly they ripped of the Trinidadians. The bartender said that this was not the case, and besides, the oil was now under control of Trinidad. Later that night Bob started to get angry with me. He wanted to fight. I said "I always start a fight with a handshake." He grabbed my hand and twisted it. At the same time he kicked with his foot, just coming short of my head. I relegated him to a psychopathic jarhead with a shrug. I didn't bother with Bob Jones after that night.

One night, I got really frightened and concerned. I fled into the night thinking the devil was after me. In the process, I had my passport and tossed it by the side of the road. In my haste I climbed a tree, believing that the devil couldn't reach me from that height. I thought I was high in the branches when in reality I was just a couple of feet from the ground. In anxious dread, I hugged the tree for a good hour. Finally, I convinced myself to face Satan. I let go of the tree, expecting to plummet a great distance and found out that I was almost on the ground. I had to laugh at myself that night.

One night I got inside a cab. I had no idea where I was going. I started telling the driver all this crazy stuff about messages to world leaders and secret plans. The driver calmly listened to my incoherent nonsense. When we reached our destination he didn't ask me for the fare. That was good because I didn't have any money. I figured he was some sort of government agent out to help me. There I was, wandering this third world country at night without a care in the world. Eventually, I was picked up by several soldiers driving a jeep. They asked me where I was staying and promptly brought me back to my residence.

One day, I was walking along and I got really tired. A bunch of local people were hanging out. I joined the group. I expressed how tired I was and they offered the services of their hammock. Grateful, I took a nap on their front porch. I must say that the people of Trinidad had a wonderful spirit.

Jammos and I would take rides on buses all over the island. On one trip, I saw a man with a purple hat. This brought a special significance inside of my mind. I would continue to speak about "the man with the purple hat" as if it held immense importance. At the time, it did. Everywhere I went, I brought up the subject. Jammos got upset with me one time on the bus because I started singing my song about the U.S. dollar going down. To add a little emphasis, I tossed a few bills out of the bus window. Jammos said the money could go to better use.

About halfway through my trip I received an unexpected visitor. It was, of all people, my mother. It seemed that the government of Trinidad had reached out to her and gave her a call. She didn't stay with Jammos' mother, but with another brother of Jammos, one who had indoor plumbing and a shower. My mom had been given some Thorazine from the psychiatrist. For the duration of the trip, she kept on slipping the horse tranquilizer into my drink. Whenever she did so, I could tell because it felt like my throat was on fire. I would simply toss out the drink. What she was trying to accomplish, I hadn't a clue. My mania would only go away if I was on medicine for an extended period of time. All my mother amounted to was being a major annoyance. I became afraid of drinking anything, because of the burning effects of the Thorazine.

In the course of my journeying I decided that Trinidad was holy ground. As a result, I tossed away my sneakers. Soon, my feet got badly cut. It was so bad that sometimes I would have to crawl for a while until I felt my strength recover and could walk once more. After about two weeks, my feet were in bad shape. I was taken to Jammos' mother's neighbor for treatment. She took a sewing needle and some ointment and splendidly fixed up the sores and cuts upon my feet.

One time we were all hanging out in a chicken place. It was Jammos, Sally, my mother, and I. After eating, I went across the street and wanted to buy a piece of jewelry. The man wanted eleven dollars. After searching my wallet, I found that I only had ten. I tried to get the man to lower the price but he refused stubbornly. I remembered the line from the Bob Dylan song, about the price being eleven dollars, but only having ten. In anger, I cast my money down and left the jewelry store. The owner came after me and insisted I take back my money.

One night, I was about the island again, and for some reason I felt very insecure about everything. I happened to come across a homeless man who was camped out in a spot. Ever intrigued by the homeless, I approached him and struck up a conversation. He started telling me about doctors and how they would experiment on him and others. Oddest thing about the man is that he had the scars to show as evidence to back up his claims.

My passport was eventually found. Jammos kept it secure for me. This brought great anger to me. I went to the police station time after time demanding that they arrest Jammos. They of course refused. Looking back on it, both Jammos and his family showed tremendous patience with me. I know I brought them a lot of worry but they were certainly entertained as well. Some of the things I did greatly upset them, like jumping inside the barrel that collected the rainwater that we had to drink. Still, we had a good time.

One day, I was walking the street and a barber called me into his shop. I had never run into the man before. He showed me the symbol of the moon and crescent as he proclaimed himself a Muslim. On all my journeys I was very vocal about Jesus Christ, preaching and teaching, and somehow this man had gotten wind of what I was about. Once he identified his faith he assured me that the Muslims were going to take over the world. It was a bizarre event, especially realizing the notoriety I had attained.

There was a man who was selling cologne. A large crowd was there hanging out. He said a couple of not-so-nice things about me, and I countered them. The gang kicking back found me hilarious and the man did a good job of making a fool of himself. He asked me to buy some cologne. I had some money, so I figured why not. When I took off the cap he said "it's poison." Then, I took the small bottle and spilled it on my feet. When I did this, he wailed, "It's not poison, it's not poison." The damage was done, though. The cologne was spilt and the crowd had the grandest laugh of the night.

Finally, the day of my departure came. I think Jammos and my mother were relieved to finally get me on the plane. However, I had one more trick in store. We didn't have a direct flight home; instead, we stopped in Caracas, Venezuela. On the layover I got up from the plane. It was my intent to defect from the United States. My mother got off of the plane with me, and I was ushered into a small security room. There, my mother gave me a drink spiked with Thorazine. As usual, I spit it out. The government of Venezuela was going to arrest me. That was fine for me, because I wanted to reform their penal system by working on the inside, but my mother didn't find that to be such a good idea. Before the Venezuelan police arrested me they contacted the US State Department. To their surprise they were instructed to put me back on the plane. They complied, so I returned to the United States from Trinidad. It was, to say the least, a memorable voyage.

SALT AND PEPPER

Some memories are locked deep inside the attics of our minds. It's amazing how going to a once familiar location or hearing a popular song from twenty years ago can spontaneously unlock these memories. Sometimes the memories are purposely locked away, because they are too painful to bear. Sometimes the days are just lost in the stream of time. When I was remembering the past, one particular day in Manhattan returned to my consciousness. It was the day I met Salt and Pepper. It was an interesting day, even by my standards.

I had just returned from Trinidad to my frat house in Hoboken. I was quite crazy. In fact, I had never been crazier in my entire life. My frat brothers didn't want me around; I was a nuisance. They had no time to deal with a raving lunatic. Yet they didn't have the heart to throw me out. It didn't matter much anyway; in a matter of days, I would be arrested, and soon after put in the psychiatric ward at Saint Francis Hospital.

One bright January day, I woke up in my frat house to find that I had the desire to visit Manhattan. Manhattan is an adventure waiting to be discovered. It's an ocean of activity, with something or someone interesting lurking in every nook and cranny. I had just bought Neil Young's new album called Life. Even though compact discs were the rage, I bought the old style vinyl. Neil Young is my favorite rock star, and on that particular album a song spoke to me: "Prisoners of Rock and Roll." The song is about how record companies exploit the genius of musicians. Apparently record

John Kaniecki

businessmen are control freaks that dictate how artists' music ought to be recorded. They're ruining the music and this disgusting interference is portrayed in Neil's lyrics about not wanting to be heard. It was my intention to fix this, so I wrote a little letter. I got the address off the album and wrote a note, nicely asking the record people not to mess with Neil's music. To prove my request was serious, I included my paper driver's license in the note. The note eventually took on a whole life of its own, with an end result of several versions and drafts being stapled and taped together into a single cluster. I was planning to mail my letters.

On the way to Manhattan, I decided it would be a good idea to get some beer. Insanity wreaks havoc with Christian principles. To get the beer, I entered the corner store. I saw a mailman there. I asked his opinion on the condition of my letter. He looked at the cluster of letters and sadly told me that it would never get delivered. I pocketed the letter and purchased my six pack of beer

I took the PATH train over to Washington Square Park. After entering the park, two black men playing a game of chess attracted my attention, so I went over and sat next to them. They were drinking beer in the normal fashion of street people, concealing the nature of their drinks by covering the can with a paper bag. I blatantly started to drink my beer without camouflaging it. A police car drove right up in front of us and the two cops inside stared, obviously upset at my illegal public consumption of alcohol. My two new companions were distraught. They didn't want to be hassled by the police, so they handed me a paper bag and I put my beer in it. Then I took another swig, but the cops were satisfied and drove away.

The two black men playing chess introduced themselves. One called himself Salt and the other was Pepper, evidently a team, like Batman and Robin. Salt was training Pepper, a fledgling professional boxer. Pepper had aspirations of a career in boxing and his hopes reigned supreme as he dreamed of becoming the world champion.

Salt invited me to play a game of chess. However, there were conditions to the game. First of all, the winner would get twenty dollars from the loser. Second, unlike regular chess, the moves had to be made instantaneously. We couldn't study and think things out, but moved in rapid intervals. After we began to play, I promptly lost.

I told Pepper that I didn't do well playing for money, so Pepper and I began a game with the same conditions, except it was only for fun this time. In a few minutes, I was one move away from checkmating my opponent. Pepper suggested we play for a draw, so I agreed and made the final move to checkmate. I technically didn't win since we changed the conditions of the game, but I impressed Pepper.

I still had some traveler's checks left over from Trinidad and they were burning a hole in my pocket. Craziness doesn't lend itself to prudent spending and I suggested that we go to the diner, my treat. I think these two characters were minor con men, because it seemed like they thought I was, in some way, trying to hustle them. A thief always sees a thief and perhaps they expected I would leave and stick them with the bill, but it was in the middle of dinner when Salt realized I was simply putting Christian love in practice. He began to weep like a child robbed of his toy. I never questioned him about it at the time; I simply let him cry. But now I wonder what it was that touched and moved him so much.

After dinner we went to a jewelry store. It was there that I used the traveler's checks to buy Salt a Batman ring. Then, while we were walking, they suggested that we pick up a couple of girls, but even mad Christians know where to draw the line. I told them, as a Christian, I couldn't do such things. As we were walking, I saw a broomstick in the garbage. I picked up the stick and started to twirl it like I knew Kung Fu or something, but Salt and Pepper were frightened and literally ran away.

I went back to Washington Square Park where I was approached by a black man whose dirty clothes and long haggard hair told me he was homeless. As offensive as the man looked, he was gentle and kind. "I wanted to warn you about those two," my new friend said, referring to Salt and Pepper.

This new stranger was from, of all places, Trinidad. He told me that back on the island he was rich and famous. He had started a brilliant political career and then the Lord touched him, so he migrated to America. The man had a fixation with Washington Square Park. He showed me the back of a dollar bill and matched the pictures off the dollar bill with the features in the park and around the park. He explained that the thirteen arrows, the pyramid and the eye each had a special meaning in regards to Washington Square Park. To me, however, it was quite amazing that I had met somebody crazier than me.

We walked to McDonald's where I was going to buy my new friend dinner. There, he told me a story. The man from Trinidad was living in the park. Another man was harassing him with a mocking tongue; small people need to put others down to feel big. Well, the big mouth didn't feel so tough when the islander picked up a metal bar in anger and chased the offender until he fell to the ground. The angry Trinidadian lifted the bar to strike the other man with a fatal blow, but at that moment the Spirit of the Lord spoke to him. "What are you going to do now?" He asked in a gentle whisper. The man dropped the weapon and spared the man's life; the bully fled in fear.

It was just another typical unusual day in my life. I never saw these people again, but I'm sure Salt and Pepper remember me. Perhaps Salt thinks of me every time he looks at his Batman ring.

My Night in Jail

Edward is a former friend of mine. We worked together for a civil engineering company that I will call Crappy Tech. Ed is an engineer who's very capable at inspecting bridges. At the previous company he worked for, he was able to inspect bridges, finding many defects in a short amount of time. One project we worked on together was the sign inspection at the JFK airport. Ed lived in Wayne, New Jersey, which, without traffic is about an hour and a half from the airport in Queens, New York. Sometimes the trip took three hours. I recall one time we were on the Cross Bronx Expressway and we literally did not move an inch for a half hour, but Ed and I didn't mind the delays. Ed was a pretty easygoing guy and we got paid by the hour anyway. We ended up making use of our time by swapping stories and experiences.

I started by telling Ed, "I have a great story."

"About what?" he asked.

"My night in jail," I replied.

"Oh, this will be good," Ed said in eager anticipation.

"Can't tell you now though," I said.

"Why not?" said the disappointed engineer.

"Just can't," I said and I cut off the conversation.

In fact, I kept Ed waiting for an entire year. He would ask me to tell the story and I would refuse. From time to time I would bring it up, but refused to elaborate. Finally, Ed said, "John, I don't care how good your story is. It's not going to live up to your hype."

A couple of months later, I told Ed the story of my night in jail. "It was worth the wait," Ed admitted.

So ladies and gentleman, without further ado I will thrill you and entertain you with my ace up the sleeve. I present to you "My Night in Jail." Remember, as unbelievable and improbable as it may seem, every word and detail is true.

I had just returned from Trinidad. It was the cold winter of January 1989. After the judge released me from Heaven's House, I stopped taking my medicine. I was in denial about my mental illness. I went down to Trinidad sane in my opinion, and took absolutely no medicine on the journey, but to say I got manic or high while there would be an understatement. If you've ever taken mushrooms or mescaline, the high I experienced was far beyond your wildest imagination. I was almost arrested for trying to enter Venezuela illegally. I had hopes of reforming the country's penal system by becoming an inmate, changing the system from within. But sadly, I returned to America and went back to my fraternity house. My frat brothers immediately knew that something was really wrong with me. In an environment that was wild to the extreme, I was over the edge, but, nevertheless, they tolerated me for a while.

One day, I went for a walk on the lovely Edwards campus when I came across a stick I had placed there two days before on a previous walk. The stick was about two feet long and blackish in color. In my twisted mind I thought it was a magical stick. As you can imagine, I was absolutely delighted that the stick had spent several days in the ground undisturbed. I happily picked up my stick and started walking down the staircase that led me to the River Road from Edwards Tech campus. The River Road was located next to the Hudson River, hence the name of the road. The descent down the hill passed through a wooded area full of trees and shrubs. At the bottom of the hill, there was a stone wall separating River Road from the wooded area.

I walked along the side of the street next to the wall. I came upon a telephone pole and I stopped dead in my tracks. The pole was about ten feet above me in elevation and behind the stone wall. I was very distressed, not because of the pole, but because of the sign on the pole that read, "NO TRESSPASSING." I immediately flew into a rage. In my delusion, I thought of myself as an American Indian. I believed I was a member of the Hopi Tribe, because its name almost spells the word "hope." How dare these foreign, pale-faced invaders put up a sign on my people's land, and such an offensive sign? This land should be free to all.

I took my wonderful, magical stick and threw it at the sign. I don't even know if I hit the sign, but losing my stick further upset me; it was very precious to me. I began to climb the stone wall in order to retrieve my prized possession and it just so happens that right then and there, campus police were driving by.

"Get down," said the rent-a-cop. The security details at Edwards Tech were indeed real police, but the students looked down on them for some reason, denigrating them to the rank of security guards. Attached to the pole was a broken guy-wire, which is essentially a metal rope. I propelled myself down the small cliff like a descending mountain climber.

"What are you doing?" asked the officer when I had safely reached the ground.

"I threw my stick at the sign and I went to get it," I confessed.

I was ushered into the security car and taken to the campus headquarters, a small room in Crystal Hall. It was the same building I had my physics and chemistry lectures in.

In the office, the police were trying to get me to volunteer to go to the mental hospital. They were rightfully convinced I was crazy. Insane people, however, lack the insight that they are insane. To them, as strange as it may seem, they are completely sane. They may babble about space aliens, dragons, demons or secret conspiracies so wild that fiction writers envy them, and they believe every last jot and tittle. So I refused to go to the psych ward, but there was an older officer there.

"What's your name?" I asked him.

"Jim," he answered.

"Gentleman Jim," I replied. I had learned that name from listening to a Bob Dylan song.

"That's what they call me," Jim affirmed.

Gentleman Jim must have looked upon me with pity and compassion. "Here, have my lunch," he offered, handing me his sandwich.

"What is it?" I asked.

"Roast beef," he explained.

I was content and happy eating my meal until I bit into a tomato. "What's this?" I yelled, my demeanor switching from calm and cool to anger.

"What's what?" asked Jim, wondering why there was a sudden commotion.

"This," I said, pulling out the tomatoes. "You're trying to poison me," I accused him.

"Well if you don't like 'em, take 'em off," said Gentleman Jim. I did as he told me and I finished the sandwich.

Moments later, the Hoboken police arrived and, at almost the same time, my mother also arrived. They must have called her, but how they got her number, I didn't know. I was promptly handcuffed with my hands behind my back and taken outside to a waiting police car. I'll never forget the stares on the faces of the people outside Crystal Hall, looks of surprise, condemnation, and pity. I was swiftly placed into the back of the police car and whisked away to the police station, which was less than a mile drive.

Upon arriving at the station, I was taken into a small room. The officer was very respectful and polite. "I'm afraid I'm going to have to strip search you," he said, seeming apologetic. My handcuffs were removed. I was undressed, bare as the day I came into the world. He searched me and even inspected my rectum.

Upon finding nothing, I got dressed. I was handcuffed again, this time with my hands in front of me. I was brought into another room. I sat in a small chair. My mother was in the room with me; she looked very distressed. Cops were walking in and out of the room, but there was an officer sitting at a desk right next to me. He had one of those old, manual typewriters on his desk

Sitting on the chair, I thought I was king of the world. I was sitting on my throne. I was, of course, in a very pleasant mood. The cop was obviously very new to the profession, so I referred to him as The Rookie. The Rookie asked me questions like, "What's your name?" or "What's your birthday?" or "What's your address?" I answered each question and, with one finger, the cop prodded the answer on the typewriter.

It took him a long time to type a single word; it seemed like it was his first time typing. The Rookie also kept asking the other cops questions like, "What does this mean?" He asked that question several times. It took a long time to finish the interview, but it's not like I was going to go anywhere but jail.

I was placed into the police car, once again, and driven to Hudson County Jail. It was a long trip compared to the one from campus to the police station. Upon being ushered into the jail, I was presented to a female officer at a desk. "Hello," I greeted her.

"Hello," she replied. "You're in jail and I'm going to photograph you," she said, while explaining the details.

I had a big happy grin as if the photograph was for my wedding or birthday.

"This is a pleasant change," the woman said, full of surprise as she took my mug shots, left view, right view and full face.

After being photographed, I was put into a small cell by myself; it was around ten feet by ten feet in size. In the cell was a yellow mop bucket with wheels. It contained a foul smelling cruddy liquid. On the wall, however, a rainbow was painted.

Across my cell was another holding area. In contrast to the emptiness of my cell, the other cell was packed like sardines. All of the prisoners in that cell were black. I assumed we were segregated by race for my safety.

After a minute I began to get upset. I began to shake the bars on the cell door. "I'm innocent!" I screamed repeatedly, continuing to shake the bars. Finally, after two minutes, I quieted down and gave up my tantrum.

I began to take the cruddy water and wash the walls by the painted rainbow. The guards peered in with curiosity. They seemed pleased.

After some time, I peered back to the barred cell door. They were putting yet another black man into the crowded cell. There were, most certainly, over a dozen of them.

"What did you do?" I screamed as they shoved him in the cell.

"Sold some cocaine," he answered.

"Was it good stuff?" I desired to know.

"The best," he assured me.

"Them cops better watch out," I said threateningly.

I later learned our conversation was not private.

About fifteen minutes later an unusual event occurred. A middle aged white man came down the hall, escorted by two guards in uniform. His hair was neatly trimmed and he was wearing a flannel shirt. He was not handcuffed. Something inside me said, "This is not right."

"I know who you are," I screamed at the man. "You run this place." I thought he was a high-ranking officer in disguise to check me out. Apparently I was right.

"Go get him," said the older man, ending the charade.

Three guards came to my cell: two officers escorting the older man and the woman who took my photograph. They unlocked my door and pounced on me, twisting my arms behind my back. They dragged me to a private part of the prison in a hurry.

One of the black inmates yelled in glee, "I've been waiting for this."

The one officer took out a large and heavy wooden baton. They began to strip me, taking my shoes off first and then my socks. The female officer looked at my bare feet. "His feet! Look at them!" she screamed in horror. My smile, I believed, had paid off.

My feet were badly cut and blistered from walking barefoot all over Trinidad and, like magic, everything changed. Instead of a beating, I was given a pint of skim milk and an orange. I peeled my orange and drank the milk, sitting on a bench outside of my original cell. I wasn't even handcuffed or being watched. I'm sure the other prisoners were perplexed and confused when they saw me well and unbeaten. I stuck the orange rind into the milk carton, concealing it; this had some special significance to me like my magical stick did.

After I had relaxed and eaten my meal, two guards took me into an elevator. We went up a couple of floors. When I got out, I walked past a group of cells. A large muscular black man in one of the cells looked at me and started yelling, "C-I-A, C-I-A."

I yelled back at him loudly, "C-I-A, K-G-B," and the man quickly shut up.

I went into a room with an older, very short, petite black

woman. She was apparently a nurse in the jail. The guards left me with no handcuffs on. The woman and I were alone. I thought she was very brave, not the least bit concerned or afraid. "A lot of the boys call me momma. I can be your momma, too," she said. The woman proceeded to tend to my feet and bandage them. I can imagine that this woman treated all sorts of prisoners. Prisoners are human beings like the rest of us. They can respect a woman like this without being a threat to her.

After my feet were repaired, I was taken up the elevator again. As I passed the large black man who had just screamed at me, he gazed at me intently.

After the ride up, I was placed in a relatively large common area behind bars. There were around a dozen individual cells within this large cell, each with the door left open. The cells all consisted of two cots like bunk beds.

After entering the cell, I went up to eight Hispanics who were watching me. I said, "I drive for Mohica Cab Company. I also worked for Gino's Pizzeria." I thought, in my madness, that I was saying I was with the Columbian crime families and the Italian Mafia and that that would provide me with protection.

Then, I asked them, "Which cell do you want me to sleep in?" They pointed out a cell.

Finally, I asked the question, "Who's the king? Who's the king?" I wanted to know who was in charge. They walked me to a small cell at the end of the larger cell we were in. There, a large black man was a sleeping. They went into his cell and pulled out a pencil sketch of Jesus.

That night I did calisthenics and other exercises in the cell. I waved my arms and feet around like a dance or some funky martial arts exercise. The Spanish men were unconcerned while they smoked a marijuana joint. Finally at night a guard came in saying, "All right, lights out, get in your cell."

We all scurried to our appropriate places. I went to the cell the Latinos told me to sleep in. The small cell doors closed one after the other: clang, clang, clang! Right before my cell door closed, I heard one of the Spanish men say, "Watch your back, little brother."

I was on the top bunk. A black man, fairly young and slightly muscular, was on the bunk below me. He seemed not to care about me at all. He didn't speak a single word. I found some pencils on my bed. Using the pencil, I wrote two things, "Jesus Saves" and "John loves Lola" on the wall. I noticed my roommate had a supply of toiletries. I stealthily reached down, grabbed his deodorant, put some on and returned it, my cellmate oblivious.

Finally, morning came. I hadn't slept and was tired. The mania, however, gives you boundless energy so I stayed up the entire night without sleeping. The cells were opened again and we all entered the large common area.

A guard came and dispensed boxes of cereal through the bars. The Hispanics took the first box, a box of Froot Loops and rushed it right to me. After all the boxes were distributed, a black prisoner started yelling, "I want mine. I want mine."

The Spanish men rebuked his yells by saying, "You sold your breakfast for a cigarette last night."

At that exact time, a white man came out of the cell that was next to mine. We were the only two Caucasians. He asked me if I wanted to trade shirts and, despite his red shirt being dirty and full of sweat, I exchanged shirts with him. I didn't believe any of the prisoners had any spare clothes.

Exchanging shirts warmed the man up to me. "I'm in here because I went the wrong way in the Lincoln Tunnel," said the other Caucasian. Then he started to brag about having connections all over America, especially the South.

I said I had connections all over America also, and Africa as well. Though I didn't realize this at the time, I believe that that cell area was where they put all the crazies. I was never certain of this and could still be wrong. Jails have a place where they keep the mentally ill. Most of these people are without insurance or family and, as a result of their impoverished economic situation, the state hospitals are the only places willing to accept them. Unfortunately, there are a limited number of beds and a long wait for them. I think I was thrown in here for a night because I was causing trouble initially.

My new friend started talking, "When I was little and in grade school we had a contest. We'd stand on a bench and whoever didn't get knocked off and managed to knock off the other kid would win. I never lost." He emphasized the last line.

I was standing next to him, so I jumped in the air, twisting my feet and repositioning them as I landed. I pushed the man over. "See? I knocked you down. I won," I said.

He stared at me in an evil way. I could sense anger and fear, but he took no action.

I took my pencils and started to write on the wall, but one of the black men got agitated and took my pencils away. I did not object.

A few minutes later, a policeman came for me. He handcuffed me with my hands behind my back and escorted me into the elevator. When we reached the ground floor, I was put in the back of a police car. Another cop came along for the ride. They started talking to one another. I said something to join in the conversation, but they told me, I'd better "shut the hell up." I was crazy, not stupid, so I listened to them and rode in silence.

I was taken to a psychiatrist when we arrived at Saint Francis Hospital. I remember the cop who escorted me having deep blue eyes. I also have blue eyes and this connection filled me with a sense of significance. When I asked him where he was from and he said Brooklyn, the eerie connection intensified. I, too, was born in Brooklyn. I felt like God was revealing an ancient secret.

"So," the doctor began, "how are you?"

"Not too good," I answered.

"You seem a little angry and agitated," he said and his observation was correct.

"You would be too if you were handcuffed and thrown in jail for no reason," I replied.

He must have agreed with my logic because I walked out of the hospital and right past the cops. It was cold and I had no jacket, but that didn't bother me. I was a free man. I was still as crazy as a loon, but I was free.

Not Alone at Bluerock

Bluerock is a state psychiatric hospital with a reputation on par with a prison. I am a graduate of dorm 62. When I arrived at Bluerock, I began thinking about the implications of my hospitalization; it was going to change my life. It was like having an epiphany while strung out on a low. After going to Bluerock, I never stopped taking my medicine again. I would sometimes cheat by cutting down the dosage but I wouldn't go cold turkey. What scared me about the institution was not the people or the environment; I actually fit in quite well. What scared me was the potential of staying for long time, and when I say a long time, I mean longer than a year. It was not a direct road from prison to Bluerock. I still had some havoc to reap on the circuitous journey.

After being released from jail, I returned to my fraternity house. I was no longer enrolled in school but I knew all the upperclassmen. My brothers really didn't like me being there. None of them had the guts to tell me to leave though. I believe they might have felt sorry for me and, perhaps, a little bit guilty. The severe hazing probably accelerated my mental illness. I just lingered on. Edwards Tech pressed charges against me for criminal mischief, throwing a stick at a sign. My mother made sure that I showed up for my court date. She spoke to the judge and said that I was under psychiatric care so another date was set for me to appear. I guess this was a preliminary hearing of some sorts.

In the midst of my madness, I went to visit my old friend

Roger, Edwards' vice president on the thirteenth floor. He was not happy to see me and was quite alarmed. I was babbling some nonsense about getting baptized in the Hudson River. I didn't feel like I was pure; I felt dirty. Roger, however, interpreted this as a veiled threat to kill myself. Taking precautions, the Edwards Tech security picked me up again. This time Roger was present. He personally went into the security headquarters. As vice president of the university he had a lot of pull. He made sure that an ambulance took me to Saint Francis Hospital in Hoboken. I, metaphorically speaking, thought that I was in the belly of the beast.

Saint Francis was a volunteer unit, so I must have signed myself in somewhere along the way. I believe Roger convinced me to put my signature on the paper. In hindsight, this helped me avoid a lot of trouble. Much of Saint Francis was a blur. I recall my neighbor visiting me. For some reason he had grown fond of me after I visited him. He brought me a large bag of oranges. I took them and gave each patient one. It was just the right thing to do. In the hospital, little treats mean so much. A fresh orange was such a blessing.

I was quite animated in Saint Francis. As a voluntary patient, I refused to take my medicine. In some hospitals they will threaten to have you committed if you don't comply, but that wasn't the case at Saint Francis Hospital. It was as if they felt I wasn't worth the convincing. Nothing chemical was working inside my body to relieve my manic high.

I recall there being a ping-pong table. The competition was fierce when I played. I somehow thought that whoever won the ping-pong game would be in charge of the world, so I gave it my all. When I finally lost, I was quite distraught but got over it quickly.

Quite a large number of ex-military people wind up in psychiatric hospitals. I have contemplated the reasons for this with deep thoughts. My first consideration is that killing a human being is contrary to how God made us. We were designed to love our neighbor and not to do ill, let alone kill. The military prepares one to terminate another's life. This is done in basic training. I have talked to veterans who have confirmed my theories.

There was one woman who suffered from depression. During this period of time Princess Diana of England got married. I thought this particular patient was a queen. As such, I would treat her as royalty. I would call her your majesty and bow before her. She really enjoyed the treatment and took a liking to me. When it was time for her to part, she was full of tears as we said goodbye. When you are locked up with somebody, you can grow pretty close to them. In addition to the constant company, you share thoughts and experiences in group therapy. Ironically enough, maintaining relationships after hospital stays are extremely difficult. Hospitals will prohibit you from returning to visit friends after your release. Furthermore, once out of the hospital, the regular ways of life come sweeping back in. It's a matter of out with the new and in with the old.

After a couple of weeks it was decided that I needed to go to Bluerock, the state psychiatric hospital. In preparation, the night before my transfer, they put me in a straightjacket. All night long I worked on that straightjacket, twisting my arms and trying to get myself free. Finally, by morning, I managed to escape from the locks. I went to get my breakfast, just like any other ordinary morning. The staff was shocked that I was free and I was quite upset that I couldn't find my usual a.m. meal.

Security and the EMT personnel had to come and take me to Bluerock. When any member of the security team or EMT personnel approached me, I would throw a punch. When I got really close to hitting one of them I would say, "See? I could have killed you there." This went on for a good two minutes, until I was secured in a straightjacket again. Needless to say, my transporters were quite upset but, as professionals, they didn't seek any retribution and simply whisked me away in an ambulance.

My first memory of Bluerock was of this large dormitory. It was like a high school gym divided by wooden partitions with a central hallway. Thus, everybody had access to everybody. There were no rooms or doors at all, except the locked door that served as an entrance or exit. I slept in the front section after my arrival. I recall lying on my bed and staring at the glaring lights high over my head. I would open one eye and stare at the light. Then I would look at another spot on the ceiling. It was like looking at the sun and then seeing spots when looking away. From focusing on the light, my eye would see a bit of light on the ceiling. I thought I was shooting laser beams.

One of the most disturbing things about Bluerock was mealtime. We would all line up to get our breakfast, lunch, or dinner. Once the doors opened, the patients would literally run as fast as they could to get to the cafeteria. It was a great competition to see who would get there first. It was puzzling to me. I didn't find the food to be all that mesmerizing, so I never bothered to run. Once in the cafeteria, we shared the dining area with patients from other wards. After our meals, every single knife, spoon, and fork was counted. It was common knowledge that if any of the silverware were missing, none of the patients would be allowed to leave.

While waiting in line, there was this muscular man behind me. For some reason I turned around and showed him a scar on my arm. It was an inch-long scar I got after being bitten by a dog in Trinidad. I said to the man, "Show me your scars." He proceeded to show me half a dozen wounds far more extensive than my own. The man kissed my hand and rubbed it saying, "You're okay. I like you."

Another time a young man around my age wanted to cut in line. I approached him and told him not to cut. He listened to me and went back with the inmates from his dorm section. After I got my food, I found the same man and offered him my desert. He refused. I have this problem of feeling I owe people something. I felt I was perfectly right in telling him what he was doing was wrong. He was, after all, violating the rules and rudely so. However, I always had a compulsion to be perfect, so I tried to reach out to make amends.

The patients were in just as big of a hurry to get their medicine as they were to get their food. When medicine was to be given out, an announcement was made over the speakers and everyone would immediately flock to the door where the nurse was dispensing the drugs. The medicine was kept in a small room, a little bigger than a closet. The nurses would go inside the room and dispense the drugs. I could see them because the door was left ajar. Instead of standing in line, I would simply wait until the others had been served and then go up to the nurse to receive my medication. I found it peculiar that nobody else took this approach.

Bluerock was, without a doubt, loosely supervised, but in other aspects it resembled a prison. There were various groups. Several of the black patients got together and sat at the same table to play cards. One of them told me outright, "See these guys?" while he motioned to his friends. "These are my homeboys." At first I didn't comprehend what he was trying to communicate, so I wanted to be a homeboy, too. Then it finally sunk in that these four were a unit and looked out for one another.

My mother had brought me a portable radio. There was a patient who asked me if he could borrow the radio. I said he could, of course, as long as he brought it back. So every morning he would ask me for it and every evening he would return it. I didn't think anything of it. He happened to be an African American. One day, a patient who was a Caucasian came up to me and said "Why do you give that nigger your radio?" This offended me, especially since the questioner and I had no relationship. I understand that things are very racial in prison.

Someone in my dorm was elected to be the president of the dorm. He took me around and showed me who was really in charge. It was some mild mannered looking patient. When my mother came to visit she brought some comic books. I gave this man an issue of Spiderman. He really appreciated the gesture. A little goes a long way when you don't have much. Later on, I would become vice president of the dorm. I was nominated for president because I had a few years of college, but, for some reason, some of the patients didn't like me and I was elected for vice president instead. I think the reason may have been because I was hyper-religious and talked about Jesus non-stop. It turned off a good number of my fellow comrades. As vice president it became my duty to dispense the snacks. Unlike my predecessor, who only gave the food to selected people, I distributed it fairly.

One time a really big man was picking on this little guy. For some reason, in my mind, I associated the small guy with the preacher at my church, so it really hit home for me. It went on for a long time and it really bothered me. I confronted the man and did a double leg takedown. The man fell to the ground and I told him to stop being a bully. My efforts were successful, but one of the two staff workers didn't agree with my interference. He took me in the back room and said, "I'm in charge here; this is my dorm." When he was talking to me I felt as though I was in the army, so I stood erect and listened attentively. The worker gave me a little shove and I fell back onto the couch behind me. I got angry, but I kept my cool and didn't retaliate. If I did, I might have been in Bluerock to this day.

The old president of the dorm actually got into a wrestling match with the other staff worker. For a good three minutes the two were at it. No punches were thrown and after the melee was over, it was considered a draw. This tactic helped calm tensions between the two individuals. As a former wrestler, both in high school and college, this event actually gave me courage. I knew that if I had to wrestle either of the two, I would easily beat them.

As far as therapy went, it did exist. One of the staff members would gather about a dozen patients. This was perhaps ten percent of the population. Everybody at Bluerock was committed. There were no volunteer patients. Some of the men just sat in their couches all day long. Though I am not certain, it appeared to me that these fellows had been lobotomized. The state hospital was, without a doubt, understaffed, at least in dorm 62.

Early in my stay I got unruly. They ushered me into a small room with padded walls. The room had a plastic window. The sun was shining bright and I was staring at it. In my delusional state I believed that I was looking at God. In my madness I cursed at the light. I was angry with God for the whole ordeal; it was a life of suffering. I didn't like the small confined area so I began to beat at the wooden door. I punched and kicked so hard that the staff had to threaten me so I would calm down. It would have been quite the disaster if I had succeeded in knocking down the portal. There would be no place to put out of control patients.

I remember telling the staff I was in training for the Olympics. I was going to win the gold medal in wrestling. I would ask the staff, "Do you want to see my takedown?" They would just laugh it off.

I would use the same line with the nutritionist in the lunchroom. She wanted me to drink skim milk instead of whole milk. I told her that I was training for the Olympics and that I needed my protein. She in turn said that I was gaining too much weight.

One time my mother came to a group therapy session. During the meeting one of the patients said, "I wish my mother would help me like yours does." This statement caught me by surprise. When the remark was made, I got up and exchanged seats with the person who made the statement. Everybody had a grand laugh over it. It is true that my mother did a great deal of helping me with my mental illness; but there was another side of the coin. I have memories of her incessant screaming. Forgiveness takes time and the pain I felt couldn't be dismissed in a moment. Sometimes, in my mania, I would not want to see my mother. I had so many mixed feelings wondering within me.

The biggest surprise and blessing at Bluerock, however, was the visit of my Uncle Sid. He was my dad's brother. Sid lived with Grandma Maggie in Brooklyn. He didn't drive or have a car. For him to visit me meant he had to take two trains to the bus station and then two buses. It was about a three-hour trip, so it was such an emotional boost for me when I saw him. He talked about how family should stick together and demonstrated his love by coming. Being committed to a psychiatric hospital made me feel like a bad person, but when Sid came that feeling went away.

Finally, my time came to go before the judge. He was going to extend my stay. I started to argue and make a case for my defense. I told him that I never attempted suicide, but only thought about it. The magistrate agreed to release me, but left me with an ominous threat: "If I ever see you back here again, you won't be seeing daylight for a long time." Those words and the bad experience of being in the state hospital really hit home. I feared being locked away for a long time.

Even though I was technically released, I still could not leave the hospital. Instead, I had to wait until a spot opened up in a group home. I turned to my parents for help and they agreed to let me stay with them. I didn't like the situation, but anything was better than being locked up. As part of the agreement of going home, I had to attend a center where psychiatric patients met during the day.

THE CENTER

I was released from Bluerock into my parents' house. As part of my agreement I had agreed to attend a day program that was known by the patients and staff as "The Center." As you shall see there were both positive and negative things about this place. The general idea behind The Center was to take seriously psychologically ill patients seriously and help them recreate a regular life. Coming from Bluerock, I fit perfectly into that category.

Just going to The Center initially caused me trauma. I would have to wake up early and wait outside at eight in the morning to be picked up by the van. My neighbors grew curious of why I had to be transported by some strange vehicle. Fortunately, though, I was soon allowed to use the family car to get to The Center.

One of the first things I did was get evaluated by one of the women who ran the place. I will call her Jezebel. Though she possessed a master's degree in psychology, that didn't keep me from viewing her as totally inept. I recall having an appointment to meet with her. It was scheduled through her secretary, although the place was small and scheduling an appointment was unnecessary. In fact, the place was small enough for me to have been readily summoned in a minute or so. Instead, I waited outside for this "important" encounter.

As we sat down to talk face-to-face, I felt like I was being belittled. It seemed she was addressing a child rather than a man at the age of twenty-one. This was all the more inappropriate since Jezebel was just out of college herself and there was probably little to no age difference between us. Her advice after our meeting was that I should "go fly a kite." I kid you not, those were her exact words. Jezebel thought I just needed to relax and this would be the thing to help.

The staff consisted of people straight out of college. I am certain of that. They tried to keep us busy by doing a whole lot of things. Some staff members were better than others. The list of things to do included recycling, listening to music, and reading. There was a lot of free time for the patients to converse with each other and just hang out. I had picked up the habit of smoking cigarettes in the hospital; it was so dull in there that I needed something to alleviate the boredom. At The Center, I was surrounded with smokers, so I picked up the habit once more.

There was this one fellow patient who shared my name, John. He was a veteran of the Korean War and was a thin wisp of a man. All day long he would sweep our cigarette butts with a broom. He would then collect the remainder of tobacco in our cigarette butts and then smoke it. We all felt sorry for Jeff and would readily give him a cigarette whenever he asked.

The best thing about The Center was the affectionate community of patients we had a connection. We would spend a long time in conversations discussing all sorts of things. I recall my friend Brenda and me reading a small Christian pamphlet entitled The Daily Bread. Every day we would get together for our reading. Sometimes other patients would join in with us. All in all, it was a place of acceptance among peers. One didn't have to worry about the stigma of mental illness; we all suffered from the same malady. Unfortunately, things weren't always calm and storms would be kicked up. There were conflicts between patients at various times. I recall Andy getting jealous of another patient named Oscar. Andy was tall but Oscar was taller by several inches. In the morning Andy walked up to Oscar and said, "You ain't so tall," in a very threatening manner. This was very out of character for Andy, as he was usually very mild-mannered. Steve did not react right away, but that afternoon, right before dismissal, the air was disturbed by Brenda's voice.

"Harvey, Harvey," she called out in urgency. Andy and Oscar

had gotten into a fistfight.

I didn't witness the altercation but the staff took it very seriously. We had a special meeting regarding it. The staff wanted to assure us that we were safe and protected. As for Andy and Oscar, they were chastised. Technically speaking, the police could have been called and the pair arrested. Instead, they were given a stern warning and life went on as usual. The two never had any more problems.

I recall one day stuffing comic books into bags with a man named David. We were stuffing these packets for some community event that The Center was hosting. The bags stuffed with goodies were to be given as rewards for those who would participate. David was very somber and talked very little. He seemed immensely depressed. In a couple of weeks it was announced that David had left The Center to go live with his wife in Pennsylvania. We all felt happy for him since we knew this was his heart's desire. He would talk about his wife all the time. Several months later we all got together for a meeting. It was announced that David had committed suicide; he hung himself. Everybody was shocked and saddened. The patients were a close group. Unlike the hospital where relationships only last for weeks, at The Center people were in contact for months, if not longer. I personally knew a lot of people who thought about suicide or who had even attempted it but David was the first of my friends to actually succeed. My heart was at a loss.

The staff at The Center would treat the clients as if they were children, like I'd mentioned before. They would tell them what to do in a demeaning manner. However, compared to the other patients I was higher functioning. A lot of my companions would simply sit around and smoke cigarettes, barely interacting with others or participating in the various events.

After attending The Center, I started to slip into a deep depression. I constantly contemplated suicide. Consequently, I found it very difficult to get out of bed or to do anything. Every morning my mother would force me to get up. She threatened to pour cold water on me if I didn't get up. Reluctantly, I got up. The problem got so severe that my mother thought I should go to the psychiatric ward to get help, but before I could get admitted, I had to see the program director Jezebel. She asked me some stupid questions and said, "Don't worry you'll feel fine. Does that help?" When I answered negatively, she agreed to send me to the hospital. I signed myself in to Solomon Hospital.

In the hospital, I was placed under the care of Doctor R. He was in many ways a bumbling buffoon. His mannerisms led one to believe that about him, especially how he would repeat questions and blink his eyes. Or how he would take a long time to respond to a question. But he turned out to be the best doctor that I ever had. This I attribute, without a doubt, to him caring about me as a person. I was more than a name on a chart and financial compensation. I was a human being worthy of care and compassion.

After the hospital stay, which I detail in a later chapter, I returned to The Center. I was forced to attend therapy with Jezebel. Doctor R had high hopes for me. It was his desire that I would return to college and finish my degree. When I told Jezebel about my psychiatrist's desires, she mocked both him and I. "Yeah right, when? In twenty years?" It felt like a cruel jab from a cold-hearted monster.

I relayed the insulting comment to Doctor R. He got rather angry and took her words personally. "She's just some stupid bitch out of college who doesn't know anything at all," was the response. Now weighing out the two opinions, evidence dictates the good old Doctor R was correct. About ten years later, I would receive a B.S. in Mathematics from Montclair State University. The rude and offensive comment actually helped me. When I desired to leave The Center, Doctor R gave no objections.

Unlike the hospital, where one lost friends upon leaving, I kept mine. I would often visit with a good number of the people. I am still in contact with two people from The Center and was extremely close to a third woman who passed away. We were so close that I was in both of her daughters' weddings. I am still in contact with that family, although my friend has sadly and prematurely departed from this life.

The Center was truly a blessing in my life, more so than the hospital. To me, psychiatric hospitals serve two reasons. When you are on a manic high it is a safe place to descend to normalcy and if you are depressed and suicidal, the hospital will keep you from killing yourself. As far as getting any good therapy or understanding anything about yourself, I have found psychiatric hospitals to be ineffective. The Center was a refuge where I could gather myself. It was like an oasis on the wayside of a thirsty trail through the desert. I met several kindred pilgrims on this similar journey.

Unfortunately, the vast majority of pilgrims feel no urgency to move on in life; they become content with their situation and decide to give up. Most of the patients are getting government assistance. To go and find a job would take a tremendous effort and would mean giving up free money from the state. Also, there is no guarantee of success. A good number of the patients lived in group homes, where they were supervised and where patients could live and were assigned various chores and responsibilities, but the most important aspect was the staff making sure that all the patients took their medicine.

I only stayed at The Center for several months but it had a big impact on my life. From time to time when I would converse with friends from the center, we would reminisce about the old times. Our conversations would always shift to the welfare of other people and I would always feel a sorrow or sadness when I was informed of the passing of a friend from the center, which was often.

Running Away

Life is a complex thing. Sometimes we do the right thing and sometimes we do the wrong thing. There are many kinds of sins. Sometimes it's a sin of passion or a sin of habit. We can overcome these by perseverance. However, sometimes things happen in a hurry. Like a camera flash going off, we have but a split second to decide and then our deeds are recorded in history.

Two separate occasions come to my mind. In both cases I fled conflict. In one case I am proud of my actions, but in the other case I feel disgrace. Both incidents happened so quickly, there was no time to carefully contemplate what the right thing to do was. I acted on instinct, but though these episodes took only seconds to occur, they have consumed my thoughts for hours.

I was returning to Hoboken from the Manhattan Church of Christ. I had taken the subway to the Port Authority. I was heading to the bus going to Hoboken and to access the buses one must travel up and down a series of escalators.

I was walking there when I saw something horrible. There was a small commotion down the platform. There were six cops, maybe seven and in their midst was one sorry black man. One officer held each limb, so both arms and legs were locked in an iron grip by the cops. The poor man was suspended in the air. The other two or three police were beating the man with their heavy wooden clubs. It made the Rodney King beating look like child's play.

Dozens of people were passing by. I could tell they had seen what was going on because, after they viewed the scene, they looked the other way and hurried off. I stopped to stare. After a couple of seconds, while I was looking, an additional cop, whom I hadn't noticed before, was standing by me. "If you don't move I'm going to have you arrested," he said. I got scared, felt helpless, and walked away.

Later, back at the frat, I told the story to my friend Al. He said his cousin was a Port Authority cop and they didn't mess around. Al was sure I would have gotten a beating had I tried to do something.

The second incident involved my friend Roy. Roy was someone whom I met at the mental health center. He was a very lonely person who found it difficult to make friends. I befriended him. I used to buy a couple of steaks for us. Roy would cook them up at my house and clean all the dishes.

On one occasion Roy asked me to take him to visit a friend in Paterson. Paterson is a rough and tough town with some very bad neighborhoods. Foolishly, I agreed to take Roy there. We went to his friend's apartment, but he wasn't there. Roy knew a bar close by where his friend often went and wanted to look for him there.

I parked on the street. To get to the bar we had to walk across a parking lot. Roy was wearing a black leather jacket. Two black men started to mock Roy. "Hey tough guy, you're a fag." I turned around and gave them an evil stare. "No, not you, him," they told me, referring to Roy.

We entered the bar that turned out to be a go-go bar. Roy looked around quickly for his friend and didn't find him. Being a former alcoholic, he wanted to stick around and have some sodas and watch the girl, who was next to naked, dance on the bar. My Christian morals kicked in and I told Roy I wanted to leave.

To avoid trouble, I thought it prudent to walk around the street and avoid the parking lot where the men were harassing Roy. As we walked around the street, we passed another bar. In front of it was a black man bothering a woman. The man was obviously intoxicated. He left the woman, who fled quickly, and approached us. "Give me a dollar," he said demandingly.

Roy gave him all the change he had and I quickly walked away. He followed and confronted me. "I need more money," he said.

I told him I was a Christian and I couldn't give him money. He announced he was a Muslim and then struck me. The blow was so surprising that I dropped to the ground. It didn't hurt me, but my glasses broke.

I knew right away that I could have easily beaten the man up alone, but he was drunk and much smaller than me and I know how to handle myself. With Roy's help, I'm sure it would have been a quick one-sided fight, but, instead, I quickly got up and went to my car. Roy followed. The thug yelled from behind us, "Don't call the cops."

I believe the world would say I did the right thing in New York but the wrong thing in Patterson. I believe God sees it the opposite way. What good would it have done to beat up a drunk man on the street? His blow wouldn't have been taken back; the damage had been done. Jesus tells us to turn the other cheek.

I should have been braver in Manhattan. No human being deserves a beating like that. Society is supposed to be a place ruled by law. To accidently hurt somebody or even kill somebody when making an arrest is one thing, but to flagrantly beat a man is another. I thought it over many times. I really don't know what I should have done. I wish I had a movie camera to film the events. I think if others had cared enough to stop, things would have been different, but even I shamefully deserted the man getting beat up. The Bible says "And the King will reply, 'Truly I tell you, whatever you did for one of the least of them you have done unto me.'"

In reflection, I believe it would have been worth getting arrested and even beat up by the Port Authority police. They would have to have justified their actions somehow. Perhaps questions would have been asked and an investigation made. Organized and systematic violence by the government is very different from a disoriented drunk. In one case, it's a frustrated and misguided drunk striking someone in anger, which may be justified somehow, but the other case is one of the greatest evils of our society.

I wonder how many people are brutalized by the police and we end up never hearing about it. The infamous Rodney King beating was only believed because a videotape was made. I believe police brutality is a daily occurrence in America. If I had made a video, it would have made all the networks. As it so happens, probably nobody remembers this occurrence, except the cops and I. And, of course, their poor victim.

Some may think they would have known exactly what to do in either circumstance, but these are split second decisions. There is no time to think, but only react.

Some of my thoughts about the Manhattan incident are to appear before a panel on police brutality. I heard recently one was being formed and I considered contacting them to tell my story, but telling the government about police brutality is like telling the fox to guard the chicken house. I did write a song about the incident but it never went anywhere.

I've told the story to other people. One of my friends told me the police were probably ashamed of what they were doing, which is why they acted the way they did.

I made some friends with the homeless people who used to live in the Port Authority. I would buy them food and sit and talk to them. They told me that the police would beat the homeless on a regular basis; cops would take them into the elevator and, once the doors closed, hell was unleashed.

I'm proud of what happened in Paterson. We need more love and forgiveness in this world.

SMOKING IN THE BACKYARD

After Bluerock I fought the greatest battle of my life. It was inside of my brain. Victory and defeat could literally mean life or death. On the positive side, I placed an enormous value in being a child of God. It brought my life meaning, gave me self-worth and put me in a group to which I belonged. All three I believe are essential for a good life. On the other hand, there was also a negative side. I wasn't a good person. My history reinforces this notion. All my violent feelings, like being an unwanted outsider, and the poor treatment by my parents. In particular, my mother's incessant screaming and my father's cold attitude and ignoring of me. This poor image was reinforced by the simple existence of my mental illness. Mental illness alone is enough to make you an outcast in our society.

Allow me to touch on my relationship with my father, as I have neglected to discuss much about it. First and foremost I am certain that my dad wanted children for the sole reason that it would prolong his existence; he believed he could somehow live through us. Whether that is rational or not is beside the point. I am confident it was his belief, as he had expressed this on more than one occasion. Thus making it a selfish concept on his part.

Also allow me to point out the good qualities of my dad. He was an excellent provider, always putting food on the table and giving me any other things I needed. As a child raised in the Great Depression, he didn't believe in luxuries. When it was time to shop for new clothes for school, the inexpensive choice was the only choice. I was never into fashion, so that was perfectly fine with me. He paid for my college education at Edwards Tech and later at County College and Montclair. My dad was a huge believer in education as he had both a masters and a PhD. Somehow this got communicated to me. I am not sure how though, especially since my dad never really talked to me. I don't recall him ever sitting down and helping with my homework or even asking about my day in school. In fact, he never sat me down and had a conversation. Especially when I was young.

In all my childhood there were two pieces of advice that my dad gave to me. That first was that if you're going into the army it's better to be an officer than an enlisted man. When my dad was attending NYU and trying to get his Doctorate in organic chemistry, he was drafted because of the Korean War. Being forced to leave school prematurely, he finished up what he was doing to get a Masters. I believe this experience severely affected my dad in a negative way. In his service to our country he experienced both being an enlisted man and being an officer.

The second piece of advice was that I should try to be a doctor, lawyer or engineer. He never indicated why these three professions, but I understood it because they all made a lot of money. As a result of this advice, in high school I pursued AP classes in my senior year. I had AP Calculus and AP Chemistry. Both of these courses would be repeated at Edwards Tech.

Dad was never involved in our lives outside of his interests. What I mean by that is that my brother and I played sports. Not once did my dad ever attend a game. I wrestled for two years in high school. Unlike my mother, who attended every single match, my dad was noticeably absent. Even when we were younger, if I spent time with my dad it was pursuing his interests. For example, he would take us fishing and playing golf, but those were two things that he enjoyed doing himself.

I recall my dad trying to teach me to play golf. He didn't have much patience and he got frustrated quickly. He really didn't put much effort into it. The focus of going golfing wasn't to teach me how to play golf, the focus was dad playing golf and teaching me as a byproduct.

When my mental illness caused me to be hospitalized, my mother was a rock. She showed up practically every visiting hour no matter how far the hospital was. My dad, however, would show up every now and then. My dad never hugged me, nor showed any emotions. I recall leaving the graveside when they had just buried his mother, Maggie. I came close to him to give him a hug and he pushed me away. Not once in his life did my dad ever say that he loved me.

If my dad had been involved in my life, I am sure I would have fared a lot better. If he had sat me down and explained life, even a perverted interpretation of reality would have been better than nothing at all. He never explained anything to me while growing up. As such, I was unprepared to make the transition from child to adult. I was very immature in a lot of ways, especially emotionally. I could excel at schoolwork but I couldn't feel a bond of love with people. It would have meant so much to me if he had given me some guidance, some wise words. Instead, I forged ahead with almost no direction.

Here I was in the backyard trying to piece my life together. I would sit outside smoking cigarettes. Our backyard was fairly secluded. There was a little garden consisting of rose bushes and other plants. Our house sat on a corner and both streets ended in a dead end. I was extremely angry with God, at least in the form of the Father. I could not relate to him at all. Jesus, I loved. I knew the stories of his mercy and compassion. The good news that he died on the cross for sinners filled me with hope. He would leave the 99 to look for that one lost soul. I was perfectly fine with Jesus who embraced the lepers, but this Father, that was another matter.

Who was this cruel overlord of the universe? Why was I going through such torment, pain and suffering? Did it bring the Almighty pleasure to crush me? If I were familiar with the book of Job I would have found myself there. Unlike Job, I did curse God, but fortunately I didn't die for doing so. Still, I knew that Jesus said, "If you've seen me you've seen the Father." Amidst the darkness and my cursing, my eyes were open to seeing something wonderful.

I felt supreme dejection at that period of time. I thought my life was over at 22. Not only would I never return to college, I would never work again. These feelings caused a lot of stress. I had this notion that I could one day do something great with my life; I was to be God's prophet and all that it entailed, but when I looked in the mirror, all I saw was a loser and a miserable failure. It was as if I was at the bottom of a pit and there was no light at all.

I refused to surrender. I thought the situation through and I thought of something peculiar. I discovered that songwriters made a lot of money. I had written poetry in the hospitals and really enjoyed doing the art. I began to write song lyrics. It was an excellent release for my creativity. Years later I would take up poetry writing once again. As it stands now, I have two published books and a couple hundred poems. I haven't cashed it in big yet, but from every seed planted comes a harvest, you just have to be patient enough to wait for the crops to come to fruition.

My neighbors really didn't know what to think of me. I had almost no contact with them at all. I isolated myself in the backyard and puffed away. I remember two of the Dutch girls from the farm passing by my house. They were a hundred yards away from my house when one girl said to the other, in really loud voice, "If anybody touches you, scream as loud as you can." They were young, but they were trying to communicate a message to me. I received it loud and clear; I was unwanted. I was a dirty pariah and I couldn't even sulk in misery in my own private backyard.

At this time, I continued to attend church in Manhattan. I had a lot of friends, but most of the people didn't know how to deal with me. Innocent questions were tossed around, like, "What kind of work do you do?" That one really stung. Was I to answer, "I suffer from a mental illness and I can't work?" Still, it was great to have an outlet, other than just contemplating in my backyard. I did read the Bible a great deal at that time as well, which was also another way to relieve the stress in my life.

As far as medically, I was seeing Doctor R on a regular basis.

My dad generously paid for the treatment and I got back on his insurance. I would float in and out of the hospital with no fault of mine. I would be taking my medicine as prescribed, but they just didn't seem to work. The hospital I attended was Solomon Memorial, or as the patients would call it: The Solomon Hilton.

THE SOLOMON HILTON

My first encounter with the Solomon Hospital, or the Solomon Hilton as the patients called it, began before any hospitalizations. My religious fervor and faith grew unchecked. Besides constantly talking about Jesus, I was reading the Bible and applying it to my life. My change disturbed my fraternity brothers quite a bit. I stopped using drugs and alcohol. I was trying to get my citizenship transferred from the United States of America to the Kingdom of Heaven. As a result, I was telling people I wanted to defect. Unwittingly, of course, they thought I wanted to join the Soviet Union. Remarkably, many were very sympathetic with my supposed wishes.

I read in the Bible where Jesus said, "If you want to be perfect, go, sell your possessions and give to the poor, and you will have treasure in Heaven." As a result of this, I began to give away money and possessions to the point where my fraternity brothers thought I was suicidal. My mother got word of my behavior as well. My dad then had a heart attack, so I left Hoboken and went home. While at home, my mother noticed a drastic change in me.

One night, I wanted to go for a walk, but my mother was pressuring me to stay. I ran out of the house and the chase began. I ran up and down the hill with my mom in hot pursuit. How she could keep up with me I could never understand. My sister called the police and, after about half a mile, I was met by cops. The police took me to Solomon Hospital.

I was ushered through the emergency room and they put me

in a small confined area. The security guard stood outside. For all intents and purposes, I was a prisoner. I couldn't leave, as the guard would not allow it. Solomon had a psychiatric ward, but it was only voluntary. Without signing myself in I could not be admitted. Solomon was in the process of trying to get me committed to another hospital. To do so, two psychiatrists had to sign off as to whether or not I was a threat to myself or to somebody else. Under the pressure I relented and signed the documents. However, I signed the documents as the Spirit of God.

When I was brought upstairs, I was very uncomfortable in the unit. I got this terrible reaction of my tongue sticking out of my mouth. It caused me great physical agony. I am one hundred percent sure this was just a symptom of being locked up. Solomon, being a voluntary ward at that time, had no lock on the door. With my tongue sticking out, I simply walked out of the ward. Once out of the ward, I felt normal. "See," I told the staff, "it's all because I'm in the psychiatric ward." They really didn't care and I was soon sent off to Saint Anna's where I was a committed patient. I was too unruly and out of control for them to handle.

The second trip to Solomon mimicked my first, except this time I refused to sign the papers despite intense pressure. I refused. I went through the painful process of being committed and, once more, they shipped me off to Saint Anna's.

I finally did get accepted and stayed at Solomon. When I felt very suicidal, they had me admitted. This is where I met up with Doctor R.

One of the greatest detriments of being hospitalized is boredom. Back in the 1980s an average hospital stay in a psych ward was around a month, which is a long time to be confined, and, depending on the hospital you stayed in, the frequency of activities varied. Solomon was pretty good in that respect though. They kept you busy, but they didn't overload you. You still had personal time as well as group time.

During personal time the patients would gather around and talk. Being locked up with a person, you really get to know them intimately. You spend a lot of time talking about a various things, pretty much everything that life consists of, such as personal problems, religion, current events, music and so on. Some people you naturally gravitate towards more than others, but you still have to put up with those that come across as obnoxious.

We had some form of group therapy every day in Solomon Hospital, with the weekend being the exception. Group therapy was basically all the patients gathering around in one room and sitting in a giant circle. There was a moderator who was always a member of the staff. There were several moderators in Solomon and they all had different techniques.

I recall one nurse, whom I'll call Donna, who seemed to be extremely harsh to me. She subscribed to the teachings of Freud; she would be looking for every flinch and move to find some deeper inner motive. For example, in our group there was this lady who was very nervous. In the middle of a discussion, the woman nervously shuffled her feet and made noises on the ground. Donna stopped the group and focused on the lady. "You just want to be the center of attention," the nurse accused her in a vicious fashion. The lady was hurt.

In group therapy the group leaders wanted the patients to reveal their deepest and innermost feelings and fears. The idea is that the patients, with the guidance of the authority, would receive the help they needed. Every group therapy session had the same setting. We would introduce ourselves, and the instructor would begin to ask probing questions, like what brought us to the hospital. The therapist, on the other hand, had the advantage of knowing all the details of each patient, so notes were taken and information was shared among the staff members and the doctors.

I recall being in a jovial mood one time. I was walking around, a common method to relieve the boredom in the hospital and the unit at Solomon made it easy because it formed a rectangle. Anyway, while I was walking, I was holding my arms out and made airplane noise. The nurses' station was in the front and the dining area was in the rear. On either length were the patients' rooms, so they had a clear view of what I was doing. Later on one of the staff brought it up to me. I acutely became aware that I was always under a scrutinizing eye.

Smoking cigarettes was allowed in Solomon. One could

only smoke in the dining room and in the recreation room, and sometimes on the roof when the weather was good. While we could have cigarettes, matches and lighters were prohibited. Sometimes, in the morning, the hard-core smokers couldn't wait until eight o'clock to begin smoking. They would take out their matches, light their cigarettes, and start smoking. Of course, the staff would then realize that somebody had matches and demanded the contraband be surrendered.

Eating was a big problem in Solomon. Not only were we served three adequate meals a day, but we also had access to the refrigerator. Whenever I was bored I would go and grab myself a snack and, as a result, I gained a fair amount of weight with each visit to Solomon Hospital.

I met a whole lot of people in my four visits to Solomon Hospital. Like I said, sometimes you care for an individual more than others. I recall a person named Gerard. He was a talented artist. There was another patient named Jack. The three of us would always sit at the same table for lunch. One day Jack asked me, "Why is Gerard hanging out with us?" I didn't respond truthfully, I just avoided answering the question. You have to be really careful about offending people in the hospital. Everyone is on edge to begin with.

There was a woman I met in the hospital named Rachel. She was a very nice woman, a few years older than me. We would sing a little song together that she had taught me. The words went, "And the Lord said let it be, and the Lord said let it be, Amen all is well, and the Lord said let it be." Singing the song would release my tensions and make me feel better. We would smile and laugh together.

Rachel was a very special case; we stayed in contact for years after our hospitalization. I tried to keep up with Gerard but he ditched me as a friend. I would go visit him where he worked in Morristown, but it seemed I was the only one interested in continuing the friendship. Gerard lost his job and faded out of sight, not bothering to inform me where he went.

Rachel and I had a long-term friendship. I would visit her and she would visit me. While we were in the hospital together, Rachel was engaged. Our relationship was purely platonic. She thought I had a romantic interest but I didn't. After the hospital she broke up with her boyfriend. At that point she began to show a sexual interest in me. I didn't desire this and made it clear that we were only friends. Despite my rebuke, our friendship remained intact. Among other things, Rachel and I saw the Grateful Dead and Neil Young in concert together. We eventually stopped staying in contact, but remained friends for many years.

Another man who I kept up with was Jose. Jose and a third young man named Robert became really close to me in the hospital. All three of us were interested in Christianity. I had the bold idea of getting matching jackets wearing the slogan "Christian Brothers." Then, we could go bowling and hang out together. The plan never came to fruition.

Robert called me several times on the phone. He would wash his hands over and over. I guess he felt guilty or dirty for some reason, but whenever Robert called me he wanted to borrow money. One day he showed up to my house without calling. I don't even know how he got my address. He said he was desperate and needed 60 dollars. When I told him that I honestly didn't have any money he got angry and left. He never called me on the phone again. Our relationship was terminated.

In the hospital, Jose was going through a very traumatic situation. I met both his wife and daughter. Jose would talk in group therapy about how he was upset because his relationship with his nephew had to end. The way he cried and mourned about it made it seem as though he were being separated from his own child.

One day Jose and I were eating in a Chinese restaurant. He told me he had something to tell me. He confessed he was in fact a child molester. He was molesting his nephew and that was the reason for the separation. In fact, he would take his nephew to church, of all places, and have sex with him in his van in the church parking lot. When I heard this confession, I felt hurt. I felt that Jose had deceived me. I wanted to get angry and condemn him, but I knew the right thing to do was to forgive him.

Jose went on to explain how he was molested as a child. It turns out that most child molesters have been molested themselves.

One would think that such an experience would do the opposite. As Jose elaborated and explained his situation, my compassion for him grew. Here was this monster that I was finding a way to love. He didn't need any condemnation, but ministering. As I talked to him about a forgiving God, I found healing in it for myself, as well.

Jose was sent to a sex offender's prison. From his prison he would send me Christmas cards and letters. They encouraged the inmates at the prison to reach out to people who had helped them along in life. I guess Jose valued our friendship and, in some way, felt that I was a positive influence. This realization helped me find self-worth. Jose eventually got a divorce and moved to New York State. I lost contact with him.

I got along very well with the staff at Solomon. I was always one to obey the rules so I never caused any trouble. Also, I think the staff felt that I had a positive effect on the other patients. Case in point was this rather large man from Paterson named Walter. Walter was a Satanist. He showed me his pentagram tattoo that proved he was beyond the initiate level. I believe that a lot of the staff and my fellow patients were afraid of the man. I just calmly sat with him and let him talk to me. At the end of one of our long conversations he would say to me, "I like you. You listen." Once more, helping another brought me self-worth. I felt good that I could contribute to the well being of others.

Sometimes the patients would answer the phone, "Solomon Hilton, funny farm." This would anger some of the patients. One made a comment that he had business calls coming in on that line. The name Solomon Hilton was found humorous by some of the patients.

My mother was a very frequent visitor at the hospital. My dad, sister, and brother would visit sometimes as well. Sometimes we would sit in the dining area talking. Often, we would sit in the TV room and watch Jeopardy and Wheel of Fortune. Just to have somebody visit is a great distraction. I felt bad for those people who had no visitors. One thing visitors did was to get things for the patients. Cigarettes, in particular, were an extremely desirable item.

I would return to the Solomon Hilton for visits after I got a lot better. Some of my friends from The Center would wind up in

John Kaniecki

the psychiatric ward. The staff was always glad to see me and years later I would offer to volunteer on the psychiatric ward. I was told that they didn't accept volunteers there though. I envisioned myself talking to patients and fetching them any of their necessities. The volunteer coordinator said she would think about it, considering my background. I never heard a response and the hospital, eventually, closed its psychiatric ward.

Trying Abe University

When I was a junior at Edwards Tech, I officially dropped out. I went to the dean and filled out the paperwork. My father was very upset, because he had paid for the semester and I wouldn't be getting a refund. He was angrier when I got hospitalized and his insurance wouldn't cover me, because I was no longer a student.

I think dropping out caused a little bit of a stir at the school. For one thing, I was scheduled to give a presentation for some professor in a mechanical engineering lab course. Every student had to appear before the professor to give a presentation. The report needed to be submitted as though we were professionals, so suit and tie were required. I simply didn't bother to show up or even send a message I wasn't coming. I heard he was quite angry.

One of my professors got word that I was dropping out and requested to see me. I had taken a course with him in freshman and sophomore years. He was a very good teacher and I liked him personally. When I went into his office, he asked me what I intended to do now that I had dropped out. I had an idea of making shirts and presented this to him. I also told him that I wanted to become an evangelist and desired to go to college for that. I was appreciative that this teacher cared about me and had taken the time to look out for my welfare.

At Edwards Tech I worked with the Development Department. As such, I was in contact with those who ran the school. At that time, I could walk into the office of the President of Edwards Tech and just say hello if I cared to. In hindsight, I had achieved a lot, but was just rejecting it. I simply didn't want to be an engineer. One of my classmates said she admired what I was doing.

I liked the sciences and, even today, I feel the desire to go back and learn. After my first hospitalization Doctor Rug advised me to return to engineering school. In fact, he attributed my not wanting to become an engineer as part of my sickness. Sometimes, when I'm reflecting on the past, I wish I could return. I don't know if I would have been successful. I have given it much thought since sometimes I have nightmares. These dark dreams involve me returning to Edwards to complete my degree, but to return to Edwards successfully, I would have to repeat my sophomore year, as I passed without really learning anything.

With the encouragement of Doctor R, I planned to make a return to school. I had long worn out my welcome with my fraternity. Also, Edwards was full of bad memories, having been arrested on campus. I considered New Jersey Institute of Technology, but decided on Abe University. In reflection, it was a bad choice.

My first bad move was not getting housing right away. I neglected to send in my paperwork after my acceptance. As such, I began the semester without any housing and had to commute. The ride was an hour each way. Not only was this physically taxing but it left me little time to do my school work.

My confidence level depleted. At Edwards, I was very detached from life. When I took a test I really didn't care too much about it. Initially, I worked very hard in my studies and it paid off. When my interest in scholastics withered, I would just cram the night before any exam. This method didn't achieve the same top-notch results, but I managed to pass my classes. Still, I cared very little what my results were. Now that I was attending Abe University, more was at stake. Not only was I seeking an academic victory but a psychological one as well. I had to prove that I could indeed handle college. To do so I had to pass my courses. It raised my concern to a high level of importance.

When I began to take my courses, I was excited and invigorated. I felt odd, though. I was several years older than most of the students. As a commuter I didn't have any base of roommates to draw friends from. I was pretty much a loner. I met a couple of people in my classes, but that was all. The campus was fairly complicated and it took several days to learn. I spent several minutes searching my map so that I could find certain lecture halls.

When I was finally assigned a dorm room, a key was given to me. When I entered the room, nobody was there, so I left a note saying I was a new roommate. Unbeknownst to me, this situation would wind up ruining this attempt at returning to school.

I returned to the dorm room later on and was confronted by a young African American man. He started to tell me that I wouldn't fit into this dorm room. He told me that one of his roommates was Muslim and that he wouldn't like me. The young man was antagonistic to the point that I thought he might get violent.

His whole demeanor changed when he saw I wasn't being intimidated. He leveled with me, telling me that the dorm room housed four people and that three of them were his friends. Since the semester started and nobody filled the fourth spot, he came into the picture. He was staying for free and not paying for the room. In fact when he saw my note he thought his friends were playing a practical joke on him. He told me that I could stay for a little while, but after some time I would tell the dean I didn't like my accommodations and would get a new room. I mentioned that we could say there were racial tensions. "Oh, no," the young man said, "we can get kicked out of school for that."

I started to explain to him that I had manic depression and that I was getting angry. He said that his roommates should have been informed of that information. I asked him if they should have been informed if I had diabetes. After all, both are chemical imbalances. This thought intrigued the young man. However, as the conversation continued, I was still heated and quite angry at how he had previously addressed me so rudely. I noticed that he took his phone and moved it closer to his person. I realized that I was getting out of control and left, never to return.

After the incident, I returned home. At that time, I was taking lithium for my mental illness with a couple of other drugs. Lithium is a good medicine, but the level has to be just right. Too little is not effective and too much brings severe side effects, like diarrhea. For me though, I noticed that if I underwent more stress I needed more lithium. Going into a new environment and returning to school was already challenging to me. This traumatic experience put me over the edge. I went to Solomon Hospital the next day. I had failed at my return to going to school.

I did get a partial reimbursement from Abe University for the tuition. My mother explained the situation and the dean cut a deal. I never elaborated to the dean at what had happened in the dorm room. To me, it was just an unfortunate incident. I held some ill will for quite a while, but I have let go since then.

CLOZARIL

At this point in my life, I was very in tune with my illness. One excellent thing that Doctor R did with me was to make me aware of the warning signs. The first of these was missing sleep and not getting tired. I am a person who always needed a good amount of sleep. Eight hours worked just fine. However, in a fit of mania, I could function on two to three hours of sleep. I would be revved up with energy and not even the slightest bit tired. The idea was to detect the mania before it was surging in my brain. So if I went three or four nights with six hours of sleep and didn't feel tired, I would have to make a note of it.

Another warning sign was religious preoccupation. I am a very religious person and I read the Bible daily. I am not ashamed of my faith. I am very happy to talk to anybody regarding Christianity. The warning sign, however, is that I think I have some special connection with God, that I'm sort of a messenger or prophet. It was a connection to God beyond the normal that others would experience, even others with zeal.

The best thing that came from mania, however, was the overflowing creativity. I often wonder if various artists suffer from manic depression. When going into a manic state, my poetry or writing seems to improve dramatically. Unfortunately, when in full-blown mania, it often becomes incoherent. A watchful eye on my artistic endeavors was another indicator that something was going wrong in my brain.

The mind, of course, is a vastly complicated connection of

chemicals and biological machinery. While a lot is known about it, there are also many unknowns. Freud proposed that the mind consisted of the ego, super-ego, and id. These three domains serve to create our consciousness. I don't reject this idea but I don't believe it's that simple.

One thing about brain chemistry is that it is not consistent. That is, certain medicines work well on certain individuals and not others. Unfortunately, there is no test that can conclusively tell which is the right medicine. A doctor cannot take a blood sample and run some tests to determine which pills one should or shouldn't take. Instead, the process is one of trial and error.

What this meant for me was that I would go into a hospital during a manic episode. Once admitted, the goal of the hospital was to stabilize me. Strong drugs like Thorazine and Haldol were given. Thorazine is actually a horse tranquilizer and is quite potent. Both of these medicines have bad side effects as well, but usually, after a period of time, these stabilizing medicines are taken away or their dosage is greatly diminished.

It is up to the psychiatrist to try various drugs in various combinations. I had been put on a great deal of medicines in hospitals. Unfortunately, for me, the voices never did go away and, based on that sole criterion, the various psychiatrists would deem the drug a failure. The idea of voices was seen as both negative and abnormal, even if the voices were positive and constructive. Once again, this is proof of how complex the human mind is. Perhaps what I define as voices is something experienced by everyone on some sort of subconscious level.

Due to the fact that I had used an abundant amount of medicines and none seemed to work, I was qualified to use a drug called Clozaril. At this time, Clozaril was being reintroduced to the United States. The drug had an ominous history. At first it was considered a wonder drug. It helped patients with bipolar disorder tremendously, but there was a very dark side to it. It killed a significant number of patients. Something called Agranulocytosis happened. In layman's terms, this is the depletion of the body's white blood cells. These cells are the ones that fight off diseases and infections. Without white blood cells in proper numbers one could get sick and die very quickly.

After being rejected for use in the United States, the drug was introduced to Europe. Once again it proved to work wonders but the deadly side effects remained. What happened is that the medicine was dispensed on a weekly basis. Furthermore nobody could get the drug without a blood test. The blood test was primarily used to look at the white blood cell count. This method seemed to work.

Doctor R presented me with the decision to try Clozaril. He told me that if I took the drug, I would most likely return to college and live a normal life. On the downside though, it could take my life. He stressed this was unlikely, given that my blood would be closely monitored. However, there was still a possibility I would die from the side effects of the medicine.

I considered a lifetime of going in and out of hospitals. I knew a fair number of people whose life consisted of nothing but going in and out of hospitals. I definitely didn't want that kind of life. I had a strong desire to make something out of my life. I refused to surrender to apathy. I would not let the mental illness win. I would fight it no matter what.

In order to get on the medicine, I had to return to the Solomon Hilton. I received the medicine in ever-increasing doses. After two weeks, I was stabilized. My blood was tested every day in the hospital and everything looked fine. Soon, I was out.

I am writing this over twenty years later. I am still on the Clozaril. Fortunately, the Agranulocytosis was discovered to only happen when a patient is first put on the medicine. However, his is not a rule without exceptions. When I first received the medicine, I had to take a blood test every week. Over time it slipped to every other week. Now I have a blood test every month.

Chemically, I had found a cure. It was a turning point in my life. The fire burning down the house had been put out. I could now focus on building back my life. I had entered a new phase of rebuilding.

That, perhaps, is one way to look at my life, but there is another. Mental illness is a trial. Silver is a metal that when dug from the earth is full of impurities. To make it worthwhile, useful, and valuable, the silver is placed in fire. This is a painful process. As the metal endures the heat, unwanted materials are burned away. When the process is over, one gets pure silver. I now look upon these years not as wasted years, but as building years. Clozaril came along to put out the flames when I had finally been refined.

Conclusion

So the curtain descends upon the first act of my story. I sincerely hope that there is some cheering and applause. It has been about nine years since I took pen in hand and have worked to produce the first scene in my story. A lot has happened in my life, but you will have to wait until the second book for those details.

I decided to end this book with when I was put on Clozaril and became chemically well to leave you with a feeling of hope. My mental illness, in truth, was tortuous and made my life and the life of my loved ones very difficult, but suffering tends to promote compassion and character. My walk of life was none of my choosing, but in the end I must say it has been a blessing.

Mental illness is not something that one simply walks away from. First of all, there is the immense amount of time spent in dealing with the sickness. If I were seeking a career in the business world, I would be ten years behind my peers. It is hard to win a race while others seem to have a head start.

More importantly, there are all the ramifications and baggage that mental illness brings with it. There is the stigma, most of which comes from a vast misunderstanding of the disease's true nature. I hope this book sheds some light on many of the skewed representations of mental illness; there is indeed more than the madness. I am, after all, a human being first.

Clozaril has given me a life without the extreme highs and lows. I live life in a "normal fashion," so to speak. Still, I had to face life with all its challenges. It wasn't anything like the first go

John Kaniecki

around. I once possessed an extraordinary confidence, especially in my academic ability. Unfortunately, this element was taken away.

There are many stories that I would have liked to include, but didn't. I tried to get the essentials while not becoming over burdensome. I once told my friend, who was a writer, that I hadn't finished my autobiography, yet. His reply was, "of course not, you're not dead yet". It made me laugh, but I realized he was right.

I keep on living and the story grows. I face demons on a daily basis, as do we all. I have put my heart and soul into this story. Many have contributed both time and effort into this work. I would like to thank them, especially my wife for giving me the time to devote countless hours. There is the fear that my tale will get swallowed up into the ocean of oblivion, that it will not touch hearts and minds and will be dismissed. If you are reading these words, that is not the case, I believe.

ABOUT THE AUTHOR

John Kaniecki is a member of the Revolutionary Poet's Brigade and Secretary for Rhyming Poet's International. John volunteers as a missionary in the inner city of Newark, New Jersey, for the Church of Christ at Chancellor Avenue. John is active in the antiwar movement. In particular John is a strong advocate of the rights of indigenous people.

OTHER WORKS BY JOHN KANIECKI

Murmurings of a Mad Man. A book of rhymed and metered poetry. A poetic companion to More Than the Madness. Where Joe Hill, Woody Guthrie and Crazy Horse assume the roles of the id, ego and super ego.

Sunset Sonnets. Life is at the heart of a poet, but what place does death hold? When love slips away, what does one say? A book of traditional poetry with a positive and wholesome message.

Poet to the Poor. Some of John's greatest works, including the award winning Tea with Joe Hill. An eclectic collection featuring the majority of the poems with rhyme, all focused on giving a spirit of hope to the disenfranchised bottom one percent. If you want to change the world it is a necessary book of art.

Words of the Future. A collection of science fiction stories only bound by a fantastic imagination. Travel into another galaxy and into nearby New Jersey and many other places.

Scarecrow, Scarecrow. A book of horror and terror. Anne McFry is following her dreams to become a rock star, but she cannot escape the sins of her past as they haunt her in the form of the Scarecrow. A memorable story with an unbelievable end.

Satan's Siren. Soon to be published by Jaded Books Publishing. The sequel to Scarecrow Scarecrow.

CPSIA information can be obtained
at www.ICGtesting.com
Printed in the USA
LVOW13s0400270217
525476LV00016B/644/P